MONTY
DoN

gardening Mad

PHOTOGRAPHS
BY
FLEUR OLBY

SOMA
san francisco

First published in 1997 by Bloomsbury Publishing Plc.
American Edition published 1998 by SOMA Books by
arrangement with Bloomsbury Publishing Plc.

SOMA Books is an imprint of Bay Books & Tapes,
Inc. For information, address: Bay Books & Tapes,
Inc., 555 De Haro Street, No. 220, San Francisco,
CA 94107.

for SOMA Books:
Publisher: James Connolly
Art Director: Jeffrey O'Rourke
American Editor: Richard Schwarzenberger
Jacket Design: Cabra Diseño / Tom Sieu

for the original edition:
Interior Design: Carroll Associates

Library of Congress Cataloguing-in-Publication Data
Don, Montagu
    Gardening mad / Monty Don ; photographs by Fleur Olby.
        p. cm.
    "First published 1997 by Bloomsbury Publishing Plc."--T.p.
    verso. Includes index.
    ISBN 1-57959-007-1
    1. Gardening. 2. Gardens. I. Title.
SB455.D579 1998
    635--dc21   97-53187
                                                          CIP

ISBN 1-57959-007-1

Printed in Italy

10 9 8 7 6 5 4 3 2 1

Distributed to the trade by Publishers Group West

Contents

Although I had always written and always wanted to be a writer, it never occurred to me to write about gardening until I was thirty-three. In my late teens I had plucked up the courage to ask an established author for advice. Just write, he told me. It will probably be terrible, but keep at it. If you can't think what to write about then write about nothing. Not until you can write badly will you learn to write well. I diligently followed his advice and wrote very badly indeed about nothing very much, but that was still in a compartment separate to the things I did like work, eating or gardening. Life and Art had to be kept apart in order to make the banality of Life endurable.

As a child I was press-ganged into helping my parents in their garden, and hated every moment of it. It seemed to be an activity composed solely of unsuccessfully keeping Nature at bay. Other than vegetables, which in those pre-supermarket and pre-freezer days were a serious link in our domestic food chain, I have no memories of planting anything at all. It was all weeding, watering, grass-cutting and clipping (endless hours and days of clipping with shears – a job that has almost vanished now, since the introduction of the strimmer). If all that effort put into hoeing and edging paths or mowing lawns to within a millimetre of scalping had been put into making something it might have captured my imagination. But the garden was seen in our household as at best a responsibility and at worst an enemy to be conquered.

Despite this, from the age of about seventeen I found that gardening had become a real pleasure. I kept this freshly discovered sense of enjoyment to myself. In the early 1970s it was distinctly uncool to announce a new-found love of gardening as a kind of horticultural coming-out. We all wanted to walk on the wild side, not down a garden path, and I wanted to keep firmly on the wrong side of the track – so much more interesting than my perceived view of the horticultural world, which then seemed to be made up of middle-aged, middle-class bores and their servile drudges doing all the hard work. And, rather embarrassingly, me.

I have always been on the side of the drudges and still enjoy garden drudgery, be it weeding, shovelling tons of muck, turning compost heaps or sweeping leaves. I like the rhythm and the sweat of it, the way that it is part of the caring for the garden's well-being as a place. But the drudges didn't like me – the middle-class bore waiting to become middle-aged – so I hardly felt at home in either camp. When my wife and I went on to make our own garden in the early 1980s we were equally out of kilter, inasmuch as we worked in the fashion business and gardening did not cut much ice in Mrs Thatcher's power-driven, champagne- and cocaine-fuelled London.

In a way this alienation has served me well as a writer. I have always been on the outside looking in and yet over the years I have developed sufficient confidence in my own garden so as not to care whether I was outside them or they were outside me. I was inside it. Since the age of eighteen gardening and writing have both been at the core of my life with work as a farmworker, dustman, waiter, jewellery designer and TV presenter all circling more or less entertainingly around those constants.

I have always felt uncomfortable about the schism between gardening and 'real' life. Why should you put aside all the influences of life around you when turning to the garden? As you get older there might be some justification in using the garden as a retreat from the grind of life and thereby in creating a deliberate unworldly sanctuary (although sterility lurks along every step of that road). But when you are younger the garden should be experienced in the same way that you experience music, film, television, books and other people.

So when I took on the job as the *Observer*'s gardening correspondent at the start of 1994, I was determined to be true to myself and not attempt to tread the same footsteps as my more illustrious predecessors in the job. I had to write about gardening from the

viewpoint of a writer who loved gardening rather than a gardener who wrote about his expertise. Big difference.

The *Observer* is the one paper with which I would like to associated above any other, and the paper that has given me almost unrestrained scope for personal expression. It is the perfect combination of freedom and the discipline of a weekly deadline. Gardening is one of the few subjects that a newspaper can carry without demanding much journalism from the writer. My column is dictated by season and weather rather than the events of the day, and the spin that I put upon it is largely domestic. I make no apologies for that. The tone is unashamedly personal and you must take (or leave) me and mine as you find us.

I am no plantsman. While I do not wear that badge with any pride and am constantly learning about plants, even when writing about a single species I remain much more interested in gardens than plants. I could easily love a garden filled with boring planting and soon become bored with one crammed with the rarest and choicest specimens. Unless there is a sense of everything coming together as a unique, stimulating and hopefully beautiful place, then there is a hole which plants alone cannot fill. I know that this contradicts popular notions of what a garden is, but for me plants are not enough.

Gardens are unnatural, controlled spaces made by and for people outdoors. They are nearly always attached to homes and must be considered in context of the household. As soon as I isolate a plant from the context of the garden my interest begins to wane. Even when I spot an amazing, hitherto unknown flower growing in someone's garden and stop to gather information about it, my first thought is where I could plant it in my garden and how best to grow it. I suspect that this puts me at a disadvantage from many other more analytical and objective garden writers, but that is the way it is.

In many ways I see gardening as an extension of architecture, in that it is about the manipulation of spaces. This is not to deny the wonder of growing things and the incredible pleasure of gardening itself. I never do enough of it to satiate that pleasure, and the irony of writing about gardening on a beautiful day when I would much rather be doing it never ceases to bite. When I do find time to garden I love the hard work and have no desire to potter about or sit admiring the place. My garden is to be lived and breathed, where there is always a new project on the go, new spaces being made and shaped and change is welcomed. It is a place of action and energy, a kind of spiritual and sensual adventure playground.

So, in every sense, the following pieces are very personal. In many ways they are a kind of weekly letter to those that I love or want to think well of me. This made choosing them very difficult because over the years that they cover there were a number of events and thoughts that I felt needed to be represented – not just for horticultural reasons but also to represent myself – and there simply was not enough room in which to do this adequately. I try to write honestly, from experience, and do not believe in the general gardening stance that dictates everyone be nice to everyone else. There are a lot of terrible gardens out there and a lot of very boring gardeners. Hagiography is insulting to everyone but saints.

In 1995 Fleur Olby provided the pictures for a series I did on colour. They were stunning and in the summer of 1996 she began to regularly provide photographs to accompany my text. I am sure that they have doubled the number of readers who would have otherwise flicked past my column.

The words are printed here as submitted to the paper, which does not necessarily mean they are the same as those first published. I have reinstated here the bits sub editors felt had gone beyond the bounds of Sunday morning cantankerousness and horticultural detail. What you get here is the unabridged Full Monty.

12.1.97 **Aconites and Snowdrops**

I'm always glad to see the back of December. As months go it is a thoroughly bad lot. There is the jollity blip of Christmas, but it always seems to happen in a dosh-free zone and is a bit of a charade (this line of chuntering can be shared on www.//bah.humbug.com). The garden is a perfect metaphor for December's clumsy life, submerged beneath the dour face of it and holding its breath against the hope of surfacing into a New Year. At last garden and I are shot of it.

You could be forgiven for not noticing any spanking changes appearing outside and the garden can still seem Pompeian, locked inside a volcanic casing of cold and grey light, but things are getting better. The days are getting longer for a start and it is surprising how quickly that shows. And quietly, quietly, there are happenings. The garden might be in a coma but beneath the sullen skin the heart is beating strongly. I love to think of plants growing underground, showing nothing above the abrasive knobbliness of frozen earth, but secretly pushing out tentative shoots and new roots, blind and mole-like but unstoppable.

The spiky shoots of crocus and snowdrop have been there beneath the fallen leaves for the past month or so, though more as an advance party than the real thing. But any day now the winter aconites (*Eranthis hyemalis*) will start festivities and from that moment on everything seems possible, however foul the weather and slow the spring to arrive. It is odd the way that snowdrops are everybody's favourite, as surefire a feel good trigger as a robin or sprig of holly is at Christmas, whereas aconites often precede them and are much more brilliantly a celebration of life and light in the desert of winter. The little yellow flowers are like jewels stitched on to an Elizabethan court dress, each gem surrounded by a leafy ruff.

Aconites prefer alkaline soils like chalk or limestone and when settled will quickly spread via their tuberous roots to make a mat. Although the plant will tolerate shade, the flowers will only open in sunshine, so plant them where they are going to get the most of it – especially bearing in mind how low the sun is at this time of year. You can sow the seed in spring *in situ* and the flowers should appear the following year, but it is best to plant some 'in the green' – just after flowering – which will almost invariably mean begging some off someone who has an established clump to spare. These will take very easily. They need good drainage and will be the better for some compost dug into the soil before planting. By April the leaves die back to the tubers and the whole thing lies dormant until the following January.

If you have acidic soil and have a hunger for winter aconites, you might

I'm always glad to see the back of December. As months go it is a thoroughly bad lot. There is the jollity blip of Christmas, but it always seems to happen in a dosh-free zone and is a bit of a charade. At last garden and I are shot of it.

To be obsessed by the tiny details of a snowdrop is as odd – and as harmless – as any other minor perversion. But it surely misses the point. Snowdrops are there to be relished – outside at least – from afar and en masse.

try *E.*x *tubergenii* which seems to be as easy in acidic as in alkaline conditions. The clone 'Guinea Gold' is particularly vigorous and has purply-bronze ruffs, a detail which may or may not be a good thing. But it is a detail only as the flowers are undoubtedly fabulous.

Aconites are somehow tough and vigorous, despite their size, but the appeal of snowdrops is centred in their seeming fragility. In ice, snow and on the greyest of days they still flower, bowed heads trembling on delicate necks, and it is their finesse and incongruity that we love as much as their absolute beauty. Yet for all their apparent vulnerability, snowdrop leaves have specially hardened for breaking through frozen ground and certainly these leaves as they appear are rubbery in their toughness.

For most people a snowdrop is a snowdrop and there's an end to it. But there are galanthophiles who collect snowdrops (the Galanthus family) like stamps. There is a huge range to collect, although the differences are likely to be measured in millimetres in the markings within the flower. There are 350 species and cultivars but for most people any form of snowdrop is better than none. *Galanthus nivalis* is the commonest self-naturalizing type, and I love the double *G. n.* 'Flore Pleno'. This is sterile, but increases perfectly well from offsets and because it does not produce seed the flowers last an extra long time. *G.* 'S. Arnott' is exceptionally successful, being tough, big and strong-scented.

To be obsessed by the tiny details of a snowdrop is as odd – and as harmless – as any other minor perversion. But it surely misses the point. Snowdrops are there to be relished – outside at least – from afar and *en masse*. For sure, a posy of snowdrops in a tiny vase is microscopically beautiful, but they have already ceased to be garden flowers at that point, the indoorness of them makes them something else. There is something repulsive and emasculating about the collector's wish to tame flowers, especially one as inherently free-born as a snowdrop. I hate the garden as zoo.

It is the outdoorness and wildness of snowdrops I am celebrating and for this they need to be planted in clumps, either to spread in large drifts composed of small clumps on open grass, or among trees, shrubs and perennial plants – again in small groups. It is important to get the size of these groups right and that can only be judged by the eye. Too big and they become anonymous; too small and they look naked and abandoned. Snowdrops will increase their spread by seed at the rate of an inch a year if left to it. If you only start with a few, that is slowish. This is also dependent upon a warm February to provide enough insect activity for pollination and different species or varieties growing close together to provide cross-pollination. Therefore most reproduction is from division of bulbs rather than seed and one can speed this process by digging them up after flowering and before the leaves die back and reclumping them to suit one's sense of balance. You may find that dry bulbs planted laboriously but horticulturally correctly produce a disappointing crop of flowers. Try to buy them 'in the green' and plant them from January through to March. They will then flower for you to the best of their ability.

No one seems to know whether snowdrops are a native or not. They certainly grow freely in the wild, but equally certainly nearly all 'wild' snowdrops are garden escapees. There is apparently no reference to snowdrops growing wild before 1770, and the first garden reference is in Gerard's *Herball* of 1597. It is particularly poignant to see the clumps of snowdrops at this time of year around the sites of long-lost cottages or farms, the stones and timbers long vanished but the tiny trembling flowers lingering year after New Year.

■ While aconites and snowdrops are hardy throughout the United States, they thrive only in cool, moist climates in rich, well-drained soil. Snowdrops in particular should not be allowed to dry out.

■ Sweet peas for spring planting should be sown indoors now. Likewise garlic.

■ Take root cuttings of Oriental poppies, anchusas, acanthus, or any fleshy-rooted perennial. This has to be done when the plants are dormant, and they may have to be dug up completely to get at the roots. Cut lengths of healthy root about a pencil thickness or a little less from the parent plant and cut the end nearest the top straight and the bottom at a slant. This is to help you insert them in the cutting compost the right way up, as the new roots will always form at the end that was furthest from the plant. The top end should be flush with the soil surface. They can be put into pots or boxes of sandy soil and placed in a sheltered spot to root. A cold frame is ideal. Root cuttings will flower sooner if taken from mature plants.

■ Heavy snow needs to be knocked off evergreens (so that they do not break), but otherwise nothing suffers beneath its protective blanket. If the weather is very cold, snow will be the best possible insulation against icy winds. Clear it only for humans and motor cars, not plants.

19.1.97 **Wind**

I had planned to spend a couple of days pruning the limes along my birthday path: a brick path 40 yards long made over forty days to celebrate forty years – eat your heart out, Richard Long – a good New Year job, cutting back the solid past and laying snares for spring. But I got caught by a lazy wind (doesn't bother to go round, just pushes right through you) and my movements got slower as my shoulders curled and my hands became oafish lumps at the ends of my arms until I admitted defeat and gave up. Although the air temperature in this country rarely drops too low to work outside if you dress properly and keep moving, the wind always makes everything unimaginably worse.

But humans can go indoors, drink whisky and have a hot bath infused with essential lavender oil. Pity the poor plants exposed to winds from every quarter. It is astonishing how many will survive in the teeth of icy gales, but gardens are about creating an environment for plants to flourish rather than merely survive. Nothing stunts a plant's development more than wind. It does not have to be week-long Arctic gusts either; even quite modest wind will make life very difficult in an exposed part of the garden. So it is worth making a mental wind-map of the entire estate, particularly if your garden is very small, because every square inch is doubly precious and cannot tolerate the slightest degree of wind-abuse. It is not so much the amount of wind as the type that counts. For something that can never be seen, something that amounts to an effect, wind is extraordinarily measurable. You can calculate its speed, its temperature, its humidity, and above all, where it blows from.

A southerly wind is always warm, and nothing dries the ground faster after a spell of rain, although this is a two-edged sword because it can wonderfully transform sticky mud to workable tilth but also make rich moisture in spring into an arid dustbowl. The Tudors thought that the southern wind carried disease, and it certainly brings a pestilent smell to my Tudor house, which stands directly north of a vast turkey farm whose acrid, factory stench means that the windows cannot be opened when the wind is in the south.

The westerlies are wet, bringing rain in from the Atlantic, and are the dominant winds right along the western side of Britain, defining our climate. The west wind scumbles across the sky, fat clouds almost tripping over each other, spilling rain and sun in equal measure. In a way the west winds are our norm because they always mean change and uncertainty within parameters of mild damp. Very British.

The north wind is invariably cold, often bitter, but the east wind is the worst of the lot. Last winter was blighted by the winds from the north-east and they caught many of us by surprise, outflanking our defences.

Although there is not much that you can do about rain, a murky sky or the way that the building next door exactly shadows your garden all afternoon, wind can be filtered and funnelled out of harm's way. You can create filters and shelters that will dissipate most of the trouble wind causes. In my garden the wind comes predominantly from the west, and I had slowly established a system of trees, hedges and fences to trap it, but underestimated the potential of attack from the east. The moral of the story is that one must think of the garden as an enclosed space set in a hostile plain and be ready for the worst, whatever direction it comes from.

In a sense a walled garden is a perfect manifestation of that horticultural paranoia, and anyone whose garden is surrounded by a high wall is lucky. But a solid fence or wall simply lifts the wind and brings it down in a swirl the other side at a distance twice the height of the wall, bashing whatever happens to be there. Once inside the enclosed space, the wind is like a berserk pinball, rebounding off the walls like a thirteen-year-old joy rider. Where it hits the side of a building the effect on anything planted against it can be devastating. Half the air is forced up and round the walls but the other half is turned to

The Tudors thought that the southern wind carried disease, and it certainly brings a pestilent smell to my Tudor house, which stands directly north of a vast turkey farm whose acrid, factory stench means that the windows cannot be opened when the wind is in the south.

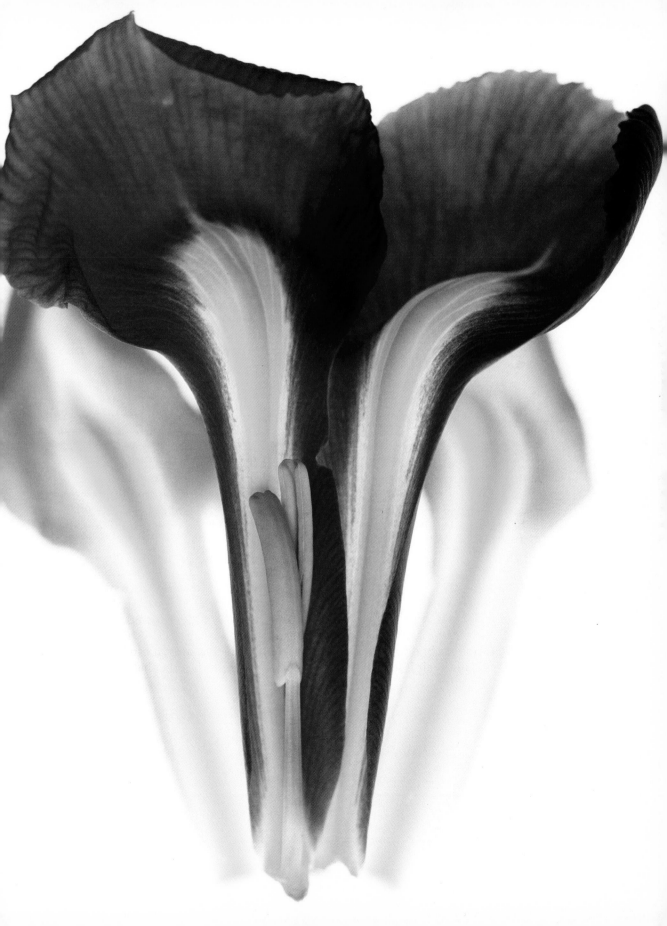

blow downwards, creating a crushing force on anything growing below.

Many town gardens have a side access which funnels the wind in a kind of tunnel so that it pummels down the side of the house straight into the garden. It is always worth creating a baffle across this so long as it doesn't unduly restrict access. The best protection comes from a thick hedge or a fence with an ideal ratio of 60 per cent solid to 40 per cent gap. This might seem too full of holes to be much use but it has been Scientifically Proven to work, so there. You can get netting Scientifically Designed specifically to act as a windbreak: every nursery now uses it and it is almost as remarkable for its openness as its ugliness. Although it is effective, it is too aesthetically challenged for any garden. A more natural solution has to be found.

The best natural protection from any type of wind is a shelter belt of large trees with another band of smaller trees and shrubs inside them and a mature hedge inside this. All would be preferably deciduous (to give sufficient gaps) although the more solid evergreens will do pretty well. The effect is that of a succession of sieves, straining the wind down to a clear broth of a breeze.

However, most gardens scarcely have room for one big tree, let alone a shelter belt the size of a football pitch. Hedges are the answer. The wind will be reduced to nothing for a distance of twice the height of the hedge and the hedge will continue to be effective for up to ten times its height. But hedges need protection if they are to grow strong enough to become protection themselves. Also, a hedge grows faster, stronger and healthier if planted when only 1–2 feet high, and is much cheaper this size too. So there is a period of about five years while the hedge does little to provide shelter and itself suffers the retarding effect of wind. Therefore there must be an interim barrier for these little plants and everything in their lee. Fences are required.

A lot of fences are pretty hideous too, especially the ubiquitous larch-lap, so you should take the trouble to exercise the full range of choice available to you. After all, you will have to look at the fence daily for at least five years, until the hedge is able to do the job unaided.

When I came to my own windswept open field four years ago and set about making a garden, I made fixed fences 5–6 feet high of hazel poles

In a sense a walled garden is a perfect manifestation of that horticultural paranoia, and anyone whose garden is surrounded by a high wall is lucky. But a solid fence or wall simply lifts the wind and brings it down in a swirl the other side at a distance twice the height of the wall, bashing whatever happens to be there. Once inside the enclosed space, the wind is like a berserk pinball, rebounding off the walls like a thirteen-year-old joy rider.

woven between chestnut stakes banged in firmly at 2-foot intervals wherever I wanted to plant a hedge. This was standard practice in the Middle Ages to contain animals and I love the basketweave of poles that pop up in all the illuminated manuscripts and paintings of the fourteenth and fifteenth centuries. The fence has the gappiness to keep out the most persistent of winds (each stretch constructed to be precisely 60 per cent solid and not a point more or less) yet is strong enough for my children to clamber all over. I then planted hornbeam hedges in the lee and three years on they seem to be growing amazingly well. Note that I planted them in the lee of the wind, not all neatly on the inside or outside of the fences. The wind is predominantly from the west, so the lee is effectively the east side of the fence. This looked odd for the first couple of years as at a corner the hedge would disappear round the other side of the woven barrier, but I knew that it would quickly grow through the fence, and already the oddness has merged into established lines. The fences will gently rot into the hedge, and by the time that it is established, only the upright posts will remain and they too will fade in time.

OK, you don't want to do that yourself. It is a fairly cheap form of fencing (about £3.50 per yard, not including labour), but you need thousands of what amount to bean sticks and hundreds of posts. It is pretty hard work and takes a fair bit of strength (a professional would split the rods, which makes them easier to work and go twice as far, and is just as effective, but the splitting is horribly difficult). The thing to do is to buy pre-woven hazel panels that serve exactly the same function, are more finely beautiful than my clodhopping home-made jobs and have the enormous advantage of being movable. Each panel is always 6 feet in length and can come in any height, although 5 or 6 feet is the most practical.

Hazel makes the best hurdles, far superior to willow, which rots much sooner and is denser, therefore failing the vital 60/40 percentage test. Most decent garden centres should sell them.

Hazel has to be coppiced every seven to ten years. If it is not cut, the coppice becomes overshaded and the hazel coarse and unusable, whilst the plants of the coppice floor – bluebell, primrose, Solomon's seal and the Early purple orchid – cannot survive in the heavy shade. Once a coppice has been left for forty years it is beyond restoration. All over England coppices are being lost through neglect. By buying hurdles you will not only protect the garden from the wind but also conserve our historic woodlands.

Within the garden, indeed within a border, you can create a series of microshelter belts by planting delicate plants in the lee of shrubs. Even a small bush will make all the difference to a tender flower downwind of it.

Finally, it is worth considering the effect that the wind has on the rainfall within your garden. Rain rarely falls straight down. It usually falls across, carried by the prevailing wind. Westerly wind will mean that anything to the east side of the house will be dry, and vice versa.

■ The effect of frost can be greatly reduced by a layer laid or wrapped around a plant or area. This might be netting, burlap, fleece or an organic material such as straw, branches or bracken. The idea is to create a warm layer of air between the ground (or plant) and the protective material. But do not put this down when there is a frost as that will have the opposite effect and prevent the cold plant or ground from warming up. Do it when the air and ground are both frost-free.

■ Wind is terribly desiccating to evergreen plants in winter and it is possible for them to die of drought in freezing conditions. If the leaves are browning, try spraying with cold water. Even in freezing weather this will water the plants and protect them from the drying winds.

■ Try to plant deciduous hedges as soon as the soil warms enough to make this possible. The importance of preparing the ground for a hedge cannot be overstressed. A hedge planted into deeply dug, well-manured soil will grow at least twice as fast as one planted without any proper preparation. Any time spent getting the ground right is always saved ten-fold.

26.1.97 **Hellebores**

Gardeners can be terrible snobs and bores, and no bore is more snobbishly dreary than a hellebore bore. If I had a pound for every time someone told me that a garden with a good display of hellebores is the mark of the 'real' gardener, I'd have about... oh, three quid fifty. As a determinedly unreal gardener I have a selection of hellebores that I value very highly, not least because they are so easy to grow and so undemanding of time and energy, for which they repay me with a performance lasting from Christmas to spring that is as reliable as frost in February.

I am of the school that considers it better to have nothing than a bad something, so performance alone does not merit a place in my garden. The trick is to have something going on that you want to see – a state of affairs that is apparently overlooked by a surprising number of 'real' gardeners. But hellebores are always lovely and if you have a garden and even just look out of your window between January and May, let alone go out of doors, you should be growing them for Maximum Pleasure.

The best way to treat a garden plant is to try to replicate its natural habitat, and hellebores are broadly woodland plants. There are different kinds from different types of wood in different places in the world, but the essence of all woodland flowers is that they flourish in a situation that has some degree of shade, shelter and rich soil (from all those years of fallen leaves) and often flower early before the canopy of leaves fills out above them, blocking all light. Many will tolerate quite dry conditions, especially in summer, after flowering. That might sound a complicated, demanding mix, but in fact most gardens are a type of mini-woodland by default and are ideal for woodland flowers like hellebores or primroses. The one thing that all hellebores hate is bad drainage, but soil that is rich enough will drain enough, and the addition of grit to even really heavy clay, as well as lots of organic material, will do the trick.

Only two hellebores are naturalized in Britain, *Helleborus foetidus* and *H. viridis*. The former is much the most common both in gardens and the wild and is one of my favourite plants. *H. foetidus* has a variety of

If I had a pound for every time someone told me that a garden with a good display of hellebores is the mark of the 'real' gardener, I'd have about... oh, three quid fifty.

The truth is that the Christmas rose is a star, and can be forgiven much because it is so beautiful and makes you feel so damn good just admiring it.

vernacular names other than the commonly used Stinking hellebore, which is neither flattering nor particularly appropriate. I prefer Bear's foot or Setterwort. It likes chalky soil best but seems to be perfectly happy on my neutral clay.

Once established and in rich soil, *H. foetidus* grows strongly, reaching 3 feet high and across, with deeply divided, serrated leaves and great panicles of yellow flowers with a crimson rim, looking as though they have been gently dipped into a pool of blood. The effect of the dark green leaves growing out from the strong stems and the much paler, yellowish-green new growth above them, rising to the greenish-yellow flowers culminating in that bloody ring, is both dramatic and subtle.

All hellebores hardly seem to grow at all for a season or two while they get used to their new site. This autumn I moved practically all mine into new, specially dug beds and they have responded by flopping tragically in the hard frosts. But they're just being hysterical. They will recover. *H. foetidus* are showing the strain least and in general they are the most robust of the species, growing almost anywhere and responding with sullen indifference to a bit of rough treatment.

The best-known hellebore, *H. orientalis* or the Lenten rose, is more touchy, and it is worth thinking long and hard about where to plant these so that you avoid the need to move them later. The Lenten rose has flowers that vary from the palest of creams to the darkest of purples, via bright green. When you buy a non-named species of *H. orientalis* there is no saying what the colour will be, and people have devoted lifetimes to breeding hybrids whose flowers are predictable. *H. orientalis* will cross not only with itself in all its various hybridizations but also with a number of other species, so garden seedlings will always be uncontrollable, which is good if you like surprises and an air of quiet anarchy and bad if you want to control your world with a tight clench. Dark flowers are considered the most desirable and this has given rise to enormously popular cultivars such as 'Queen of the Night' and 'Philip Ballard'. As a rule, seedlings showing dark stainings on the stem will produce the darkest flowers.

The only real fault of *H. niger*, the Christmas rose, is that it rarely flowers at Christmas. However, in my experience this is one of the more touchy hellebores, and is the main reason for the fallacy that hellebores are somehow a plant you can only aspire to once you have passed through a series of horticultural hoops. For a moody, sensitive performer it is surprisingly muscular, the flowers clear and strong as well as curiously pure and refreshing to look at. The truth is that the Christmas rose is a star, and can be forgiven much because it is so beautiful and makes you feel so damn good just admiring it. And of all the posies in the world, I have never seen anything to match a small bowl of Christmas roses – they are the florist's equivalent of truffles or perhaps Château Yquem. So it is a treat to have them in the garden for about the same price as a bag of mushrooms or a bottle of plonk.

I have very few *H. niger* – for the lazy reason that no one locally sells them and I am hopeless at ordering plants – but I have a number of plants of a hybrid species called *H. nigercors,* which is a cross between the Christmas rose and the Corsican hellebore, *H. argutifolius* (which you might see described as *H. corsicus*). It has a hybrid vigour, the flower almost as good as *H. niger*, and a long flowering season. It is perhaps a more viable goer than the Christmas rose, especially if you live on acidic soil.

H. argutifolius has pale green stems and veins on especially shiny, dark green, big, leathery leaves divided into three leaflets. I have seen it growing wild in the woods in the north of Corsica in the stoniest, most unlikely of places . Like *H. foetidus*, it is very vigorous, growing to 3 feet or more on good soil and there is something meaty and shrubby, almost mahonia-like, about its solidity. It will take any amount of dry shade without batting whatever plants bat in lieu of eyelids, but to allow it to thicken out and reach its full stately potential it is best to grow it in part shade, perhaps facing east so it gets early morning sun. The flowers are a mass of up to thirty apple-green cups that will last into April. They set seed easily, often in unlikely places and odd corners, but the mature plant only lasts about five years so you should encourage seedlings as they emerge around the parent plant to fill the gap that will inevitably be left when it dies back.

If you have the space, hellebores are best planted in groups of hybrids or species. They are more expensive to buy than most plants – expect to pay up to £8 for a 9-inch Christmas rose – so establishing a mass of them is perhaps best done by preparing the ground as though you were going to fill it with plants, planting what you can afford spaced widely across the whole area, and letting the alarmingly big gaps between plants fill themselves over the years with self-sown seedlings. The only real price will be in extra care when hand-weeding as you sort the delicate little seedlings from the weeds.

■ With the exception of *Helleborus lividus,* hellebores can be grown anywhere in the U.S. In areas of coldest winters, they should be amply mulched in the U.S. In areas of coldest winters, they should be amply mulched with shredded bark. They grow best under trees, and some *(H. foetidus, H. corsicus lividus, H. x. sternii, H. orientalis)* tolerate some drought.

■ It is a good idea to dig in plenty of mushroom compost before planting any hellebore and to give the plants a mulch with the stuff every autumn. This not only feeds them and improves the structure of the soil but also makes the ground more alkaline, especially if the compost is fresh. It is a bad idea to mulch hellebores in spring with anything other than really well-rotted mushroom compost because a crop of seedlings will sprout around each plant, which, when dug up and planted out in autumn, provide the easiest and cheapest way of propagation. A thick mulch would snuff them out if put on after germination, and be too coarse a seed bed if applied uncomposted, and ordinary garden compost would have too many competing weeds in it.

■ It is best to remove any damaged or dead leaves of any type of hellebore as they are noticed, but a general tidying of leaves should be done in autumn with removal of all the old leaves as the flowers emerge. New ones will grow back as spring unfolds. Flowering stems should be cut back to the ground after the seeds have dropped, although there will be a tatty phase between flowering and the seed leaving the plant, so if tattiness is abhorrent, you can tidy earlier and forgo your seedlings.

28.1.96 **Camellias**

It is curious that gardening can make the mildest-mannered liberal (me) into a seething mass of bilious prejudice. For no obvious reason there is an eclectic selection of plants that I cannot abide. Take camellias (and you most certainly can): I read in one well-known gardening guru's works that camellias are 'almost universally admired'. Well, not here they aren't. I can't abide them. What disturbs me as much as anything about them is that I don't know exactly what it is that disturbs me about them. It might be the colours of their flowers that tend towards the sickly pink and glaring, almost hostile magenta, but then there are other plants, notably roses and peonies, which can match them for ugly colour, shade by shade, which do not bother me the least. It could be the shiny, beetle-back hardness of the leaves that always seems to me so unspringlike and aggressive at a time of year when in the main the plant world is making a concerted effort to be soft and gently glowing – although you could argue that this provides a welcome diversification. It certainly has something to do with the way that camellias appear to be neither shrub nor tree, gangly affairs without shape, and even more, I think, with the relationship between leaf and flower. They appear so hard, so set in their unloving ways, like lipsticked Tory ladies with fiercely lacquered hair setting out on grim do-goodery. But prejudice is bred in the bone. I was raised on chalkland and the only camellias I came across in my formative years were freaks, growing in peat-filled tubs (I can remember the residual smell from the alcohol soaked into the wood when I was knee-high to a camellia). Although more lime-tolerant than rhododendrons, they need an acid soil to thrive and at least a neutral soil (a pH of 6.5) to survive. By the time I was old enough to express well-schooled prejudices for myself, my opinions were enseamed with lime: there was no room for camellias, rhododendrons, heathers or any of the acid-loving shrubs that dominate the acidic badlands.

There is a patch of London, around Knightsbridge, where the various squares surrounded by impossibly expensive houses are made the more forbidding and gloomy by the camellias that bloom each spring as unrealistically as real flowers can, their deep green leaves blackened by fumes. It is quite a feat really, all that gaudy colour exerting such a powerfully gloomy influence.

Having got that off my chest, I have to admit that occasionally camellias can look not bad. Invariably that is in woodland and almost invariably that will be in Cornwall, on the West Coast of Scotland, or in Ireland where the air

I read in one well-known gardening guru's works that camellias are 'almost universally admired'. Well, not here they aren't. I can't abide them.

is suitably moist and mild. The great gardens at Crarae do a nice line in camellias, along with rhododendrons and nothofagus, where they become part of an extraordinary, surreal landscape, brilliantly coloured, almost tropical despite the freezing rain that fell all the time I last visited. They are, of course, woodland plants, and should always be planted with some shade to protect them. Famously intolerant of early-morning sunshine on frost, they perform best in the lee of a north or west wall – never on an east wall.

The original *Camellia japonica* has been so diversely bred into a family of hybrids and cultivars that it is lost. But *C. reticulata* from Yunnan in China is still available and has also created its own web of offspring. It was one of the first horticultural benefits from the trade links with China, and John Reeves, an inspector of tea in China from 1808 to 1831, sent back cultivated plants – as opposed to the wild specimens that most plant collectors were gathering – to the Horticultural Society at Chelsea. By 1825 there had been sufficient breeding development for E.B. Buckingham to publish *Camellia Britannica*, which illustrated plants raised following crosses made in 1819.

The semi-double form of *C. reticulata* 'Captain Rawes', introduced by Robert Fortune in 1820, was thought to be the type plant until George Forrest sent home the single wild form in 1924. 'Captain Rawes' should be coming into flower about now and is one of the earliest camellias.

Both *C. japonica* and most forms of *C. reticulata* are pretty hardy although originally all camellias were thought to be tender and their survival of harsh winter weather – such as the great frost of 1837/8 – was recorded with incredulity. This supposed tenderness was probably due to the fact that they came by way of Johnny Foreigner, and because the flowers certainly dislike frost, but most camellias can be grown outside in a reasonably sheltered spot. The boom in conservatories that came with cheap coal to heat them, cast iron to build them and, most significant of all, the railways to bring the coal to them, meant that camellias were enthusiastically grown under glass throughout the Victorian years.

However, although *C. reticulata* and especially *C. japonica* were bred with such enthusiasm, they had faults which even the most ardent admirer had to recognize and which persisted in all the many cultivars and hybrids. The chief failure is the way that their flowers fade on the tree, hanging on like a used paper tissue wiping out the memory of any virtues the flower might have had. At a time of year when

There is a patch of London, around Knightsbridge, where the various squares surrounded by impossibly expensive houses are made the more forbidding and gloomy by the camellias that bloom each spring as unrealistically as real flowers can, their deep green leaves blackened by fumes. It is quite a feat really, all that gaudy colour exerting such a powerfully gloomy influence.

everything else in the garden is bursting out with new flower or new leaf the camellia looks like the morning after a particularly dissipated party. The only way to deal with this is to deadhead the bush as the flowers fade. A bore and a chore.

But then John Charles Williams applied himself to the case. He was a toff of the kind that keeps cropping up in the history of gardening, an enthusiastic amateur blessed with enough money to pursue his enthusiasms. He was born and spent his life at Caerhays Castle in Cornwall where he planted eclectically but particularly magnolias, camellias, daffodils and rhododendrons. He crossed *C. saluensis*, collected by George Forrest, whose plant-hunting Williams helped to finance, with an unnamed form of *C. japonica*. *C. saluensis* has little to recommend it, being another variation on the impossibly garish white-to-pink flowers that afflict most camellias, backed by dull green waxy leaves. Pretty forgettable really. But when wed to this unnamed *C. japonica* it produced a hardy hybrid called *camellia* x *williamsii*. The main advantage of this over its parents is that it drops its faded flowers good and fast, with the net effect that the ground below the shrub, rather than the plant itself, looks as though it has been littered with coloured tissues. The cultivar 'Donation' has become ubiquitous in all garden centres, which is probably more a tribute to its ease of production than any other virtues over other variations of the *williamsii* group, although it is exceptionally floriferous. It makes a pretty large, almost tree-sized shrub. *C.* x *williamsii* 'Anticipation' is smaller and neater, not growing much over 10 feet.

To end on a positive note, if you must grow camellias, avoid all forms of pink. Stick to blood-red or white, and preferably the latter. Of the *williamsii* camellias, 'Sea Foam' is a double white and 'Francis Hanger' a single. *C. japonica* 'Madge Miller' (doncha just love these flower names?) has the faults of all japonicas but is tough and looks pretty good. Skipping hastily past all the possible pinks, try *C. japonica* 'Kouron Jura' which is one of the darkest red of all camellias and one of the most resistant to frost damage.

■ Your camellia may fail to produce flowers even though it seems to have plenty of buds. The buds may swell healthily and then drop off for no apparent reason. Both problems are likely to be due to the buds being frosted with no outward sign of damage. Assuming that the plant is well protected from cold winds and the early morning sun (absolutely essential), the only thing you can do is to ensure that the plant remains moist at all times. Give it a good mulch of peat twice a year, to help maintain acidity, damp and root warmth.

■ Sow sweet peas, four or five to a pot, and germinate on a window-sill or in a greenhouse. They can be put outside to harden off in a month or so and planted out at Easter.

■ Move aconites, while they are still in flower. They will take much better than from dry bulbs and you can immediately measure the effect of their new position.

4.2.96 **Drugs**

As a rehabilitated ex-*Archers* addict, I avoid exposure to it whenever practicable, but trapped in someone's kitchen the other day, I could not avoid Brian Aldridge's unmistakable supercilious tones tempting me from the radio. Unable to resist, I was amazed to hear that he was being nicked for growing cannabis in a pot on his fridge. Blimey! Is nothing sacred? But I suppose that the average young farmer is as likely to swap stories of adventures on the reversible plough over a spliff as a pint of bitter. And there are plenty of people whose interest in horticulture is focused on the performance of a couple of gro-bags sporting healthy plants of *Cannabis sativa*. It combines the worthiness of gardening with a naughty-but-nice frisson of illegality. Hemp seed is a component of birdseed and used to be sold as bait for fish, so is not that exotic. In their book *Garden Flowers From Seed* (Viking) Christopher Lloyd and Graham Rice quote this recommendation from Suttons' seed list of 1915: 'the Hemp seed you sent me has produced plants which attained the height of 10ft 6ins to 11ft, with grand foliage.' This vigour of habit makes it a good plant to foster horticultural interest because it responds so well to nurture, reacting almost instantly to increases of light, heat, water and feed, making grand palmate foliage. Unfortunately the powers that be deem it illegal to cultivate it in any way.

Nevertheless, hops, *Humulus lupulus*, are part of the Cannabaceae family, and it is no coincidence that hops are the vital part of beer's attraction. Henry VIII forbade brewers to use the hop in ale, describing it as 'a wicked weed that would... endanger the people' – which is exactly the sort of talk you would expect from a Tory MP helping himself to his third G&T. You can perfectly legally dry hop leaves and crush them before adding them, half and half, to Ceylon or Indian teas, for a 'calming' drink. A bag of hops under the pillow is supposed to help sufferers from insomnia as well.

The garden is full of drugs of one sort or another, all of them perfectly legal to grow and nearly all sanctioned by society. After all, what is an infusion of camomile but a drug to soothe and calm you? Folk medicine is ripe with potions made from plants picked from the garden that change or enhance mood. So in Gerard's *Herball* we learn that borage, when slipped into wine, makes 'men and women glad and merry, driving away all sadness and dullness'. Basil, taken with alcohol (i.e. as a tincture), is a nerve tonic that is also a stimulant. The alcohol just might be part of this effect, but Gerard also says that chervil alone lifts the spirits and gives courage. Germander and Milk thistle will lighten the spirits if merely chewed. I have no doubt that our Tudor forebears would have regarded cannabis – which they would have taken as a tincture – as just another calmative, and not a particularly potent one at that.

The dried root of valerian, *Valeriana officionalis*, has long been used to ease anxiety, a sort of herbal valium. It does best in moisture-rich soil, becoming about 2 feet high, with pinkish-white florets. (The Red valerian, *Centranthus ruber*, that you see growing on walls and banks all over the West Country, has no narcotic value at all.) Apparently the potency of the root is affected by the time of year that it is dug, but I have been unable to find out when it is at its most potent. Answers on a postcard, please.

Papaver somniferum, the Opium poppy, is one of the loveliest of the annual poppies, and I certainly would not be without it in my garden. The latex from the ripening seed pod is the raw material for morphine, opium and heroin. It is

I suppose that the average young farmer is as likely to swap stories of adventures on the reversible plough over a spliff as a pint of bitter.

quite legal to grow but tricky to harvest much of a morphine crop from, as we do not really have enough heat here for the seed pods to ripen sufficiently to produce the active ingredient. I went to the Golden Triangle recently, expecting to see fields of Opium poppies, but the Thai government has cracked down on the trade and now all the peasant farmers grow cabbages instead.

Theodore Zeldin, in his wonderful, fabulously polymathic book, *An Intimate History of Humanity* (Minerva), points out that the great common enemy of mankind was always hunger, and when this could not be defeated by food, the escape was through drugs. 'The most common European drug in the Middle Ages was probably poppy seed…and it was used to make bread, as was hemp seed, spiced with coriander, aniseed, cumin and sesame…Restless children were given infusions of poppy to keep them quiet… When hunger turned to famine they slowly withdrew into dazed stupefaction, oscillating between narcosis and neurosis, but dreaming that they were eating.' So the next time you get that restless, hungry feeling in the garden, snack on poppy seeds.

The seeds of Morning Glory (*Ipomoea hederacea*) are hallucinogenic. I confess to having tried them in my misspent youth and being severely underwhelmed by the results. Better to put the seeds in compost rather than your mouth. Soak them overnight and sow individually in 3-inch pots in a temperature of 23°C/75°F. After they have germinated they will need to be carefully hardened off before planting out. Rightly is *I. tricolor*, 'Heavenly Blue', called heavenly. Distinctly trippy.

From about the age of nine I used to smoke what we called baysvine, the dried stems of Old Man's Beard or *Clematis vitalba* (looking spectacular at the moment, looped like crazy cobwebs across the trees and hedges). We stripped off the bark and cut it into lengths between the nodes. They smoked well and were a lot cheaper than fags, although I don't recall getting much of a buzz from them.

There is nothing other than climate stopping you from growing your own tobacco. The tobacco plants that we grow primarily for their scent will not do the trick. You need *Nicotiana tabacum* and a greenhouse to provide the right moist heat, and then the dried leaves can be smoked or snorted to produce a high of the most addictive kind yet devised by man. But it is not a patch on the scent of *N. sylvestris* inhaled deeply on a warm August evening.

■ It has been pointed out to me by a number of readers that I wrongly ascribed inedibility to the fruits of *Chaenomeles japonica*. This was a result of stupidity and ignorance. Many thanks to those of you who wrote to me with various recipes for these maligned fruits.
■ Improbable as it may seem, spring and the really busy time of year is coming up soon. It is becoming urgent that you get any deciduous trees and hedging material planted very soon so that the roots can establish before new growth appears above ground. Make this a priority for the coming few weeks.

A single, thorny, dewy, centifolia rose, stolen at dawn from a beautiful garden, intensely fragrant and with massed petals almost dissolving under your gaze, is when roses get sexy.

9. 2. 97 **Valentine Roses**

I once visited a rose farm on a Christian kibbutz in Israel where the flowers were grown in long polytunnels before being shipped for sale in Holland. I got up early to watch the daily harvest of thousands of identical buds on long stems snipped off the production line of bushes growing through black polythene. They only grew one variety, chosen for its ability to produce identical red flowers on long stems and its resistance to disease. The only fragrance in the tunnels came from bodies. Production rose to its peak at about this time of year to meet the coyly romantic demands of St Valentine's Day. But although there may be real romance in declaring love via a dozen red roses, a mass-produced, fragrance-free rose is not a sexy thing.

A single, thorny, dewy, centifolia rose, stolen at dawn from a beautiful garden, intensely fragrant and with massed petals almost dissolving under your gaze, is when roses get sexy. But for that you must wait until July, and the commercial celebrations of romance will wait for no man, or rose.

The red rose is, of course, heavy with symbolism beyond the limitations of Romance. The rose was the symbol of Venus, who, before she took on the attributes of the Greek Aphrodite, was the goddess of gardens. Indeed Aphrodite, whom we regard as a symbol of Eros, was also the goddess of gardens and fruitfulness and the rose was sacred to her. The blood-pure flower, so universally accepted as a definition of loveliness, was adopted by early Christians as the symbol of the Virgin Mary, the five petals representing the five senses and the thorns the pricks and tribulations of life that have to be braved to reach the flower. One legend has it that the Virgin Mary was born when St Anne inhaled a rose. No colour is specified, but this does not diminish the wonderful zaniness of the image. A red rose, with its obvious association with blood, fitted the early medieval confusion of romance and lust which lies behind courtly love and characterizes the Christian attitude towards the mother/madonna. So frail, so beautiful, so fragrant, but so bloody and fleshy and real, and so confusing.

St Valentine's Day is properly the Feast of Fowls, the day when birds mate. It is not difficult to see the romantic association that rides along with this, especially when we have endless television films of birds going to fantastic evolutionary lengths to choose a mate. It makes sense, too, in any analysis of the avian calendar: they have to make the eggs, lay, brood and hatch them, at a time when there will be maximum food around to rear them, in time for them in turn to feed sufficiently on their own to survive the subsequent winter. Put all those needs together and the middle of February is about the only weekend free.

Certainly every February I watch crows tumbling out of the sky in seemingly kamikaze spirals in order to impress the corvine object of their passion, whilst the songbirds get noticeably more vocal from St Valentine's Day onwards. There is a real feeling that the garden is coming alive, that soon evenings will stop starting mid-afternoon, and that the odd stab of sunshine has some heat in it. Nevertheless, the first rose is not even making buds, let alone flowering. And when they do arrive, in May, the first roses are nearly all yellow, with *Rosa primula*, 'Canary Bird' or the climber 'Lawrence Johnston' leading the xanthic pack.

But yellow will not cut any Valentine mustard. Come 14 February your rose must be red or it counts for nothing. Love and sex are both universally red. Excitement and passion can only be coloured red – to the extent that the human metabolic rate is supposed to rise by 13.4 per cent on merely seeing the colour. Holidays are Red Letter Days when we paint the town red or for really special visitors roll out the red carpet. Scarlet Women are wicked but a lot of fun, and in these post-Desmond Morris days we all know that bright red lipstick mimics sexual arousal. This is all red and good, but the middle of February has no red flowers that I know of. For St Valentine's Day, the festival of couples that falls between the Christmas festival of families and Mothering Sunday, we cannot look to the garden for suitable red decoration.

(As I was writing the above my dog jumped up, banged my face and split my eye open. Blood everywhere. The dog's name is Red. So life mimics, um, art.)

Although the rose is the English national flower, this has been adopted from roses brought back from the Middle East by crusaders, rather than from our fourteen native wild roses. The Romans brought roses to the gardens of the Arabs and they had kept growing them after the Roman Empire got its come-uppance in the Dark Ages. We know that *Rosa gallica officinalis*, or the Apothecary's rose, was being grown outside Paris in the thirteenth century and this eventually became the red rose of Lancaster a couple of hundred years later. It seems probable that *R. alba* and *R. damascena* were also grown in Europe's gardens by that period. The white rose of York is almost certainly a hybrid of the damask rose *R. x damascena* (from Damascus) and the native *R. arvensis*, our pure white field rose. *R. gallica officinalis* is more of a dirty pink than a lover's red, but the choice was limited, and needs must when red drives.

The evolution of the Feast of Fowls into a human celebration of romance seems to have been invented in the slightly mannered affectations of the English court of the early 1400s, perhaps on the back of the French poem *The Romance of the Rose*, written a century earlier. Soon it became customary to exchange Valentine gifts and tokens with an existing or would-be lover. By the seventeenth century people would go out in the morning with a long strip of paper and write down the name of the first person they met (having arranged the night before that they would meet the person they fancied) which they would then wear in their hats as an emblem of love.

Valentine cards evolved from this, and by 1825 the Post Office was handling 200,000 more letters on 14 February than any other date in the year. By the mid-nineteenth century these cards had become very elaborate, with artificial flowers, lace decorations and real feathers stuck on. Here, I think, is the origin of the Valentine rose. It was never a real flower. That romantic red

Certainly every February I watch crows tumbling out of the sky in seemingly kamikaze spirals in order to impress the corvine object of their passion, whilst the songbirds get noticeably more vocal...

rose is simply another version of a Valentine card. Only the development of mass-produced 'artificial' real flowers in the post-war years enabled us to replace paper flowers with living ones, although to all intents and purposes they are as fake as their Victorian predecessors. So the bunch of a dozen red roses bought at the wildly inflated price of a dozen rose bushes should not be unfairly judged in comparison to 'real' roses: they are merely a symbol, a token confusingly similar to the thing that it represents.

There is a way to transcend the limitations of this artificiality. Last year my wife gave me a Valentine's present of a dozen red rose bushes, which was both preferable to the conventional phoney bunch and just as loaded with significance. Every year that they flower I will see each red rose as an individual Valentine and a token of love far better than a barrowload in February. So this year both give a red rose bush to your love and plant one at home in their honour. On St Valentine's Day they will show merely the bones of love, but come June and July they will flesh passion with colour and scent and continue to do so for many years – perhaps long after the original romance has faded away.

■ Red, shrub (i.e. not Hybrid Tea) roses that will grow easily and smell good include 'Charles de Mills', 'Conditorum', 'Tuscany Superb', 'Henri Martin', *R. rugosa* 'Hunter', 'Dupuy Jamain', 'Empereur du Maroc', 'Eugene Furst'. All these are 'old roses' and will mainly flower for one four-to-eight-week season.

■ 'English' roses are a modern breed developed by David Austin, which in general do not have the subtlety of old roses but do flower for a longer season and are extremely beautiful as well as robust and generally more healthy than many other roses. Good red, scented English roses include 'Prospero', The Squire', 'Othello' and 'The Prince'.

■ When you plant roses it is important to take trouble and treat them as though you were planting a tree. Dig a hole a yard in diameter and take out the top 9 inches. Break up the subsoil to the depth of a fork and mix in plenty of manure. Unless your topsoil is very good, mix some mushroom compost or well-rotted garden compost into it before planting the shrub. Spread the roots out and plant it deep enough so that the union – the knobbly bit where the rootstock is grafted to the above-ground rose – is below the surface. All potted roses are sold with this above ground, but that is to save money on pot size and not an indication of how it should be planted in the garden. Tread it in firmly and water it.

■ *Always* prune roses hard after planting, whether rampant climbers or miniatures in a pot. This promotes strong basal branches, vigour and flowering and will be the only hard prune a shrub rose ever needs.

■ Roses are best pruned about the time the daffodils are blooming, but do not get obsessed by the technicalities of this. Just cut out weak growth and tidy it to suit your eye. Remember the basic principle that the harder you cut back, the greater the resulting vigour will be.

■ The best way to ensure repeat flowering through the summer is to deadhead regularly, cutting the spent flower back to a bud or leaf rather than just pulling off the dead petals.

16.2.97 **Chalk**

I have dug graves in chalk, their sheer white walls blotting up blood from my hands as they were nicked by the embedded flints, making a curiously delicate pink. Most were neat little holes for caskets set with sad, inarticulate headstones in the little grassy churchyard I tended that was set around a knapped flint

The plants in the gardens, crops in the fields and flowers along the hedgerow, with their specific scents and colours, are all determined by what goes on below ground. Our past is rooted deep in the ground. So to love the soil, to luxuriate in it is to try to know the thing that made you.

church, but one was a deep, circular chalk tomb on a hilltop for my lovely dog, marked by a cairn of huge field flints as organic as steely tree roots.

Although I have not lived on chalk for twenty years now, whenever I drive through a chalky piece of England I am stabbed by a homesickness that is rooted entirely in that soft, starchy stone. It is the ground I know most intimately and the one least like any conception of what stone might be. But most people are hardly aware that chalk could be underfoot and are amazed at the vast whiteness of it so thinly covered by lawn, soil or street. In that it is invariably covered by a layer of topsoil, albeit often very thin, chalk is not truly a soil type. It is a subsoil or stone. But its influence over anyone that gardens above it is all-pervading. English chalk (there is no Welsh, Scottish or Irish chalk) is made from billions of shells and skeletons of tiny sea creatures, that began to be laid down 135 million years ago when the south-east corner of England sank. The resulting chalk belt covers a triangle from the Wash in the north-east across to Dorset in the south-west, with another outcrop in the Lincolnshire Wolds and on Humberside. Although these boundaries are strictly defined, the chalk belt covers millions of gardens.

We are all a product of our geology. The soil that we grew from shapes the way that we see the world as much as any other factor. It influences the material our homes are built of, the smell of the dust in summer and the extent to which puddles linger in winter. The trees that tower over our childhood and stalk the edge of adult myths and dreams are specific and shaped entirely by geology. The plants in the gardens, crops in the fields and flowers along the hedgerow, with their specific scents and colours, are all determined by what goes on below ground. Our past is rooted deep in the ground. So to love the soil, to luxuriate in it is to try to know the thing that made you.

I was raised on Hampshire chalk. It dictated the way that I knew the world and as much as anything else it *was* the world. I carried a lump of it in my pocket always, as much part of essential kit as handkerchief, string, penknife, a few old sweeties and perhaps a conker in season. Dry and dusty in summer, Hampshire chalk became a sticky white in winter. It was a rolling landscape covered with beech and hazel woods, yew, ash and elm (until 1976). Oaks hung on but never thrived, and birch and rhododendron were unknown.

The fields were good for barley, not wheat, so one had that extraordinary silken shifting of the green corn in June that the sturdier stems of wheat cannot mimic. The buildings were of brick and flint and in places greensand. Gardens were filled with flowering shrubs of all kinds but especially clematis, philadelphus, weigela, ceanothus, deutzia, forsythia and hebe. Roses never really prospered, herbs loved it, and all ericaceous plants were aliens.

In the main chalk is fast-draining, which makes it quick to warm up in spring, quick to freeze (bobbles of chalk like opaque ice-cubes) and easy to work. But it is thin soil and you need to add as much heavy organic material as possible to beef it up. Because it is so light and because the high lime content breaks humus down very fast, it is best to mulch any ground to be dug as thickly as possible in autumn, digging it in early spring just before you start sowing. The main chalk belt that runs diagonally across the south-eastern corner of the country is also the main area for riding stables, all of which have a vast surplus of strawy manure. This is perfect for chalky and limestone soils.

Occasionally chalk lies above a belt of clay, as in London and parts of Hampshire, deposited 70 million years ago and lying submerged for 55 million years until the emergence of the Alps pushed it surfacewards. The result is that although the chalk drains quickly, the water collects on top of the clay and makes the chalk above it into a white, sticky paste. Bramdean House, just outside Alresford, is a much-visited garden with exactly this soil type. Whilst the borders could be left alone during the sticky winter months, the kitchen garden, which supplied fruit and veg all the year round, became a white quagmire. The head gardener attacked the problem with raw barley straw. Now that straw-burning is illegal, this is not hard to get hold of. He used it in two ways, partly by laying it directly on all open ground that would be trod over in winter, creating strawy paths to mop up the mud which would be dug into the ground in spring, and partly by making huge compost heaps made solely of fluffed-up straw bales. He kept them moist and in twelve months they had rotted sufficiently to dig in like manure. There is one singular bonus to gardening on chalky clay: it is the ideal medium for earthworms which can reach a population of 300 per square yard, doing nothing but good, aerating the soil and pulling leaves down into the ground to eat, leaving decomposing plant material to enrich the soil and providing fodder for fungi and bacteria which the soil needs to recycle carbon and nitrogen which, in turn, plants need to grow.

The one quality that all 'good' gardens share is lavish attention to their soil. You may not be able to alter its basic character, but you can mollycoddle, bully and cajole it into a fertile ground for your garden. Most people under-estimate how much organic material they need to put back in each year, and no garden is so greedy for extra goodness as a new one being made over chalk. Every scrap of compostable material, from grass-cuttings to tea-bags, must be kept and composted, and enough mushroom compost or manure bought in to mulch the ground thickly twice a year in spring and autumn. For the average garden this is no big deal, and no more expensive than a night out twice a

The one quality that all 'good' gardens share is lavish attention to their soil. You may not be able to alter its basic character, but you can mollycoddle, bully and cajole it into a fertile ground for your garden.

year, but it is a mind-set that has to be taken on board.

Chalky soil is very alkaline. This means that its pH will be above 7, which is neutral. pH is a measure of the concentration of hydrogen ions in solution, so a pH of 7 has a hydrogen ion solution of one in ten million, or 10 to the power of -7. When the pH goes above 7, you enter a zone where many plants cannot survive, many flourish and many, such as vegetables and fruit, perform OK but not as well as they would at their ideal of 6.5. The main feature of alkaline soil is that phosphate, which encourages strong root growth and is important for crop ripening, is less available, so needs to be added as an annual light dressing in spring in the form of bonemeal, or fish, blood and bone.

It is not possible to make alkaline soil significantly more acid. I have nothing but contempt for the absurd attempts to make acidic peat beds for plants that grow awkwardly like circus freaks in a chalky environment. If you want a container, then grow stuff with specialized needs in pots, but the only practical response to a garden with chalky soil is to eliminate entirely all acid-loving plants such as heathers, rhododendrons, azaleas, many camellias, lupins and most lilies, and to make the most of the huge range of plants, especially flowering shrubs, that relish the given conditions. It is, for example, clematis heaven. Nothing becomes them so well as chalk, so long as lots of manure is added when they are planted and the roots are kept shaded and cool – which applies to any clematis planted anywhere. Lavender loves chalk, as do rosemary and all Mediterranean herbs. Chalk provides exactly the right balance between good drainage and hot, stony resilience for their shallow roots to feel completely at home.

Although most vegetables prefer a slightly acidic soil with a pH of 6.5, this is too nice a difference to be significant for the average gardener. Spinach, however, and all brassicas (cabbages, broccoli, cauliflower and brussels sprouts) actually prefer an alkaline soil so perform best on chalky soils. Mulberries thrive, and whilst most other fruit will only show discomfort in chalk by a slight yellowing of the leaves which is a symptom of lime-induced chlorosis and indicative of a failure to take up sufficient iron and manganese from the soil, raspberries and pears are traditionally not at all happy on chalk. Certainly I do not remember a decent crop of pears from the orchard at home but raspberries grew OK. The answer, to the point of repetition, is to add loads of muck. You can also top-dress annually with sulphate of ammonia, but there is a strong element of pissing into the wind in this.

Structurally, most garden hedges do very well on chalk. Yew and box are in their ideal environment. Beech grows very much better than hornbeam. Grass prefers more acidic conditions and quickly turns yellow in drought.

One last thing: chalk is curiously like cheese. When damp it has exactly the same brittle springiness as fresh parmesan.

Plants that will relish chalk:
▪ **Trees** Beech, yew, maple, horse chestnut, hawthorn, sorbus, Japanese cherry, mulberry.
▪ **Shrubs** Berberis, buddleia, box, ceanothus, cotoneaster, cornus, deutzia, euonymus, forsythia, fuchsia, hebe, philadelphus, potentilla, sambucus, senecio, lilac, weigela.
▪ **Perennials** *Acanthus spinosa*, anchusa, bergenia, cowslip, *campanula lactiflora*, *Clematis rectifolia*, dianthus, eremus, bearded iris, *Geranium pratense*, gypsophilia, hellebores, heuchera, linaria, paeonies, *Salvia nemerosa*, verbascum, veronica.

■**Annuals** Most. Wallflower, snapdragon, dianthus, linaria, convolvulus, echium, etc.
■**Climbers** Honeysuckle, a number of clematis, *Celastrus scandens*, *Eccremocarpus scaber*, ivy, *Hydrangea petiolaris*, jasmine, lavender, sweet peas, passionflowers, vines, *Solanum crispum*, wisteria.
■ **Herbs** Most.
■**Vegetables** All brassicas (cabbage, brussels sprouts, cauliflower, etc.)
■**Fruit** Most, but not blueberries, raspberries, pears.
■Chalky soil has a pH of 7.5-14.
■ **Pros:** drains fast, warms fast so good for early sowing, high calcium and lime content, organic material rots fast so responds very quickly to mulching and manuring, excellent for flowering shrubs.
■**Cons:** cools fast, can get very dry, nutrients leach fast, can make deep planting (for trees and hedges) hard work, not ideal for fruit or vegetables, a range of plants will not grow at all.

25.2.96 **Snow**

I don't care if you read this sitting outside in early spring sunshine sipping your Sunday morning coffee. I am writing with 9 inches of snow on the ground and however inappropriate, I'm not going to let the opportunity pass. The truth is that it is rare for us who live at an altitude of less than 1000 feet to get a good fall of snow despite all our Christmas card images of a Winter Wonderland. This year's fall was the first snow of any substance that my five-year-old son had been in. Every seasonal gardening book and columns like this are full of dire snow warnings and instructions on how to cope with it, but one rarely has a chance to put these skills to use. The last time that we had 6 inches or more of snow over a garden of mine was in 1990/91. My house had been sold and there was a two-month gap between exchange of contracts and completion. Every minute of those two months was marked by freezing temperatures and thick snow. My real concern was with the plants I wanted to take with us – which was almost impossible because of the frozen ground – and not with the very few evergreens that I would never see again.

So I went out the other morning and was for the first time in a position to practise what I have often preached. I solemnly knocked the snow off the branches of my box, yew and holly. It took ages and was boring. I have some seventy topiaried box plants, a couple of longish box hedges, a holly hedge, ten topiaried hollies, some yew hedges and twenty pieces of yew topiary. The snow was frozen so did not puff off like talcum powder. It stuck and had a habit of taking the end of the branch that it was stuck to. I began to wonder if one was not doing more damage clearing the snow than letting it be. What was worse, I made a staggeringly beautiful scene utilitarian and philistine. I felt like the Roundheads in Yeats and Sellars' *1066 And All That*, Right but Repulsive (as opposed to the Cavaliers, who were Wrong but Wromantic). In fact a lot of gardening advice is distinctly Roundhead in tendency, sacrificing beauty and romance for efficiency and control as if the garden is a New Model Army. But despite my zeal, I was unable to make the snowy garden ugly.

We all think that we know what snow looks like, know all the possibilities that it has to offer visually, but nevertheless it always comes as an entirely fresh delight. Nothing transforms the ordinary and familiar into the magical quite so reliably as snow. It glorifies the humble and commonplace, elevating the bare branches of hawthorn, hazel and birch into shining wonders as beautiful as a medieval cathedral and makes hedges and evergreen bushes flow anarchically. Almost all the rest is smoothed over, hidden, so these few wonders become the centre of our amazed attention. Of course one is always aware, in this country at least, that it is transient. Put off going out to have a look for an hour and the moment has passed. The sun goes in and the temperature rises and you are left with slush and another bleak winter's day with potentially years before the coincidence of a thick cover of snow, a garden and you all come together.

Snow is curiously like darkness in the way that it imposes a monochromatic blanket on the garden. Everything is made astonishingly simple; you can have your garden any colour you like so long as it is white. Actually that is too simplistic. So long as it is white and black. Snow is the only way that we get to notice black in the garden other than the odd exception like *Ophiopogon planiscapus* 'Nigrescens' (which I see the *RHS Encyclopedia of Garden Plants and Flowers* classes as purple. I don't). Just as Wittgenstein's white piece of paper seems to become grey when laid on freshly fallen snow, so the bare branches of most deciduous trees seem black against a snow-laden sky with the reflection of white from the ground. Water becomes mirrored tar and all shades of brown and grey are flattened to black. It is lovely, a visual representation of the simplification of life's complexities to, to... er, black and white.

There are a few black plants other than ophiopogon, or at least plants that have bits that are blackish. The bamboo *Phyllostachys nigra* has wonderful polished black stems as it matures. The dogwood *Cornus alba* 'Kesselringii' also has black stems. Ivy berries turn black and those of *Ilex crenata* are always black. The name of *Iris* 'Black Knight' gives a hint as to its colour, and *Iris* 'Sabre' is also a deep enough purple as to appear black. The viola 'Penny Black' is fabulously dark. I have never seen them, but apparently the catkins of *Salix melanostachys* are black. It is difficult to use these plants as part of a colour harmony as they get lost in a summer garden. But a corner that has them as novelties would be good fun.

I have used black slate as a surface for paths, seats and a table in a previous garden and it looks good in those capacities, although psychologically people shy from the thought. I have just been interrupted by my aforementioned five-year old son, ruddy-cheeked from making a snowman. 'What are you writing about?' I told him. 'Tell them about the rhyme,' he said. 'What rhyme?' 'You know, the one about Mary had a little lamb' (sweet, lilting singsong here) 'it was as black as charcoal, and when it stood upon its head, it whistled through its...'

'No, they don't want to hear about that.'

Oh, the snow, the driven snow, symbol of all that is pure and innocent!

A lot of gardening advice is distinctly Roundhead in tendency, sacrificing beauty and romance for efficiency and control as if the garden is a New Model Army.

Water becomes mirrored tar and all shades of brown and grey are flattened to black. It is lovely, a visual representation of the simplification of life's complexities to, to... er, black and white.

■ It is very nearly spring. The keen gardener will be like a sprinter in the blocks, desperate to get out there and be doing. As a rule there is nothing to be gained by rushing things at this stage – but you can start sowing seeds in seed trays. A propagator is ideal, but a warm, sunny windowsill makes a good substitute. No seed needs light to germinate, but once they are through they must have a reasonable light source to stop them growing spindly. Use seed compost rather than general-purpose and *never* use a peat-based compost for seeds. Buy the most rigid seed trays that you can find – flimsy ones are a waste of time. Water but do not drench and keep at a steady heat.

■ Most compost heaps lie unattended all winter. Now is a good time to turn them again so that they can reheat before being called upon for use as a mulch. Mulch your borders, trees and hedges at any stage in the next couple of months, as long as the ground is clear of perennial weeds, not frozen and damp. As with most rules of gardening, don't go by the chronological calendar but by the conditions: when they are right so is the time.

■ If you grow tomatoes, peppers, cucumbers or melons directly in the soil in your greenhouse, get on now with trenching. This means taking out a trench, putting in plenty of manure and replacing the topsoil, bringing in new if you have not done so in the past three or four years. This will give the ground time to settle and the manure to rot down a bit before you plant out in May and June.

2.3.97 **Clay**

Scoop up a handful of clay soil and it becomes a smear, a brick waiting to happen. It is heavy and lumpen, sullenly defying you. The simplest planting involves excavations of red putty that has to be chopped and beaten into small enough pieces to fit around roots. In summer it bakes hard so that a dug plot can be like the detritus of a brickyard, and in winter it saturates, its solid wetness gleaming like purple slabs of liver on a butcher's tray. And yet, of all the soils, clay is the most fertile. Treat it right and you can grow almost anything. In drought, it holds moisture well beneath the crusted surface and it is slow to cool down in autumn. It takes huge labour and skill to manage but returns this with a dividend of astonishing fecundity.

If you are uncertain whether you have clay soil or not, pick a dry handful up and squeeze it. If it holds together, it has clay in it. If it can be moulded and squeezed and holds the various shapes, then it is mainly clay. The trouble with clay is all to do with its structure. Clay particles are tiny, less than one sixteen-thousandth of an inch in diameter. To put that in some context, particles of sand are a thousand times bigger. These tiny bits of clay pack tightly together, leaving little space between them for air and organisms and roots to move through them. This compressed characteristic is also clay's greatest strength because it means that nutrients will not wash through the soil and there is a large surface area for the roots of plants to come into contact with and absorb the goodness, ensuring high fertility.

Technically, any soil that has more than 25 per cent clay particles is a clay soil. The balance should ideally be a mixture of clay, loam and sand. Loam is another of those words bandied around that is heavy on description and light on meaning. In horticultural jargon it describes soil that is both rich in organic matter and light and open. The proper, non-jargon meaning of loam is 'a rich soil comprised chiefly of clay and sand with added organic matter'. So if you start with clay you are nearer to a loam heaven than those poor unfortunates on sand or chalk, even if, in its loamless state, it is as near to garden hell as can be conceived. The seventh circle of loam can only be achieved through a combination of bacterial and root activity and the addition of organic matter. Regardless of the type of soil, loam will be created if you grow lots of plants and mulch or dig in plenty of organic goodness each year. Do not underestimate the simple value of roots in opening out a soil and providing organic material to enrich it. Beneath each square yard of a turnip crop is, so I am reliably informed, 12 miles of root. Even the roots of weeds do good as long as they are cut before they set seed.

My current garden is clay over gravel, which is an almost perfect combination, but the previous one was red clay over more clay. Coming from the chalklands of Hampshire, it was a shock to my system. The weather could be beautiful for days but the soil remained sticky, and every spadeful had to be chopped out of the ground as a solid cube. A wise neighbour who grew herbs commercially put me right. 'You have to humour it,' she said. The struggle I was having in trying to look intelligent without having a clue of what she was talking about must have been too transparent, because she explained patiently: 'Work it, feed it, put in as much organic material as you can at least once a year. Pander to its every whim. Ignore the calendar and do what it needs when it is ready. And when it is ready, you had better drop everything and get on with it, because it will bake hard in days. It will break your back and occasionally your spirit, but if you humour it, it will never break your heart or your bank balance.'

'Humouring' clay soil means fundamentally altering its structure. Those tiny particles have to be levered apart. There are two ways to do this and ideally one should do both in tandem. The first and most important is by adding manure or compost. It does not matter what you use but you simply cannot add too much. It has been calculated that you need at least 10 lbs per square yard just to maintain the organic content of a soil, and obviously more to improve it. The second is by digging in horticultural grit or sharpsand. This is incredibly effective and to all intents and purposes permanent, so only needs doing once. But the tiny bags of grit that are sold at garden centres are hopelessly inadequate for the task. You need to fork in a layer 2–4 inches deep, which works out at a cubic yard or ton for every 3–4 square yards

Waylay a gaggle of narcissistic lads on their way to the gym and give them a spade each with a promise of pain in return for your gain. And the calories! My dear, they just fall away.

covered. You have to think big. If you have access for a lorry to tip a load that can be barrowed to the relevant sites, then this is the only viable way to set about it. Buying in bulk like this is cheap, too.

There is much debate (well, in certain rather sad, isolated circles) about the relative virtues of applying organic material to clay soils as a mulch or dug into the ground. I think that one should do both. Dig new sites well, mixing in manure to the subsoil. Easily said but very, very hard work. Waylay a gaggle of narcissistic lads on their way to the gym and give them a spade each with a promise of pain in return for your gain. And the calories! My dear, they just fall away. This will improve the drainage of the soil but also stop compaction. If you avoid standing on the earth, then it should only need doing every ten years or so. In the vegetable garden it is best to dig bare soil over in the autumn with a spade, leaving it in slabs so that it has all winter to weather before breaking it into a tilth that you can sow in the following spring.

When it comes to spring cultivation of clay, timing is absolutely of the essence. You have to be intimate with the soil so that you know when it is ready for you. This is always at most a matter of days and often one of hours when it is dry enough to be worked and soft enough to respond to you. If you cultivate when it is too wet you will compact it, making the situation steadily worse. If it is only a tiny bit too wet it will 'work' but you are liable to be left with masses of round lumps both the size and hardness of golf balls. If it is too dry it breaks into curiously angular, square-edged lumps, mocking the vain notion of a viable tilth. Do you catch the voice of bitter experience here? Reader, listen well, I know whereof I speak by dint of bitter experience.

Getting it right means going out every morning and testing the ground, spotting the signs and watching weather forecasts with the intensity of a deep-sea fisherman. You have a job, other interests, a Life? Get your priorities right. Clay soil will brook no such feebleness. Go sick, ignore the wedding/child's birthday/football match or ravages of flu. Be ruthless or be condemned to a season of rock-hard, untillable soil. I am not exaggerating about this. Clay is the most demanding of taskmasters.

The only way round this is to build up a loam that is an artificial layer above the clay, not dependent on such a tyrannical timetable. The best way to do this is by mulching really thickly each autumn and spring. It is better to do this with anything organic, be it straw, bracken, bark, grass cuttings or whatever, than not to do it at all, but good garden compost or mushroom compost is best. You will find that all the most evangelistic compost-makers have experience of the demands of clay, forced by brutal necessity to manufacture as large a quantity of good-quality compost as quickly as possible.

For vegetables or herbs in particular it may be best to focus this process on

Getting it right means going out every morning and testing the ground, spotting the signs and watching weather forecasts with the intensity of a deep-sea fisherman. You have a job, other interests, a Life? Get your priorities right.

a few clearly defined areas and to make raised beds. This is really no more than a self-conscious application of the process above. The basic principle of raised beds is that, once prepared, they are never, ever, stood on. In consequence they must be narrow enough so that you can comfortably reach the middle from either side, which, in practice means a width of no more than 5 feet. The ground should be dug as deeply as stamina and strength will allow, with huge quantities of goodness mixed in. Then the soil from the paths between the beds is piled on to the beds themselves, raising them up. This can be an informal mounding, or the edges can be defined by boards or bricks. A mulch is laid on top of this, which is renewed each year. The result is a growing area as much as a foot above the path level and a loose, well-drained soil.

It has to be stressed that it is only worth going to this trouble – and all this mulching, manuring and digging is a serious amount of hard work – because the end result is soil that everything luxuriates in. The rewards are overwhelmingly measurable.

One can apply finesse to the details of this process. Horse manure is better than cow manure for lightening the soil. Lime spread thinly over a clay soil helps to break it down. Grazing rye sown in October and dug into the ground the following April will have developed a huge network of fibrous roots that open the clay, as well as the green top providing nutrients as it decomposes. But finesse presupposes you are doing the right thing anyway. If you are not doing so with abandon already, put all your energies into mulching and getting together sufficient material to do the job.

If you are not accustomed to its ways, it is surprising how slow clay is to heat up in spring, and mulching on to cold soil will only insulate the coldness in and delay that heating process. Nevertheless, better to mulch at the wrong time than not at all. Slowly you will build up a loamy topsoil that will be subservient to your whims rather than being left to the imperious tyranny of Mistress Clay.

A lot of plants grow very well in clay. This list is a selection.

Trees

■Deciduous: maple, chestnut, alder, birch, hornbeam, hawthorn, ash, holly, crab apple, poplar, oak, cherry, willow, lime.

■Conifers: firs, larch, juniper, pine, yew, thuja.

Shrubs

■ Abelia, berberis, chaenomeles, choisya, cornus, corylus, cotinus, cotoneaster, deutzia, escallonia, forsythia, genista, hypericum, mahonia, magnolia, osmanthus, philadelphus, potentilla, pyracantha, ribes, roses, skimmia, spiraea, viburnum, weigela.

Perennials

■ *Acanthus mollis, Ajuga reptans, Aruncus dioicus*, astilbe, caltha, *Cardamine pratense, fitipendula, Gunnera mannicata*, henerocallis, hosta, inula, ligularia, Lythrum, *Peltiphyllum pelatatum*, phormium, polygonum, rheum, rodgersia, troilus.

Climbers

■*Campsis, Celastrus scandens*, clematis, *Euonymus fortunei*, Golden hop, sweet pea, honeysuckle, *Parthenocissus*, passionflower, *Vitis cognetiae*, wisteria.

Annuals

■ Love-Lies-Bleeding, foxglove, sunflower, impatiens, *Limnanthes douglasii*, lobelia, mimulus, forget-me-not, ornamental maize (*Zea mays*).

Bulbs (despite the adaptability of the following, plant with extra grit)
■ Snowdrops, daffodils, Darwin tulips, *Anemone memorosa*, camassia, *Crinum* x *powellii*, *crocosomia, eranthis*.

3.3.96 **Species Roses**

A year ago I wrote in this column of my growing fascination with species roses and my desire to acquire some and grow them in my garden. On St Valentine's Day I received not only a present of two dozen red rose bushes (twelve *Rosa. moyesii* and twelve *R.* 'Scharlachglut', both with flowers as scarlet as arterial blood) but also, as a kind of supplement, three plants each of ten different types of species rose. I loved the thought of the bloody two dozen but the species roses are the things that best feed my hungry horticultural heart.

What is it with species roses that makes them so alluring? They do not have great voluptuous flowers like centifolias, do not last long like almost all modern roses, for the most part confining their flowering to a brief June flurry. Many are lax or sprawling of habit which makes them sound like a degenerate bachelor uncle. But like a DBU, they are easily loved.

This present came bare-root and hot-foot from the nursery, bony, spiny bundles tied together with string, sticking out of used fertilizer sacks. No marketing budget or packaging or point-of-sales devices – just the actual thing itself in spiky evidence. It was rather like receiving a tired and emotional porcupine as a present. Gingerly the plants are lifted out of the sack and laid out for admiration. There is not much to see. But what there is is informative and vital, and invisible if you buy your plants in pots from the garden centre. Roots. Healthy, strong roots. Everything that happens above ground is entirely dependent upon this. Too often one buys what seems to be, judging by its upper storey, a flourishing plant, only to find that it fails, and on a post-mortem you discover that the roots were inadequate. Bare-root means just that: the plants arrive buff-naked with roots exposed. This is good for the eye, good for reassurance, but bad for the roots if left exposed for more than a brief moment of inspection. The first thing to do is to stand them in a bucket of water while you prepare a trench to heel them into. It is the tiny, hair-like roots growing off the sturdier bits that one is trying to protect, rather than the solid anchors that are more apparent.

Once heeled in alongside the leeks, my species roses stuck out of the soil like ten bare posies. There was *R. hugonis*, just a bunch of brown twigs,

This present came bare-root and hot-foot from the nursery, bony, spiny bundles tied together with string, sticking out of used fertilizer sacks. No marketing budget or packaging or point-of-sales devices – just the actual thing itself in spiky evidence.

R. cantabrigiensis, stems covered with baby bristles and the occasional vicious thorn, *R. sericea pteracantha*, a curiously drab brown all over, giving no hint of the glorious red fins that its thorns are to become, catching the light like a medieval stained-glass window. *R. wilmottiae* has weird and beautiful thorns when bunched all together, each zigzagging away from the one above and below, making a graceful geometric pattern. *R. moschata* and *R. complicata* are both green-stemmed, even in the heart of winter, but *R. californica* plena is orange, *R. wintonensis* red and *R. farreri persetosa* 'Nan of Painswick' a deep alizarin. Finally there was *R. pimpinellifolia* 'Double Yellow', so prickly that it was almost bristly. These roses used to be called *R. spinosissima*, which more accurately describes their appearance. Unless you are an expert, only *R. sericea pteracantha* instantly gives itself away for what it is in this raw, unfledged state, so if they are not all clearly labelled (which they should be) you must do it straight away.

These were a gift, remember, so I did not choose them. To have an influx of unasked-for plants on this scale transforms things and instantly introduces a key I had failed to provide. Species roses are tough and easily grown and should last for at least twenty-five years. They will reach 'maturity' in three or four years, but will flower this summer and go on increasing in size for perhaps ten years, all becoming substantial shrubs. So they will make a lasting difference to this place, just as a new wall or staircase would indoors.

There is no reason why species roses should not be mingled carelessly in with other plants just like any other shrub rose, but I shall plant most of these all together on the edge of the bit that is called the Wild Garden. It is actually rather a Tame Garden at the moment, but a bit of spiky, sprawling, lax habit might make it wilder. Of course species roses have flowers, wonderful, delicate flowers, and that is the main reason one grows them. All of my lot will flower just once, although this brevity is compensated a little by the hips that the flowers become.

The first in bloom will probably be *R. cantabrigiensis*, which has pale, primrose-yellow flowers towards the end of May. The foliage is unusually long and fern-like, turning bronze in autumn. This was a chance seedling between *R. hugonis* and *R. sericea* found in Cambridge Botanic Garden in 1931, and is tougher than either of its parents. *R. hugonis* is pretty similar to its offspring, but has smaller leaves and slightly darker yellow flowers, also in spring. Both plants genuinely belong to spring, having the freshness of flower and leaf that is rare in a rose. They are single-flowered, but the Scotch burnet rose, *R. pimpinellifolia* 'Double Yellow' is, as its name indicates, double. The flowers are small and bright yellow, becoming hips that are a wonderful black.

R. farreri 'Nan of Painswick' is identical to *R. farreri persetosa* or the

Curiously drab brown all over, giving no hint of the glorious red fins that its thorns are to become, catching the light like a medieval stained-glass window.

Threepenny-bit rose and was, according to the grower, Lindsay Bousefield of Acton Beauchamp Roses, found by chance in a garden belonging to 'Nan' in Painswick, Gloucestershire. So there you are. According to Peter Beales it has 'fern-like leaves that turn purple and red in the autumn, and hips, produced in profusion, are bright orange-red. These features, together with its habit of growth, are perhaps more important than its small lilac-pink flowers.'

The sum of any individual species rose tends to amount to less than the whole. That is the great charm of these roses. In this respect they are the exact opposite of Hybrid Teas – which is what most people still think of when putting a picture to the word 'rose'.

R. wintoniensis has glaucous foliage, rather like the much better-known *R. glauca*. The flowers are shocking pink, balanced by the bright red stems, and will, in turn, become great clusters of flagon-shaped hips that have a curious purplish bloom.

R. wilmottiae has tiny flowers but they have a big scent, and the tiny leaves are also scented when crushed. Its hips are, like everything about the plant, delicate and miniature. Having said that, it will eventually make a bush about 6 feet round, so it is not a miniature rose, just fine-boned.

R. californica 'Plena' is much more robust, becoming perhaps 10 feet around, and has substantial, almost hollyhock-like dark pink flowers, looking a bit like a *gallica*. Although still commonly labelled as *californica*, it is properly *R. nutkana* 'Plena'. By either or any name it is as sweet. A tip is to prune one-third of it right to the ground each year, encouraging it to throw up red stems, rather like Dogwood.

You can do this with *R. sericea pteracantha* as well, although the new stems will make translucent, bristly shoots. This shrub is famous for its huge, webbed thorns, and that is the best thing about them, but *R. sericea* is most remarkable for the fact that it is the only rose with four petals. Every other rose has five. The flowers are white, flushing yellow.

Last, but not least, will be *R. complicata*, which I have grown before in amongst gallicas which are the dominant part of its parentage, crossed with a Dog rose. It has shocking pink flowers and can be treated as a climber, getting up to 15 feet or so if supported. I am longing to be duly shocked by it, round about my birthday at the beginning of July.

■ Heeling-in is a term describing the temporary planting of bare-root plants to protect them until they can be placed in their final planting position. I use the vegetable patch for heeling in because the soil is rich and deep and well dug, so the process is very straight-forward, but wherever you choose, make a trench sufficiently deep and wide to completely bury the roots of whatever it is, be it tree or small herbaceous plant.

■ Species roses are ideal for both the novice gardener and less than perfect soil. They are robust and unfussy. Nevertheless, they must be planted in a decent-sized hole with some manure, making sure that the union of rootstock and stems is well below the ground level. Always prune a newly planted rose right down to a couple of buds above the ground. This ensures strong growth from the base and will quickly make for a much healthier, bigger plant, however drastic it seems at the time.

17.3.96 **Allotments**

Allotments are never still. They flicker past, always from trains, strange slivers of cultivated sidings with scarecrow sheds, from cars as you skirt round a town, appearing suddenly at the turn of a street as an unlikely corner of patchwork urban horticulture. Modern allotments have the tattered monochrome of a stage-set for an Ealing comedy, a throwback to a time when men cycled to work with bicycle clips and wore raincoats rather than blousons against the wet, when a cap was flat rather than baseball, and deep-freezes belonged only in cold stores. It is an age tinged with back-to basics nostalgia and stained with the dreary predictability of a black and white Sunday afternoon. Yet this is real end-of-the-millennium life. Allotments belong to the age of the Internet, Aquarius and women priests. They are not even called allotments but are officially known as (wait for it) 'leisure gardens', a nomenclature about as likely to catch on as the Community Charge. Even the jumble of sheds made up from old sash-windows, salvaged corrugated iron, doors and tabletops look less like a collection of outdoor privies than a New Age settlement.

Allotments by any other name have a long tradition founded on dramatic changes in the English countryside. Until the eighteenth century much of lowland Britain was farmed under the open-field system. This meant that people farmed strips of land, often dotted widely around the local landscape, in common fields undefined by hedges or boundaries. It allowed for a peasant system of life whereby a household could raise their own crops as well as work for and with other people. It gave them a stake in the rural landscape and economy. Then the combined process of enclosures and industrialization, especially in the 100 years between 1750 and 1850, removed most people from that stakeholding and put enormous power into the hands of a few landowners. For example, between 1760 and 1818 there were 3500 Acts of Parliament enclosing 5 million acres of land. It was a form of disenfranchisement, and led to an increase in rural poverty alongside the better-documented growth in industrialized slum towns.

The poor became subject to poor relief, payable by parishes, and the allocation of land for inmates of poorhouses to grow their own vegetables was a means of defraying the costs of supporting them. Gradually, throughout the nineteenth century, more and more land – although a tiny fraction of that which had been enclosed – was allotted to the 'labouring poor' as a means of feeding them. So we

Modern allotments have the tattered monochrome of a stage-set for an Ealing comedy, a throwback to a time when men cycled to work with bicycle clips and wore raincoats rather than blousons against the wet, when a cap was flat rather than baseball, and deep-freezes belonged only in cold stores.

should see allotments not as the remnants of the 1950s, along with warm beer, maiden aunts, church bells and cricket on the village green, but of a medieval system of agriculture and society and millions and millions of acres of strip-fields.

The Victorians latched on to allotments as a means of keeping the degenerate labouring classes away from demon drink. If a man could be encouraged to spend his evenings on an allotment, despite having worked physically for twelve hours during the day, he might be discouraged from indulging himself in drunkenness. To an extent, there was a logic in this as the allotment provided a place to go other than the pub, to escape the impossibly cramped conditions of the home. But it was a patronizing, inhumane stance.

Food was always the motive for allotments, from their earliest form. As ever, the need for colour and aesthetic pleasure in the lives of 'The Poor' was underestimated. People used their allotments to grow flowers as well as turnips. In the 1860s it was estimated that as many as 30,000 people gardened 10,000 plots on Hunger Hill in Nottingham, and they staged the first rose show in Britain on Easter Monday, 1860. Ever since, the tradition of growing flowers for cutting, particularly dahlias and chrysanthemums, has been part of every allotment holding.

At the start of the First World War there were half a million allotments in Britain. By 1918, as a result of the attempt to starve Britain into defeat with U-boats, this number had trebled. It was estimated that over 2 million tons of vegetables were produced on allotments in 1918. This huge increase in allotment gardening had a profound social effect. Until then allotments were specifically for the 'labouring population' and were seen as a kind of poor relief, focused mainly on rural areas. Now the urban middle class had been introduced to vegetable gardening and they found that they liked it. Since then, allotments have had an urban emphasis. There has been a steady decline since 1918, and at the last count, in 1978, there were 49,000 acres and 490,000 plots. The National Society of Allotment and Leisure Gardeners guesses that this has fallen to 35,000–40,000 acres, although numbers are holding steady.

An allotment allows the tower-block descendants of the medieval peasant to farm their own piece of Britain. While they do so they are freemen. This is important. It is empowering. Nobody now believes that it is a form of poor relief (even if it were politically correct to do so) because growing your own veg is an absurdly expensive pastime. The rewards are in peace of mind, fresh air, hard work, an atavistic connection to the earth and perhaps, at the end of it, a product that really tastes, as opposed to most supermarket pap. I met a man some years ago who said that he had been a 'farmer' in his native Uganda, but had fled from Idi Amin. Now he lived in a room in London's East End. Every day he made a fifty-minute journey involving three buses to his allotment. I found out later that he was chief of a large tribe and 'farmed' tens of thousands

So we should see allotments not as the remnants of the 1950s, along with warm beer, maiden aunts, church bells and cricket on the village green, but of a medieval system of agriculture and society and millions and millions of acres of strip-fields.

of acres. This had shrivelled down to 300 square yards of black soil, but, for the moment it was enough. It provided him with his sanity, he said.

Until very recently allotments resisted Eurocentricity and were measured in poles. Rent was determined by the pole, perch or rod, all synonymous for a piece of ground of about 30 square yards. Whilst there was no determining size, most plots were 10 poles or 300 square yards. There were 40 poles to a furlong, which was the standard length of a field strip. An acre is 40 x 4 poles. Only connect.

As a result of the original parish poor law funding, allotments have always been under the control of local councils. An allotment is allocated as an Act of Parliament and councils have a legal obligation to provide the land. If they wish to move an allotment they must exchange it for land of similar quality in a similarly suitable location. In this Brave New World of fag-end Torydom, some councils have been 'tendering out' allotments. In Hereford, the allotments closest to my home, this has had the happy effect of the allotment holders setting up their own cooperative to run the 286 plots that the city has spread over ten sites. Given that the rents are still paid to the council (at a mean of about £15 per year per 10-pole plot, although this varies enormously from region to region) and that there are no amenities of any sort other than the land itself, allotments hardly present a business opportunity for the Enterprise Society.

It is, of course, the land itself that matters, not as potential, but as its cultivated self. We may not need the food it produces but we desperately need to feel that we can till our own piece of earth, albeit rented from the council, and it is as a link to our shared agricultural past that allotments are most valuable. The cabbage stalks and ranks of runner-bean poles and squatter camp of sheds are not a hangover from quaint post-war Britain, but the last shreds of peasant independence clung to from medieval unenclosed land.

■ The nearest equivalent to the allotment in the U.S. is the community garden. The community garden is primarily a phenomenon of densely populated cities since most suburban and small town homeowners have space enough for vegetable and flower gardens. Often community gardens are municipally sponsored, and some cities have included them into their master plans. Financial sponsorship is usually necessary because the potential problems of turning an abandoned city lot into a garden are numerous: pollution, theft and vandalism, lack of an irrigation supply, questions of security and insurance, to cite some of the most vexing. Moreover, the would-be participant may not have the required tools nor the basic gardening skills to achieve success without which a commitment is not sustained. Educational programs, generally staffed by volunteers, have in many cases helped to overcome start-up hurdles. Despite these difficulties, community gardens are thriving in many U.S. cities.

■ Now is an excellent time to start any kind of vegetable garden. Do not attempt to double-dig it now – save that for the autumn if you must. By all means add well-rotted manure or compost, but not strawy, unrotted stuff – leave that for the winter too. Do not worry if it is very weedy – that is a good sign, showing that the ground is fertile. Clear the weeds and turn the topsoil over, working up a good tilth. Sow a green manure such as rye grass or mustard over areas that you are not ready for, which will keep the weeds down and enrich the soil.

■ The real secret of vegetable gardening is to keep on top of the situation, doing a little often rather than in great bursts of enthusiastic activity followed by weeks of neglect. I would say that if you cannot guarantee at least one visit during the week and a few hours each weekend regularly, then it is not worth taking an allotment on.

30.3.97 **Paradise**

The Garden of Eden is the archetypal Paradise, and presumably, assuming that no one intelligent enough to read the *Observer* is stupid enough to be a Christian fundamentalist, Eden was taken from the Greeks who we know derived the notion of Paradise from the gardens and parks that surrounded the Persian royal palaces. This immediately raises the inherent contradictory aspect of Paradise in that it is the absolute property of all who dream and yet is private and exclusive of anything that – for whatever reason – offends us, which in the case of the Persian court was just about everybody. In fact the whole point of Eden was that everybody – both of them – was excluded. More than any other human activity, gardening is a struggle to manifest and re-create this lost perfection.

Gardens are a hunt for that state we once knew – in childhood. This theme has fed poets for centuries, but none with better results than the seventeenth century Metaphysical writers. In his poem 'Corruption' Henry Vaughan writes: 'Man...sighed for Eden, and would often say/Ah! what bright days were those?/... and still Paradise lay/ in some green shade, or fountain.' Thomas Traherne – lovely, Holy Fool Traherne, wrote in his *Centuries of Meditation* of the existing world as Paradise, transformed to Eden by the power of love. His whole thesis is that we are born with 'open Eys' and lose the power to see as we are corrupted by the ways of the world.

Gardens have a simplicity and purity unsullied by the vileness of man. There is a sense of rhythm that is all but lost in modern daily life. Without that annual rhythm we live in limbo, cut off from the cycle of life inevitably flowing all around us.

This is fine, yet has the faults of coyness inherent in the biblical Eden story. The truth is that Adam and Eve were booted out of Paradise for acknowledging each other's sexiness. Lust, that terrible enemy of Christianity since Augustinian times, precluded Paradise. But that is the central flaw in Christianity. Any half-decent Paradise would include lust – and lots of it. Good gardens – Paradise gardens – must be about sex. Not fucking exactly, but we are in that territory. It has long been my theory that a branch of our more celebrated gardeners of all three sexes garden with such vivacity and verve in lieu of sex, whilst the very best – such as Derek Jarman – do so as a sexy celebration. A really good garden should turn you on. A garden at its perfect pitch of beauty is a celebration of fecundity in its most sensual and sensuous form. To divorce this from human sensual response is almost perverted and yet, astonishingly, gardening has managed to be hijacked by

In fact the whole point of Eden was that everybody – both of them – was excluded. More than any other human activity, gardening is a struggle to manifest and re-create this lost perfection.

Gardens have a simplicity and purity unsullied by the vileness of man. There is a sense of rhythm that is all but lost in modern daily life.

the loin-dead. Half the self-styled good gardens of this country are dull as Hell, dried up, thoroughly unsexy places.

Yet it is pointless to try to agree on what Eden should be like – it must be idiosyncratic and quirky if it is to work. My sexy Heaven might be your Hell. Paradise cannot be configured by rote, which is why all the books pouring off the presses telling you how to put your garden together should be read for titbits of information and then thrown away. Anything other than your own thing is not worth doing.

But we in the temperate north do share a generalized view of exotica, and most northern people will approximate an earthly Paradise as featuring heat, tropical lushness, turquoise sea and palm-fringed stretches of beach. Whilst I am innately suspicious of attempts to re-create holiday experiences in general, there is no reason why the very otherness of sub-tropical planting cannot do the paradisical trick if that is your bent. The essence of it is a luxuriance of foliage with splashes of vivid colour and you can achieve that perfectly well in an ordinary back garden.

Foliage first. You want plants with leaves as big as possible. If you have naturally boggy conditions, then this is going to be easy. None grows bigger in our climate than the Brazilian *Gunnera manicata*, whose leaves will reach 6 feet across and 8 feet high. They grow best in boggy soil but can be restricted for a small garden by the simple device of planting them in a border, whose comparative dryness will curtail them without losing the essence of the plant. Gunnera is tenderish, and must be protected from frost by a covering of straw or a carpet. Hostas are also bog-lovers but are as untropical as you can get, relishing cool, wet shade. Nevertheless they have the right lushness. Go for the biggest ones like *H. sieboldiana*, *H.* 'Blue Piecrust', *H.* 'Devon Giant' or *H.* 'Elata'. *Rodgersia podophylla* can be grown in a shady border or by water's edge and has flowery plumes above horse-chestnut-shaped leaves. *Astilbe rivularis* is much bigger than the common or garden astilbes that one ordinarily sees with 6-foot plumes and dark green leaves with red veins. The American Skunk Cabbage stinks like rotten cabbage but looks divine, with bright yellow banana-like spathes growing out of wet mud in spring, followed by great leaves like spinach on steroids. *Peltiphyllum peltatum*, or Umbrella Plant, also starts out quite differently to its final form, with the pink flowers growing on bristly stems bare of any leaf. But when the leaves do come they are spectacular, great scallops 12–18 inches across. I have none of these plants in my current garden because it is essentially dry, but I grew all of them by a large pond we used to have. Just writing this list brings back the incredible pleasure they gave me then.

If your garden is dry, then you can still get big foliage, although you will have to water more than usual. The most exotic of the lot is the banana, *Musa ensete*. After a few years it should develop leaves 14 feet long and nearly 3 feet

wide from a stubby trunk, finally getting to about 18 feet high. It grows incredibly fast and can easily be grown from seed. It needs full sun and a very rich soil with really lots of watering in summer, which is tough on all those within the controls of the more incompetent water authorities. *M. basjoo* is hardier but is not so wind-resistant as *M. ensete*. Both types will need heavy protection from winter frosts and are ideally grown in large pots which are sunk into the ground for summer and brought indoors to a conservatory in winter.

Cannas have become dead trendy of late, a Hawaiian shirt among the brogues and tweeds of conventional gardens. Having both large, lush leaves and extraordinarily bright colours, they exemplify paradisical exotica. They are herbaceous, but their rhizomes will need protecting from frost and in cold areas they should be treated like dahlias. Plant them in full sun in very rich soil. *Canna* 'Firebird' has red flowers that shout, and *C. generalis* 'Wyoming' dark purple leaves with apricot flowers. *C. lutea* has bright yellow flowers. Altogether more refined, though still literally fantastic, is *Melianthus major*, which comes from South Africa and is grown for its deeply cut, chalky blue-green leaves. It will reach 8 feet by the end of summer and will survive winter in a sunny and very sheltered site, but is best cut to the ground around Christmas, mulched with straw and allowed to grow back again in spring. It is one of those unfortunate plants that people are snobbish and elitist about (talking a load of bollocks about 'real gardeners') but one can hardly blame melianthus for that stigma. I do not grow it (though I would like to) but I do grow a vaguely similar plant, *Cynara cardunculus*, the cardoon, which is almost as lovely and terribly easy to grow. It is tough, will reach 6 feet, and although a mainstay of kitchen gardens and herbaceous borders, can be extremely exotic.

Bamboos are an easy way to mimic a garden Paradise. I was on Tobago (Robinson Crusoe's island) a few months ago and the bamboos there were staggering – 50 feet high and as thick as my waist. You cannot grow those here, but you can grow a range of good ones. Remember, bamboos are grasses and tend towards the moist, sunny condition that grasses like. Given the right situation, some can spread as voraciously as couch-grass too, so be choosy. If you want to contain bamboo, avoid species of sasa and pleioblastus. The phyllostachys varieties lose their sheaths early, so the stems are visible and grow from the ground up, whilst arundinarias produce their leaves and branches from the top downwards once they are full-grown and hang on to their sheaths longer. *Phyllostachys nigra* is rightly regarded as the Black Prince of bamboos, with its shiny ebony stems growing to 8 feet. *Indocalamus tessellatus* will only reach 5 feet, but is good for a shaded site, fast-growing, and has broader leaves than most, so fits the exotic bill. No bamboo flourishes in wind and the phyllostachys are particularly touchy about this.

Last but not least in this brief list of a phony exotic Paradise are the ferns. If you are lucky enough to live in the shelter of the Gulf Stream you can grow (probably already are growing) tree ferns, *Dicksonia antarctica*. This is instant tropical rain-forest, Jurassic Park out the back door. But you must have very high rainfall and warm winters. If you do not have those climatic provisos but live on acidic soil, then you could grow *Osmunda regalis*, the Royal fern, which will grow to a majestic 6 feet if planted near water's edge or in exceptionally rich, well-watered soil. It is a native, perhaps proving Thomas Traherne's point that 'We need nothing but open Eys, to be Ravished like the Cherubims'.

■ By far the greatest enemy to exotic or tender plants is cold wind. You cannot change the climate but you can provide shelter, particularly from winds that blow from the north or east. Protection is greatest if you filter wind rather than block it.

■ Any plant with large leaves will need a lot of water. But there is a big difference between a plant like a banana that needs a lot of water to replace the evaporation from its huge leaves and a plant like gunnera that likes bogginess. A hosepipe replaces rainfall that will be quickly washed away, whereas wet ground is a much more permanent state of affairs that the plant has evolved to make the most of.

One of the best ways of conserving water is to minimize evaporation from the ground by mulching. Anything is better than nothing, but an organic compost is probably best of all. Keep mulch clear of the bark of trees and shrubs as this can damage them. Gravel is particularly good around large-leaved succulent plants like hostas because it deters slugs.

■ April is the month to plant or transplant evergreens. Take stock of the structural evergreen plants in the garden and consider moving. A minor adjustment can make a big difference, and now is the moment to do it.

3.4.94 Novice Gardening

If the weather is good, crowds will pour into all the gardens opening up again to the public after the winter closure. I am likely to be among them. But I wonder if any of them share the same conflicting emotions of wonder and iconoclasm? Somehow visiting grand, cathedral-like gardens, with their slow-moving huddles of hushed supplicants, seems a long way from the easy prayer of actually gardening.

It is surely a form of prayer to be wholly absorbed in a physical process, aware of all the sensations and details of the job but free from all the burdens and constraints of time, human pettiness and suffering. This is my experience of gardening. I am not a Christian. But in my garden at Easter I know that I can be closer to a real meaning of the Passion story, and to God, than in any church service I have attended.

I realize that I have just lost half my readership. The British get shifty-eyed as soon as God comes into things. Too bad. Take the spirituality and poetry out of gardening, and what is left behind makes train-spotting look racy.

Whilst I might be forgiven for this line on Easter Sunday, I know that it will not do when I am stopped in the street by someone my own age wanting help in their garden. They want practical answers. But they very rarely ask me specific questions that require specific answers. The underlying question is always 'Where do I begin?' I have received hundreds of letters from people asking me to 'solve' the problem of their garden. I suppose one way of stopping these would be to write back urging them to Dig and Pray. Praise the Lord with a Fork.

The questioners want directions ('Can you tell me the quickest way to a beautiful garden please?') and I just want them to garden. I don't care what their

Somehow visiting grand, cathedral-like gardens, with their slow-moving huddles of hushed supplicants, seems a long way from the easy prayer of actually gardening.

Take the spirituality and poetry out of gardening, and what is left behind makes train-spotting look racy.

beautiful garden please?') and I just want them to garden. I don't care what their garden looks like as long as they love it. Everything follows from that. So here is a practical list for the novice that should take you to the point when the doing of it – which on Easter Sunday I am allowed to call prayer – is more important than the form that the doing results in.

1. Go outside. Notice things. Where is the sun? Which bit of the garden feels most pleasant? Why? What is growing already? What are the neighbours growing? It is not necessary to know the names of these things, but enough that some things are clearly more successful than others.

2. Stay outside as long as possible and return as often as possible. There is more to do than you can ever find time for. Both give in to and be driven by this. Stop seeing the garden as a place to order and conquer by rote. Forget quick fixes. You are in this for life.

3. Choose a small piece of ground and dig it. It doesn't matter where it is, although it would make life easier if it got the sun for at least half the day. Notice the soil. Pay attention. Break it down until you can run your hands through it like gathering hanks of hair.

4. Buy some seeds – all the different types of lettuce that you like to eat – radish, carrot, hardy annuals such as sunflower, poppy, nigella, anchusa, herbs like borage, parsley, chives. Sow them in drills – lines ruled in the soil and then covered over, or scatter them at random.

5. Care for them. Trust your intuition and common sense. They will need thinning. All that means is creating a reasonable growing space – perhaps 3 or 4 inches – between each plant. Most people start out by thinning too cautiously. You'll learn. Pull up the weeds. If you cannot tell the difference between weeds and emerging plants, wait a while.

6. Resolve to cultivate the whole garden. Not by digging it all or even by doing anything to all of it. Cultivate it in your mind. Think of all the possibilities. I know someone who did this and decided to concrete the entire surface. A bit perverse, but reasonable. To cultivate the garden you have to know it. You have to spend time with it, see how it reacts in all weathers. It is a love affair. Give it your heart.

7. Be ambitious. Do not be satisfied with the second-rate or the ugly. Gardens are places where we build dreams. Overreach yourself.

8. Don't be mean. People are absurdly tight-fisted with their gardens while indulging their houses with overblown, over-priced productions in kitchen and bathroom. If you have money, spend some of it. If you don't have money, spend time. Think of a wedding feast – the table should be overflowing with good things. Sliced bread and a microwaved Dinner for Two will not do.

9. Work hard. Be wary of the trend towards labour-saving gardening. Why save labour? Save it for what? Give labour to your garden. Work until your muscles ache and your hands are blistered. You will harden up.

10. Never lose the poetry.

The rest is experience.

17. 4. 94 **Damsons**

Every spring I fall in love with the English countryside but every year I am surprised and caught unawares – seeing it as though for the first time.

This time it was the damsons in Worcestershire that seduced me. The twisting road from Bromyard to Worcester is flanked by damson trees in the hedgerows as are the fields on either side. The repeated effect of the delicate blossom – no blowsy voluptuousness here like the apple orchards to come, just a dainty sprinkle like powder snow – builds a rhythmic beauty as you go past, a kind of visual clattering of a stick along railings. Yet the damson is a scrubby, untidy tree, hardly worth its place in the garden for aesthetic reasons. It is the massed effect, planted every 5 yards or so in a hedgerow, that works so well.

There is no reason why one could not include damsons – and crab apples – in a mixed hedge, just as they do in these West Country hedgerows. They stand above the hedge like sturdy Cinderellas, waiting for their brief week of glory

The repeated effect of the delicate blossom – no blowsy voluptuousness here like the apple orchards to come, just a dainty sprinkle like powder snow – builds a rhythmic beauty as you go past, a kind of visual clattering of a stick along railings.

They stand above the hedge like sturdy Cinderellas, waiting for their brief week of glory when they are the belles of the ball.

when they are the belles of the ball. And sturdy they are. Tough as nails. So they will act as a good windbreak as well as fruiting reliably for 100 years in any soil, although they prefer a heavyish loam, are uncomfortable in too acidic a soil and respond to a good manure mulch every spring. They will fruit much better in an open, sunny site above a frost pocket that might nip the early buds, but all these conditions are refinements upon the damson's basic ability to thrive anywhere.

Damsons were planted as much for their use as a dye for wool and leather as for eating, as anyone who has picked damsons will know from the rich crimson stain on their hands and the tell-tale smear of damson lipstick around the mouths of children swearing blind that they have not been raiding these intense little plums. But they make wonderful eating. Damson jam is the richest and best and damson cheese very good with lamb or game as well as bread and butter. Damsons work well in pies and crumbles as well as being delicious on their own, stewed. They are one of the few fruits better preserved in a kilner jar than frozen and the rich red fruits swimming in crimson liqueur are an ornament. Of course, all of this needs a degree of preparation and trouble which will deter most people, which is their loss.

Damsons are not difficult to grow and will produce fruit within fifteen years. They will come true from a stone – 'come true' means that a stone from a 'Bradley's King' will produce a 'Bradley's King' tree. This is not the case with apples, for example, which must be grafted to predict how they will develop). Alternatively one can buy a tree grafted on to a rootstock that will control the amount of growth. The latest introduction, Pixy, is described as 'a real space-saver', which immediately raises my hackles, but would, I suppose, mean that it could be grown in a container. 'St Julien A' is a larger rootstock making a tree up to 12 feet, but unless you intend to train it to a particular shape, try to grow damsons on their own roots as standards – they do not make intrusively large trees and their sprawl is part of their character.

Despite this, it is perfectly reasonable to train damsons to a fan shape against a wall, as with any other plum. After planting cut back the main stem until you have at least three lateral buds or branches, left and right, but no lower than 18 inches. Prune these lateral growths to one bud. In about June tie the top lateral to a vertical cane and select two of the strongest shoots on either side to train, cutting the rest back to the stem. In August tie the side shoots at 45 degrees to canes secured to horizontal wires. In late winter the following year cut the laterals back to a healthy bud so they are about 18 inches long. In summer choose two shoots, one below each lateral, so that the fan shape begins to evolve. All other growth is reduced by a third, pruning back to a downward-pointing bud. Select three new shoots from each branch and tie them to the wires, covering the wall. Prune all other shoots to a single leaf.

This sounds intricate, but spread over two seasons it is pretty straight-forward. Once the shape is established it is thereafter a question of pruning back forward-growing shoots and general thinning. By pruning any plum

like this you do make the most of the warmth from the wall behind it and the inclination to fruit on lateral growth.

You need not worry about cross-pollination with most damsons. Of the self-pollinating varieties, 'Merryweather' produces the biggest of all damson fruits and is a heavy cropper, the fruit lasting well into autumn on the tree. 'Bradley's King' was first recorded just over 100 years ago and has fruits sweet enough to be eaten raw, covered in bloom when ripe from mid-September on.

'Shropshire Damson' (confusingly also called 'Cheshire Damson', 'Westmoreland Damson' and 'Prune Damson') is a variety known since the sixteenth century. The range of names implies that it was widely grown and is perhaps the nearest taste we can have to the fruit of the Tudor dining table. For this reason alone I would recommend it above all others.

Damsons have been largely ignored by modern plant-breeders. Because it comes true from seed it has quietly carried on down the years so that the fruit you eat from your slightly scruffy tree in the back garden tastes the same as the fruit the crusaders brought back from Damascus, and the tree in the central London garden is pretty much the same as the thousands that made my heart leap on the road to Worcester.

■ Damsons are not common in the U.S. Nurseries that offer some: Hines Nurseries, P.O. Box 11208, Santa Ana, CA. 92711 (714) 559-4444; Tsolum River Fruit Trees, Box 68, Merville, B.C., Canada V0R 2M0 (604) 337-8004; Barnes and Son Nursery, P.O. Box 250L, McMinnville, TN. 37110 (615) 668-8576; Greenmantle Nursery, 3010 Ettersburg Rd., Garberville, CA. 95440 (707) 986-7504.
■ Like all plums damsons flower early, so netting might be needed to protect against birds.
■ Thin fruits when they are the size of peas, so that each fruit has a chance to swell.
■ Do not be tempted to prune a standard damson as you might an apple tree. It is a more cluttered, tangled tree. Just cut away diseased or crossing branches.
■ To make damson cheese: Simmer 3 lb of fruit in ½ pint of water until tender. Sieve the mixture to remove the skins and boil with 12 oz sugar to each pound of seived pulp until the mixture is nearly solid. Pour into small jars or saucers and leave to cool.

20.4.97 **Hawthorn**

Even the most city-bound, subterranean person will have noticed by now that spring is tuning up nicely, the hawthorn all in leaf, and in some stretches of hedgerow threatening to burst its buds into flower. Unless you live in agricultural countryside – which most of you don't – the best place to see hawthorn nowadays is alongside new town bypasses, as it is inevitably planted as a hedge to soften the roadscape and absorb some of the attendant pollution. You might have also noticed that one quite short stretch of road will have hawthorn in several clearly defined stages of development, although the climate, soil and situation are unchanging. This is because most commercial hawthorn has been bred from stock that originated from the Balkans, where spring comes suddenly after a harsh winter and before an equally harsh summer. This means that it has adapted to use the sliver of spring to break into leaf fast and produce viable seed as quickly as possible. This genetic disposition remains the trigger dictating the cycle of the plant. So a mile of hedging that comes from three different gene stocks will obey three different genetic time-switches, coming into leaf, blossom and fall independently of each other.

All of the 200,000 miles of hawthorn hedges that were planted across the agricultural landscape in the great enclosure periods of the eighteenth and nineteenth centuries came from home-grown stock and so react from parish to parish, county to county, within the same climatic zone, as if by one prearranged signal, although the flail hedge-cutter that has meant that one man can smash miles of hedge every day regardless of season or growth means that much of it never flowers nor consequently produces haws. The machine age has imposed a tyranny of sterile neatness in its labour-saving wake, a state where flowers are not permitted to bloom. Nevertheless, there is still enough untrimmed hawthorn to turn much of the countryside into a delicious froth of May blossom above and cow-parsley below, and at its best it is one of the great unsung glories of the planet.

The expression 'Ne'er cast a clout till the may is out' refers, as everyone knows, not to the end of the month but to the blossoming of the may tree or hawthorn, because that is the moment that truly measures the advent of summery weather. Until 1752 the may blossomed on 1 May or thereabouts but the introduction of the Gregorian calendar and the ensuing 'lost' eleven days has meant that the May Day of tradition is now actually 12 May, which is when the hawthorn can be counted on to start to flower. But it is not coincidence that the month and the tree share the same name. Hawthorn is called may because it is the most important plant of spring, the most important and vital season of the year. This utterly commonplace piece of planners' visual jargon is one of the living princes, a mysterious, strange sorcerer of a tree.

Before the mass hedge-planting, hawthorn was either a component of mixed hedges or a solitary, scrubby tree, marking boundaries far older than churches or existing shapes of many fields. It was believed to protect from lightning, ghosts, witches and fairies, and was an instigator and symbol of fertility. The scent of its blossom has a curiously foetid tang which grows stronger as the blossom fades. This is also a scent of visceral sex, encouraging fertility at this fecund turn of the year. In fact the flowers contain trimethylamine, which is an ingredient of the smell of putrefaction – a fitting aside to the Christian ambiguity about sex and death. The raw sexuality of the plant, with its hint of rotting flesh, merely added to the richness of its magic – all life, love and death in one breath of Maytime air. This also led to the idea that it offered protection against the plague, and the 'nuts in May' from 'Here We Go Round the Mulberry Bush' is actually a corruption of gathering knots, or posies, of May blossom.

But strong magic can harm as well as protect. Physically the tree is armed with thorns that bite deep. It was the tree that supplied Christ's crown of thorns, the bush 'that pricks my heart so sore', and bringing may blossom into the house is still considered to bring bad luck on the household.

The plant that all this refers to is *Crataegus monogyna*, the quickthorn. *C. laevigata*, the Woodland or Midland hawthorn (although Richard Mabey, in

The machine age has imposed a tyranny of sterile neatness in its labour-saving wake, a state where flowers are not permitted to bloom.

his *Flora Britannica*, rather crossly calls this description 'unfortunate and misleading...'), has different magic. It is one of the prime indicators of semi-natural woodland, which means that a hedge or patch of scrubby woodland with this in it is very likely to have been continuously woodland for man's history, older than any cathedral, older than any Roman remain, older, in all probability, than Stonehenge.

The easiest way to differentiate between the two types of hawthorn is when they flower: *C. monogyna* invariably has white blossom whereas *C. laevigata* can flower various shades of pink and tends to do so rather earlier. It is from this that most of the garden cultivars, such as the famous 'Paul's Scarlet' are bred. The flowers of woodland hawthorn smell more distinctly of decomposing flesh, and before the mass planting of hedges this species would have been at least as common as *C. monogyna*. In all probability it was the original mayflower and instigator of the superstition of bad luck that attends its presence in the house.

It is a pity to see the beautiful and magical hawthorn reduced to public hedging, whether it be road – or field-side. It will grow in almost every garden, has lovely flowers, cuts to any shape, is ideal cover for birds, bears fabulous berries or haws and is about the cheapest tree, if not plant, that you can buy. It grows very fast, making an unpassable barrier 6 feet tall within as many years and is the perfect foil for wind as well as being completely hardy. Perhaps its field association is so strong that this has passed into a collective subconscious veto, although if you asked a gardener why he did not plant hawthorn as internal hedging I am sure he would not give that as the answer.

Hawthorn also makes a very good topiary specimen because it responds so well to cutting, becoming denser every time it is clipped. Standard hawthorns are very good for smaller gardens, making a mophead or lollipop on a straight stem, and the tightly tangled bare branches in winter look rather like the 'clock' seed-head of a dandelion, making a change from the more usual evergreen of holly standards.

For hedging or topiary there is no need to go further than *C. monogyna*, but there are another couple of hundred varieties that are used as specimen trees. The Cockspur thorn, *C. crus-galli*, has very wide-spreading branches and particularly long thorns. *C. x lavallei* has glossy green leaves that last right into midwinter and orange berries that linger on longer still, whereas most hawthorn berries get gobbled up by the birds after the first really hard frost. *C. monogyna* 'Biflora' or the Glastonbury thorn will occasionally flower in midwinter as well as in spring. The legend of the Glastonbury thorn is that Joseph of Arimathea happened to be down Glastonbury way and either stuck his walking stick in the ground, upon which it grew leaves and flowered every Christmas Day, or brought with him the original crown of thorns which did likewise. Harmless codswallop, but interesting, because this legend only

The raw sexuality of the plant, with its hint of rotting
flesh, merely added to the richness of its magic –
all life, love and death in one breath of Maytime air.

originated in 1722 and seems to have been a deliberate attempt by puritans to dissociate the hawthorn from the pagan and sexual mythology that clings to it as closely as its scent.

You can have your magic sanitized if you want, but I prefer it pungent and obscure. For the same reason I feel much less inclined to plant fancy-pants varieties in the garden, when *C. monogyna* is such a superb small tree. Either plant it as an untrammelled, flowering, fruity specimen, or use its extreme cheapness to play with hedging. If you buy it by the hundred it will cost between 25 and 50 pence each and can make straight, crinkle-crankle or circular hedging. It is all about making spaces where gardens can happen, transforming boring outside uniformity into private magic.

■ If you do want to plant a hawthorn hedge, either get on with it as soon as possible or else wait until next October, as the growing plant places great demands on the root system of deciduous plants. Nevertheless, if you are prepared to water each plant at least a pint a week, then go ahead. Just because it is tough do not stint on the preparation. Place the hedge in a single row 12 inches apart. When it has developed a set of leaves you should cut each plant down to 6 inches. This might seem like butchery but will ensure a really strong hedge with branches right down to the ground.

■ Early June is probably the best time to trim an established hawthorn hedge. If you want it to flower next spring, do not cut it again. If you want neatness above floriferousness, give it another trim in autumn to reduce the number of mildew spores that overwinter in the outer buds.

■ Hawthorn is a member of the rose family, as is the pear, and could well suffer from the same canker that is afflicting my espaliered pears, withering the tips of established growth. Clearly this is a disaster for any attempt to train a tree and not good news for one growing untrained. It is caused by a fungus, *Nectaria galligena*. The only answer is to cut back to good wood wherever it appears, picking up all the prunings and burning them. Keep the ground clear of fallen leaves and, if practical, improve the drainage.

■ I learnt the name of the fungus from the new *RHS Book of Pests and Diseases* by Pippa Greenwood and Andrew Halstead, published by Dorling Kindersley. This is not a subject that usually enthrals me as I tend to take the view that it's a jungle out there and good husbandry will deal with most problems in time, but I recommend this book.

■ Another problem that has arisen from my pears is the use of wire ties when training any woody tree or shrub. My advice on this is simple: Don't. It is amazing how fast the growing bark envelops the wire, causing a wound for nasties like fungus to get in. Only use wire on soft growth like clematis that will be pruned away annually. For training anything that will last for more than one season always use soft green twine or raffia.

23.4.95 **Smaller Gardens**

I work on the assumption that most of you live in a town and have smallish gardens. I know that there are plenty of exceptions to that, but I presume that these prove the rule. So I gear this column towards the 100 x 30-foot back garden. To do this I hark back to the ten years that I also lived in a town with a garden of that size and convert my current experience into urban, small garden mode.

The truth is very different. I live deep in the country surrounded by open land. My gardening is focused on the 2 acres of field that we moved into two years ago, with a house tucked into one corner. For the four years before we moved in it had been abandoned and was filled with burdock growing as tall as a man and with countless velcro seeds that clung to your jersey as you brushed past.

I laboriously cut and raked all this and then Brian came with his Bobcat and pushed a huge pile of horsemuck over it. The horsemuck was from Eric's horse that was in the barns next to us and had a load of anthracite mixed into the bottom section which we discovered too late to stop spreading that around too. I'm still digging bits of it out every time I plant something. Then Eric Hyde – another Eric – ploughed it with a huge reversible plough, the unused half shining and flashing in the sun like a marching medieval army. That was two years ago almost to the day, no garden, but a ploughed field and Big Ideas.

Brian is back now, buzzing his Bobcat around at an unbelievable lick. Bobcats are small bulldozers, like a Mini with a bucket on the front, and Brian is a small man too, so they go well together.

The reality of making a largish new garden on a shoestring is made up of the rigmarole of the last few days. It goes like this: Brian was booked to clear away the huge pile of rubbish we dug up when making a new border, path and grassed area in front of the house. At the same time he would bring in his lorry a load of topsoil to sow the grass seed into.

The day began bright and beautiful, I went off to London at dawn to earn the money to pay for this, leaving my wife – who is frantically busy herself – to 'be around in case anything happened'. If she knew what a short straw that was she was too noble to show it. The problems began at once. In order to tip the topsoil Brian had to move the rubbish. And to move the rubbish he had to put it in his lorry, and to put it into his lorry he had to tip the topsoil... My mobile phone rang on the train. Where should we dump the topsoil? In a neighbouring field. That would need permission from the farmer and the farmer was not answering his phone – probably due to the more pressing demands of farming. I said that I would keep trying him and finally got him somewhere between Charlbury and Oxford, and got the go-ahead. No problems.

Then I got another call, this time in a taxi going to Television Centre. The people from the mushroom farm have just rung: they can deliver the 24 tons of mushroom compost we ordered in an hour's time. Was that OK? One of the beauties of gardening on a largish scale is that you can employ the economies of scale, so that things like mushroom compost can be bought in bulk at a fraction of its normal price. A thick mulch of this was exactly what we needed now that we had finished our spring weeding. Yes, of course it was OK, the timing was perfect. Sort of.

The 24-ton lorry apparently only just fitted down the lane, but having negotiated its narrowness couldn't turn the corner into our yard where the

Rose, who had come to help spread the vast pile of mulch, had got stung in the face by an unknown insect and her cheek had swollen like a football. She had to be taken to the cottage hospital for attention. Other than that, everything was fine.

compost was to go. Another phone call: Where should we put it? In the field. Would I ring the farmer, he knew me... I would, I did, he said yes, by now bemused. Make a mental note to show material, liquid, thanks.

So the field by our house now had a pile of topsoil and a pile of mushroom compost, with Brian, small and fast, tearing backwards and forwards distributing both. I rang to see how it was going. Swimmingly apparently, although Rose, who had come to help spread the vast pile of mulch, had got stung in the face by an unknown insect and her cheek had swollen like a football. She had to be taken to the cottage hospital for attention. Other than that, everything was fine.

I suppose that I ought to admit that I want this sort of operation to be a drama. I want to relish the change and excitement of it. This is one of the great attractions of making big gardens: it must be a Performance.

When I came home I inspected the work by torchlight and saw that it was good. Half the topsoil was spread, all the rubbish was moved, and the field was well and truly carved up by the Bobcat's wheels. I went to bed wondering if the farmer had noticed.

Brian was back by eight with another load of topsoil which he dumped *in situ* this time. We decided to move the mushroom compost and tidy up as quickly as we could. The only place that the compost could reasonably go was where we park our cars and over the wall by the back door. This latter spot was occupied by a ton of firewood that Chris had delivered. Chris is the strongest man I know. When I was young, that role was filled by Tommy Ball, with the mind of a child, sleeves rolled almost to his armpits and hands like shovels. He was a woodman as well. Tommy had a speech impediment and would come into the pub and order a pint o' cherry brandy in an almost incomprehensible Hampshire burr. Just you behave now, the landlord would say, or I'll tell your mum. Tommy must be an old man now. It is unthinkable. Chris had tossed the oak in cord lengths from his truck, over the wall into the back yard as though they were bean sticks. I now had to move it to make room for the mushroom compost and it made me squeal with effort.

The rest was dumped in the car park so the cars had to be moved, blocking the lane. At that point, Eric Hyde came down with his tractor to feed the lambs. He volunteered to walk the last quarter of a mile across the fields and we watched him guiltily as he stumped off, a half-hundred weight sack of nuts over one shoulder.

Brian finished early and as we had booked him for the day, whether we used him or not, I got him to turn a couple of compost heaps – usually the work of a distinctly sweaty hour or more – and take out a low stone wall where we are to plant a yew hedge. It was all done in a trice.

I suppose that I ought to admit that I want this sort of operation to be a drama. I want to relish the change and excitement of it. This is one of the great attractions of making big gardens: it must be a Performance.

Then, and only then, did we begin gardening. The mushroom compost was spread 3 inches deep over all the borders and the topsoil raked and sown with grass seed. This last operation was interrupted by a call from daytime telly asking me to do a live item on their show. I asked what they had in mind. Oh, anything, they said, whatever it is that you would be doing in your garden now.

■ Even if you have a very small garden, do not discount using machines. They can often do the job better than you and make time for things that humans do well. If you have 3 feet of access you can get a small digger in and do a surprising amount of work in a day.

■ Mushroom compost is an ideal mulch, especially if you have heavy soil. It fertilizes, suppresses weeds and improves the soil structure. Mushroom growers have to replace their growing medium regularly and are only too keen to sell off the waste. It is usually sold in bags but many growers will deliver a load, which is much cheaper.

■ If you buy a load of topsoil, be very discriminating about it. Mine came from a vegetable garden that was having a bungalow built on it. I remember the vegetables. But often you receive an anonymous mishmash of subsoil, topsoil and weeds. If in doubt, go and see where it comes from.

1.5.96 **Apples**

I used to have an orchard, 4 acres of apples on a Herefordshire hillside, and at the beginning of May they frothed like whipped cream, the tangle of unpruned branches laden with blossom. In the last summer we were there a pair of young owls grew up in the orchard, screeching to each other appallingly throughout the August nights, hiding among the 30-foot Bramleys during the day. Most of the fruit was eaten by the foxes and fieldfares as it lay on the ground over winter, tons and tons of apples uncollected. There was a particularly memorable tryst beneath the pink flowers of a Blenheim Orange which strongly influenced my attitude to apple trees. Every gardener should plant at least one apple tree in their life with the fervent prayer that one day love might be made beneath its branches without offending the neighbours or frightening the horses.

But when you turn to the gardening books, almost all exhort one against growing a standard or even half-standard apple (or pear) tree as being unsuitable for most gardens because they are too big, have too much fruit, are difficult to spray, difficult to pick from, and so on. Almost all fruit trees sold in garden centres are dwarf trees or bushes. With the exception of a handful of good nurseries, it is almost impossible to get a standard apple tree.

At this point one has to take a deep breath and leap into the jargon of fruit -tree growing. A standard is what might be called a proper tree. In fact it is a precise definition and can only be used of a tree that has a trunk of at least 6 feet 6 inches. A half-standard has a trunk – or stem – of at least 4 feet 6 inches. A bush has a stem of 2–3 feet. To achieve this degree of predictable growth the apple variety is grafted on to a rootstock, which is always a type of crab apple. This is categorized according to its vigour by a number with an 'M' prefix. Apples do not grow true from seed, and do not take readily from cuttings. So grafting is the easiest way to propagate an apple. By grafting the bud of a variety on to the rootstock of a tree with a measured vigour you achieve the type of fruit you want on the size of tree you want. When the graft has taken, the crab-apple above the graft is cut off so that you have the apple tree growing on crab-apple roots. This is how apples are universally grown.

This use of rootstocks is quite separate from the training of fruit trees by pruning so that they grow as cordons, espaliers, dwarf pyramids or fans, although it is normal to use dwarf rootstocks for trees to be pruned in this way.

The critical prefixes are M111, M25, M26, M9 and M27. They represent a descending vigour of growth. This means that only trees grown on M111 or M25 rootstock will grow into proper trees – or technically, standards.

All gardening books seem to work on the assumption that people want to produce as much fruit as possible in as small a space as possible and that they want their fruit to be as unblemished as possible. I am sure that this misses the point by miles.

Of course most people have limited space. Of course one wants a fruit tree to be productive. To that end I think that trees trained to shape by pruning, especially cordons, espaliers and fan-trained trees, are an excellent thing in any garden. But the pygmy bushes that are sold as 'trees' are a travesty. They are usually ugly in form and seem to be a stunting of the spirit. Commercial fruit growers never plant the standard trees of traditional orchards, but grow their trees like vines or gooseberry bushes. An orchard used to be synonymous with rural peace. Now an orchard is an agribusiness unit of row after row of stunted trees chemically coaxed into a few frantic years of fruiting before being bulldozed.

But no gardener nowadays grows an apple tree for the fruit alone. Almost everyone in this country has access to apples in a shop. It is a moot point whether the apples on sale are worth eating, but that is another issue. You grow apples to enjoy the appleness of the thing, for the blossom and the leaves, the colour and texture of the bark and the sense of an orchard in one's garden. The fact that the fruit might be small and a bit scabby doesn't seem to me to lessen any of this. I rang a couple of (very good) nurseries supplying fruit trees and was assured that dwarf rootstocks were the only ones suitable for a garden because half-standards and standards were too large to spray easily. I might be very wrong, but I doubt if many people spray their apple trees, big or small. In a small garden the apples from an apple tree are a by-product, whereas the tree is the thing itself.

There are nurseries who seem to appreciate this. I spoke to Graham Deacon, of Deacon's nurseries on the Isle of Wight, who specialize in grafting on to any rootstock to order. He pointed out that the best way to grow a standard apple is to buy a 1st Maiden Whip on M25 rootstock. This sounds as though it might be a treat peculiar to Tory backbenchers, but translates as an

Every gardener should plant at least one apple tree in their life with the fervent prayer that one day love might be made beneath its branches without offending the neighbours or frightening the horses.

All gardening books seem to work on the assumption that people want to produce as much fruit as possible in as small a space as possible and that they want their fruit to be as unblemished as possible. I am sure that this misses the point by miles.

unpruned two-year-old tree, about 6 feet tall. If the leader – the topmost upward growing branch – is left unpruned and the lateral branches cut off until a sufficient trunk has established, an apple tree will grow itself.

I should like to plant a standard Bramley in the middle of an urban back garden and let the garden evolve around and under it as it grows. After thirty or forty years it will come to dominate the whole space. But I think I would rather have my back garden dominated by the branches of an apple tree than by a lawn or a Leylandii hedge. My grandchildren could climb in it, we could eat at a table beneath the blossom, there would be so many apples we wouldn't care that it was impossible to spray or even pick them all, and perhaps the owls would nest in it.

■ For apples, try Sonoma Antique Apple Nursery, 4395 Westside Road, Healdsburg, CA. (707) 433-6420.
■ Plan your orchard now and order your trees for November delivery. Container trees are more expensive, you will have less choice, and there is nothing to be gained by planting now rather than next November.
■ We can still get late frosts for another week or so. Watch the weather forecast and use fleece to drape over blossom and tender flowering shrubs.

12.5.96 National Trust Gardens

The National Trust has 162 gardens that attracted nearly 8.5 million visitors last year. Next week it is publishing a new guide called, slightly predictably, *Gardens of the National Trust*, written by Stephen Lacey, a much respected garden writer and plantsman. He clearly loves gardens of all kinds and is genuinely filled with admiration for the Trust's work. On the whole I agree with that stance, although I think there are central criticisms of the Trust that affect our entire view of gardening.

I have been a dedicated member of the National Trust for over twenty years now and in my twenties spent most of my holidays visiting their gardens (those days are now behind me. I am now firmly on the straight and narrow and have not inhaled a National Trust flower for at least two years). Often my wife and I were the youngest visitors by about fifty years. Even if that statement is not completely true, it at least rings true. There is no doubt that the Trust does have a very staid, geriatric image, conjuring gaggles of

slow-walking pensioners in cardigans and fawn blousons attended to by bossy tweed and corduroy-clad volunteer members of the local WI or British Legion. It is all about age, reverence and not a little snobbery.

But if youth and spiky iconoclasm are not welcomed there can be no growth, no future. Every shuffling pensioner once had a mind filled with sex and limbs springing with energy. Why does all that have to go before a National Trust garden becomes interesting? To be fair to the Trust, it does have a very positive educative drive to attract children, but it seems to write off people between school age and thirty-something. I put this to Stephen Lacey and he said that people in their twenties were not interested in gardening. The gardens would be there for them when they did get interested later on in life. This seems to me to be wrong. I would say that the age-group between eighteen and twenty-eight has never been so aware and sensitive of ecology, the environment, food and nature as it is today. People in their twenties would be interested in gardening if it were not presented as such a retrospective, middle-aged activity.

It is significant that National Trust gardens inevitably have a tea room. Why? No one under the age of fifty actually chooses to go to a tea room except in desperation or a spirit of irony. Why not a restaurant or a bar?

It is also significant that all the gardens in the National Trust are retrospective. Where are the wacky, shocking, revolutionary gardens? The one that most closely fits that bill is Biddulph Grange, made just on 150 years ago. Why should we not visit and admire modern gardens? Stephen Lacey pointed out that there are no contemporary gardens available to the Trust. They simply do not exist.

I wonder why? Some of the blame must be at the door of the Trust for holding up nostalgia and retrospection as the epitome of excellence. What other art form (and I passionately believe gardening to be a major art form) would celebrate the past with such vigour? What other industry would at its premier trade show (Chelsea) have cod-pastiches of sentiment-soaked nostalgia as the prime exhibition pieces?

Yet the strength and importance of the Trust are in its historical guardianship. If it were not for the Trust, scores of sites would have been lost for ever. To my mind, the more obviously 'historical' the gardens are, the more satisfactory the Trust's stewardship. By visiting a careful and accurate reconstruction of a seventeenth-century garden we have a brilliant insight into seventeenth-century life. This is the nearest we can ever get to time travel, better than any BBC costume drama. You can smell, touch, see and taste what our periwigged ancestors sensed. This is an aspect of the Trust's work that cannot be praised too highly.

So gardens such as Westbury Court, Biddulph Grange or Stowe are the real gems in the Trust's crown. The more conventionally admired gardens,

Every shuffling pensioner once had a mind filled with sex and limbs springing with energy. Why does all that have to go before a National Trust garden becomes interesting?

All great gardens are the product of the whims and inconsistencies of at most two people and usually just one. To raise a garden from the ordinary someone must be a despot.

like Hidcote and Sissinghurst, are inspirational to practising gardeners and the mindless admiration of cruising trippers, but in the end are just some people's back gardens. The people are always more interesting than the plants – witness the frantic cult of Vita worship, and the empty space where Lawrence Johnston should be at Hidcote. People tiptoe round these gardens with the reverence normally reserved for Royalty or Cathedrals, treating the living – the garden – with the hushed respect of the dead.

Although the Trust is institutionalized to a timeless degree, it only started to deal with gardens (as opposed to houses with gardens attached) in 1948. After the war teams of gardeners were impossible to finance for all but the very rich, although all large gardens made over the previous 300 years had depended on large teams of cheap workers to maintain them. The Trust stepped in at this historically crucial moment to preserve gardens that would otherwise now be grassed over and mown once a week.

All great gardens are the product of the whims and inconsistencies of at most two people and usually just one. To raise a garden from the ordinary someone must be a despot. No organization can be run this way. The NT has an impossible task. To hold a garden at a fixed point, either that of the moment of the creator's departure, or of its supposed peak, is to fossilize a living art and anyway is all but impossible. Things grow and die. So decisions on style have to be made, important changes agreed and executed, and inevitably this is all done by a committee, although it is, of course, personal prejudice that is the vital ingredient of a great garden.

It is a great pity that the decision was taken with this new publication not to review the analytical side in the style of Graham Stuart Thomas, looking at each historical period, the process of garden visiting and the work of the Trust itself. It limits this new work to a very well-written, glossy guide.

For all my reservations and discomfort, I have to finish by stressing that the gardens of the National Trust are the greatest collection of gardens in the world and every gardener should belong to the Trust. I shall certainly continue to break long journeys by dropping into whatever NT gardens are on my route, shall dutifully consume my cups of tea and walnut and coffee sponge and shall no doubt continue to be delighted, irritated and informed in equal measure.

■ *Gardens of The National Trust*, by Stephen Lacey, published by the National Trust, £29.99.
■ Spring may have been late coming but everything will catch up very fast, especially the weeds, so get on top of them now. If at all possible dig up perennials now and burn the roots. Pull and cut annuals before they seed. The important thing is to reduce the weed problem to a manageable level at this stage and keep on top of it for the rest of the season.
■ Water-lilies and other aquatic plants can be planted now that it is warmer.
■ Keep wary of frost if the weather is dry and resist the temptation to plant anything

remotely tender for a week or so yet. A frost will set everything back much more than a week's delay in planting.

■ Stake your herbaceous plants now, before they need it. The supports look a bit overpowering for a couple of weeks but will soon be hidden.

26.5.96 **Firstborn**

Today is my first son's birthday. This day two years ago I was walking with a smiling, square-shouldered, white-haired man on the westernmost cliffs of Europe looking out to the Blasket Islands, bright sun and wind bouncing off the sea and much good talk between us. We had met only an hour earlier, both willing victims of a television programme. His people had lived on the Blaskets and the Dingle peninsula for at least ten generations. That's about 400 years. 'But I am walking,' he told me, 'with four thousand years of history, walking with my ancestors in the walls and the stones. My feet in their footsteps.'

Sea pinks and primroses grew in the lee of dips and hollows in the tightly cropped grasses of the clifftop, fragilely sheltered from the winds and sheep. I loved that place, felt exhilarated and honoured to be there with this man who was solemn and wise beneath the steady flow of banter and jokes, yet I was torn because it was my son's birthday, the first I had missed. I wanted both, to be here and with my son, walking with us and gathering flowers. I said as much to my companion.

He told me a story.

This was the first time that he had been on these cliffs for ten years to the day. It had been his youngest son's birthday too, his ninth. He was a busy man in those days, urgent, very involved in local politics. He did not often have time to spend with his children. His boy was hanging back, collecting these same sea pinks and primroses to make traps to catch butterflies, enticing them with flowers. 'Sure I was busy and took no notice,' he said, still smiling.

'I took him home and he ate a good dinner and was well, as full of life as the day. I had to go off to a meeting and had no time to say goodnight but went up when I got home. He was sleeping, just snoring a little. The wife went up around midnight just to see that they were all right and he was dead. He had had a brain haemorrhage in his sleep.

'We didn't know what to do. We did nothing, nothing at all for half an hour. I didn't take the other children from their beds. You cannot imagine it. You cannot possibly know these things. And now my life has changed. Nothing can ever be the same.'

We walked back, nothing more to be said. As we parted with a handshake he slipped me a bottle of home-brewed poteen. 'I make it for the old folks,' he said. 'Purely medicinal, of course.' The public twinkle was in his eyes. Then

As we parted with a handshake he slipped me a bottle of home-brewed poteen. 'I make it for the old folks,' he said. 'Purely medicinal, of course.'

he leaned forward and whispered, 'Put your arm round him once in a while. That's all that matters.'

All.

The day my son was born, the same day his son was born and died, another year, treading the same footsteps, I was overwhelmed with a sense of homecoming. My child had returned home and after thirty years he had found me. The stories of elderly couples laying the extra place for a child that disappeared half a century before now made sense. We brought him home and instinctively I took him outside to show him my garden.

Unlike this year, spring '86 was fine and bosomy, and by the end of May the garden was spilling with growth. Half mad with love and terror for this delicate bundle, we slowly had a look around. It made sense. This was the best I could show him. Of anything I had done or was, this was the most intimate.

When he was safely swaddled in his mother's arms indoors, I went out to pick him a bunch of flowers. For all the abundance, there was not a lot of choice. I am looking at a bad snap of that bunch now, taken exactly ten years ago. No sea pinks on these Islington cliffs and the primroses were over. But there was a spray of the early honeysuckle *Lonicera japonica*, a couple of tall, violet-blue flowers of *Iris germanica* (almost certainly one of the many clones), the white, heart-shaped drops of *Dicentra spectabilis* 'Alba', *Alchemilla mollis* and a few violet aquilegias, looking like upturned tables. I remember choosing slowly and carefully, aware of the paucity of choice, aware of the loss of these best specimens to the garden and aware that I wanted only the most beautiful in the vase in his room. I also picked clematis, which were dominant in the garden on that day. My favourite, *Clematis armandii*, had finished flowering, its glossy leaves entwined amongst the incipient buds of the rose 'New Dawn', but the two *C. montana*, one white, the other, *C. montana* 'Elizabeth', that blushed a slightly unnecessary pink, were at their frothy peak. Much more refined was the spiky purply-blue of *C. macropetala*, and the splashes of *C. alpina* 'Francis Rivis', the flowers almost submerged in foliage. We had then a superb *C.* 'Vyvyann Pennell' which has wonderful double flowers, but I had foolishly pruned it hard a couple of months previously, so there were no flowers at that time. The pruning had the effect of making its second flush of single flowers, in August, much more effective. But I would have traded this for the few magnificent doubles. There were also 'Xerxes', 'Marie Boisselot', 'The President' and, almost inevitably, 'Nelly Moser', all in flower. I put this mismatched posy on a pedestal next to the cot, a long strand of the white montana spilling down to the ground.

That was ten years and three gardens ago. My current garden has no walls and the only clematis I have are late-flowering varieties such as 'Gipsy Queen' and 'Perle d'Azur' and the species *C. jackmanii* and *C. viticella* grown on tripods in the borders. But I have all the other plants, some literally the same,

Like any parent I am still filled with overwhelming love and terror, raising children, raising plants, getting it mostly wrong, but trying to remember what matters.

lifted from London to here via two other moves. If it had not been such a blasted and chilly spring I could have picked almost the same bunch of flowers today as ten years ago. The tiny baby is an iconoclastic lovely boy with his own garden within the garden, more in love with the lawn as football pitch than plants. Like any parent I am still filled with overwhelming love and terror, raising children, raising plants, getting it mostly wrong, but trying to remember what matters.

I want my gardens to include this, to continue beyond me through each year's cycles, to have the spirit of the Blaskets, spirit of the Shiant Isles walking carelessly through them. Each time I set up home and garden I am trying to make a thousand years of settlement out of the life and death of plants. I want it to last forever while relishing its transience and change. We all long for a permanence that makes home, where, just like plants, one season's living and dying matters so much less than the footsteps traced across the years. I want my children to walk in the garden after I have gone, not with reverence but with laughter, walking on the edges of understanding in the garden, collecting flowers and knowing the cycle of death and promise of return, season by season through a thousand years, out in the islands with the sea pinks and primroses, out in the garden where laughter, football pitches, stolen posies and an arm around a shoulder matter more than plants, technique or the bundle of conventions most gardens are lost inside.

■ Memorial Day Weekend gives a chance to tackle some longer jobs spread over a few days. This is a good time to clean out a pond, remove all plants in baskets and lift all planted marginals. Pump or siphon the water out and carefully dredge the sludge off the bottom. Divide and replant all the aquatics and marginals.

■ Cut box hedges and topiary now. The idea is to give new growth as long a period as possible to harden off between the last frosts of spring and the first frosts of autumn. Use a line to keep the top of the hedge straight .

■ Sow biennials (such as wallflowers, forget-me-nots) for spring bedding in rows in a seed bed or vegetable garden.

■ Resist the temptation to cut back any leaves of daffodils for at least another month, however much the tidying urge sweeps over you. They need to use the green leaves to make next year's flowers.

■ Take soft cuttings from fuchsias, potentillas, philadelphus and viburnums. The thing to remember with soft cuttings is that they 'take' very easily but also die very easily. It is a race for the new roots to establish and support the cutting before it gives up the ghost, so put it in a propagator if you have it or in a polythene bag to retain the moisture and keep it warm.

29.5.96 **Umbellifers**

May has all but passed without me. The garden is rank with neglect but, although it's slightly daunting, I know that I can reclaim it with a few days' blitz. But May is gone for a whole year and nothing can bring it back. If you live in a city – as I did throughout most of the 1980s – there are triggers that fire the blood in spring, *Clematis montana* sprawling along a thousand garden fences, wisteria hanging in opulent lavender bunches in the first warm sunshine of the year, the glaucous green of the whitebeams as their leaves unfold along back-streets (by the middle of June they become nondescript and scruffy). But it is hard to be enraptured by an urban May, whereas it is almost impossible not to be transported by the countryside, where thousands of miles of hedgerow and bank froth with cow parsley, the mass of tiny white flowers almost floating above the freshest and most delicate billows of leaves. Just as it reaches its moment of perfection you can guarantee that the local councils will send out tractors with flail-mowers to reduce it to a damp pulp in the name of bureaucratic tidiness.

Nothing in the garden gives me the same thrill of pure pleasure as I get afresh each May from cow parsley. This May I have been in America, West Africa, Israel, Corsica and Ireland and seen nothing as lovely. It is one of the great glories of the British countryside. If cow parsley is so beautiful, why do we not grow it in our gardens? It is clearly easy to grow, occurring on all soils in all situations.

To a certain extent, we do. Although cow parsley is strictly *Anthriscus sylvestris*, it is also a broad term to describe a whole group of naturalized umbellifers. These include Sweet Cicely (*Myrrhis odorata*), chervil (*Anthriscus cerefolium*), hemlock (*Conium immaculatum*), angelica (*Angelica archangelica*) and rough-chervil (*Chaerophyllum temulentum*). With the exceptions of angelica and hemlock, these are much better as a group, relying on the massed froth of their flower-heads for effect. If you had a mixed or hawthorn hedge running along the edge of a paddock or rough grass, a yard-wide ribbon of cow parsley would be wonderful but I have never seen it done. It is pointless to imitate nature laboriously – you might as well just leave the thing alone and let it get on with it – but one can intelligently borrow.

We tend to restrict umbellifers to the herb garden (no 'we' don't: most people do not have distinctions as clear as that within their garden, but you know what I mean) and dot them about as part of a generally fluffy composition rather than grow them in great drifts. Angelica, however, is big and majestic enough to stand alone in company with anything in a mixed border and should be planted there. It will reach 6 feet in its second year with hollow stems 2–3 inches across. Angelica likes shade and a rich soil but grows pretty easily. Collect the seeds as soon as they ripen in August or September and sow them in a seed tray. They will be ready to plant out next spring. Otherwise you can divide plants in autumn, chopping through the roots with a sharp spade.

Chervil is altogether a modest affair. It appears like a green doily before the stems grow and produce the small dusting of white flowers. It has a delicate, parsley-like taste and, like parsley, will grow the year round if sown in April and August.

I have hemlock growing in foul-smelling clumps in the far corners of my garden. It stinks like a mouse's cage that has not been cleaned for a month.

It is almost impossible not to be transported by the countryside, where thousands of miles of hedgerow and bank froth with cow parsley, the mass of tiny white flowers almost floating above the freshest and most delicate billows of leaves.

I have a feeling that it is illegal to introduce Giant Hogweed into a garden, which makes it all the more tempting to grow.

Nevertheless, if you can keep upwind of it, it is very handsome, with purple blotches all over its stem and growing almost as strongly as angelica. It is famously poisonous but my children do not seem to have tasted it yet. Given its smell they would have to be in a particularly perverse mood. I would not recommend putting it in any sort of border for risk of poisoning the air more than offspring, but it looks good in a wild patch.

Some years ago my wife casually admired the Giant Hogweed (*Heracleum mantegazzianum*) growing like angelica on steroids in a friend's garden. About two months later we received a torn brown envelope, wrongly addressed, with half a dozen flat seeds loose in it. It got put in a drawer and forgotten about until the following spring when the seeds were scattered in a dark corner of our Hackney garden. They all germinated and within two years we had our own ineradicable forest of umbellifers, lovely but a bit overpowering. They are also dangerous, the juice of the stems causing bad blisters on the skin if exposed to sunlight. I have a feeling that it is illegal to introduce Giant Hogweed into a garden, which makes it all the more tempting to grow.

Sweet Cicely is both legal and harmless, despite the cloying name. The leaves are used to remove the tartness from stewed fruit and the boiled roots are, according to Mrs M. Grieves's *A Modern Herbal*, supposedly good 'for old people that are dull and without courage', as well as being a tonic 'for girls between fifteen and eighteen'. (The euphemisms flap like sheets in the wind.) Again, it is easy to grow, liking a bit of shade and preferring a rich soil, but bung it in anywhere and it will make the best of any conditions. The leaves appear early, in February, and can be picked from then right through to November. But if you are growing it for the virtue in the leaves then you must cut the flower-heads back as soon as they have flowered or else all the goodness goes into the seeds. These remain a beautiful lime-green before ripening, so it seems a pity to decapitate them.

■J.L. Hudson, Seedsman, has a wide range of umbellifers. Catalogue requests: P.O. Box 1058, Redwood City, CA. 94064.

■If you have been away or have not had time to get into the garden, do not panic. The situation is retrievable. Weeds at this time of year pull up easily and many have not yet seeded. An excellent tool for crisis weeding is a mattock, with which you chop all the weeds, however terrifyingly rampant, just below the surface. Rake them up and make a heap of them. In twelve months they will have composted down. This creates a physical and psychological space to manoeuvre in.

■Now the soil has warmed up it is time to sow the second batch of vegetables, such as sweetcorn, dwarf and runner beans, okra, salsify, scorzonera and chinese greens, straight into the ground.

■ If you are buying bedding plants, do not be seduced by too many flowers. It is best to buy strong, healthy plants with bright green leaves. The flowers will come after you have planted them out.

■ Trim the foliage of *Iris unguicularis* with shears when it has finished. This lets sun and air in to ripen the roots for next year.

■ Prune *Clematis montana* and *C. armandii* now, cutting back only as far as tidiness and size-limitation dictate. They will flower on the growth produced in the remainder of the summer.

2.6.96 **Past and Future Gardening**

Three weeks ago I wrote about the National Trust in this column and it provoked a postbag of more vituperative hate mail than anything else I have written.

I like getting feedback, even if in this case it was very much of the spluttering variety ('You poor Americanized ill-cultured little shit'). The most direct conclusion is that some people feel very threatened by the suggestion that gardening could do with some re-evaluating and injection of fresh blood. ('Who but you wants "shocking revolutionary gardens"? Grow up.') It also suggests that the gardening establishment as represented by the National Trust and its gardens is a fragile thing and fears the thin end of any wedge. ('I suppose you want rock music... or Madonna look-alikes' ... 'Piss off to some drunken druggy eighteen-to-thirty bar, preferably abroad.')

Apart from the utopian vision of Madonna look-alikes serving me home-made crumpet in a drunken, druggy bar to the accompaniment of suitable rock music, with a wonderful garden to visit outside the door, it does seem that I touched upon a genuine raw nerve. Why is it that we, the British, are so uncomfortable with innovative gardens? In part it is because we are slow, treacly people, so congealed with our past that we cannot move forward. But mainly it is the result of great success. British gardening believes itself to be the best in the world. This is a residue from the imperial power that we once exercised when we believed that we were the best human beings in the world. Both attitudes are absurd.

Our colonial power has had a vast influence on modern gardens. It has enabled plants from all over the world to be plundered in the perfectly honourable guise of plant-collecting. Arguably this has produced great cross-cultural integration but in the context of gardens it has meant a number of deleterious things. The most obvious effect is that it has placed a greater accent on plants for plants' sake than on the artistic disciplines of organizing objects in space. Even the landscape movement of the mid-eighteenth century, barbarously sweeping away all the wonderful formal gardens so tantalizingly represented at Levens Hall and Westbury Court and in the drawings of Kip and Knyff, used the organization of objects and the landscape itself rather than the exhibition-like display of plants.

Some people feel very threatened by the suggestion that gardening could do with some re-evaluating and injection of fresh blood. ('Who but you wants "shocking revolutionary gardens"? Grow up.')

Then our Empire and energy delved into the unknown and brought mementos, exactly as the first visitors to the moon did. Plants were grown because they were a curiosity – not for their beauty or effect in the general scheme of things. We became philistines via acquisition of power.

Science has become the new colonialism. Plant-breeding for colour, size, shape and longevity are all new continents to plunder. Micro-propagation, hydroponics, ultra-violet light, computer-controlled humidity and temperature systems: these are the colonial administrators now. We grow things because we can, not because it is the most just thing to do.

The other factor that has a bad influence on our current garden design is our climate. We boast that our frosts prevent disease, our summers are not too hot, our rain the right sort and in the right amount, and our changing seasons a joy. Take the grey glumness of nearly half the year out of the equation and it is all true. It has meant that the plant collectors could scour the world for stock, bring it home, bung it in the ground and more often than not it would flourish. Rhododendrons from the Himalayas, hellebores from the dry shade of the Mediterranean, tulips from Turkey's mountains, firs from the Pacific seaboard, gums from Australia – the list is very long. This reinforced our absurd sense of moral virtue. It served to prove that the British were Best. The truth is that it made us lazy as well as philistine. Because so little skill was needed to grow a collection of plants, everyone was doing it. By the end of the nineteenth century every back garden became a kind of mini-Kew.

The other disastrous influence on modern gardening has been money. It is not a simple effect. Until the mid-nineteenth century garden design was the province of the fabulously rich. Alexander Pope is an exception to this, but he proves the rule. Land was the currency of success. So they laid out their gardens as an expression of newly acquired wealth and power over the landscape and man. They hired designers to do this, just as they hired architects to build their houses. The result was a patronage of the new in both artistic disciplines. Between 1600 and the advent of neo-gothick at the end of the eighteenth century it would have been unthinkable for anyone to have created a house and garden that was locally retrospective. The classical influence became overwhelming but there was never an instance of gardens aping those of previous generations as we glutinously do now. When money rather than land became the currency of worldly success (although the two inevitably run hand-in-hand), it abstracted gardens from their location. You could now make anything anywhere, like larger versions of the show gardens at Chelsea Flower Show. Admirable gardens became synonymous with money and power. The more the Empire slid away and Britain became a minor little nation, the more gardens became aspirational, a stale relic of the longed-for days of greatness. Gardens that open their doors to the public invariably belong to the great

Our Empire and energy delved into the unknown and brought mementos, exactly as the first visitors to the moon did... We became philistines via acquisition of power.

and the good, pillars of the *status quo*. Anyone making money since the last World War has gardened with a nostalgic lack of invention. We have lost the gift of patronage. Money now buys us the past rather than the opportunity to celebrate the present.

Many of the best gardens being made now are good as a result of necessity and wit rather than cash. Derek Jarman's wonderful garden on Dungeness Beach shows what is possible in the teeth of the most unlikely conditions. Ian Hamilton Finlay's garden at Little Sparta is confirmation that gardening is still capable of poetry rather than just rhyme. Poverty of resources inevitably produces things cobbled together from what is available. It is the difference between a child with a brush and three colours and an adult laboriously painting by numbers. Poverty is never a virtue. But being thrown back on one's resources without the cushion of cash is more likely to produce fresh, creative work. At the moment people tend to garden when they have a house and steady income and their bank balance is as padded as their waistline. Of course, innovation and creativity are not the sole province of youth – witness the work of Sir Geoffrey Jellicoe, still revolutionary in his nineties – yet youth and iconoclasm are poor, therefore have the will to innovate, but also therefore have no horticultural canvas to work on. This conundrum is not decreed by nature, even though that is the received opinion. Why not provide allotments free for students? Could not the National Trust finance a country-wide design competition focused on radical innovation? Where are our patrons?

I am not rejecting history. We must absorb and learn from the past and make something new from it in a contemporary idiom in order that we may see the world afresh. I saw a French garden in a magazine the other day that used blocks of wheat to create a modern parterre. This is tremendous. Immediately one feels inspired and invigorated rather than cosily confirming a lifetime's prejudices of taste.

I think that the virulence of the letters provoked by my criticism of the National Trust proves that we are in danger of becoming sterile unless energy, excitement, and above all failure are actively sought out. If there are no failures it means that there can be no great success. If you love gardens, then you must want this. If age and experience cannot provide it, then clear out the way for those who can. Play safe and you must expect the vultures to circle, because you are already dead in your head.

Keep writing. I love you all really.

■ Drought is becoming part of our calendar. If you have not done so already, mulch everything that you can, particularly trees, shrubs and hedges. Use anything organic if possible, although newspaper laid ½ inch thick and then covered by a layer of soil works well. Always mulch after the ground is thoroughly wet as it will then retain dryness as well as moisture.

■ Avoid using a sprinkler except on lawns and fine seedlings. The water falls on the foliage and much of it evaporates before reaching the roots – which is where it is needed.

■ Concentrate what water you have on individual plants and direct the water at their roots.

■ A good soak once a week is better than a drizzle every day.

■ Water in the evenings or early mornings so it will not evaporate before it reaches the roots.

■ If you have spring-planted trees, put a length of piping down to the roots and water directly into that. This will also encourage the roots to grow deeper.

16.6.96 **An English Country Garden**

When I read other people's gardening columns the main thing that strikes me is that my gardening life is either bloody odd or very different to theirs. I know that most people live and garden in towns, but for those of us out in the sticks, things can be very different. My garden is bounded on three sides by pastureland, which from March to November contains grazing stock. The BSE crisis has meant that there are more unsold, full-grown cattle this year than ever. The cold has meant that there is less grass than ever, with the net result that there are a lot of big, hungry animals eyeing my luscious garden. Yesterday they made their move.

The phone went at seven-thirty in the morning. It was a neighbour, wondering if I knew that there were six – Ooh no, seven now – large cows in my garden. The milk curdled in my cornflakes. This is the country gardener's worst nightmare. Half-a-dozen cattle breaking in from the neighbouring fields can outdo all the combined damage of a year's frost, hurricane, drought or blight in twenty minutes' slow munching and a few playful passes across the lawn and flowerbeds.

I ran outside, the dogs at my heels, liking this unexpected game, to see that yes, there were seven – Oh my God, eight now – cattle tasting the delights of the Wild Garden. They had got there via the orchard, the new hornbeam hedges, the kitchen garden and the avenue of limes with juicy young leaves. I barely resisted the overwhelming urge to sit on the ground and cry. The dogs saw the cattle and decided to chase them. This had the immediate effect of stopping them eating the Wild Garden, but also made them turn on their heels and run in a curving, rumbling canter through the growing willow circle, through the hedges, across the newly sown and levelled grass, back towards the orchard. For those of you unfamiliar with the effects of rampaging cattle, imagine Sumo wrestlers performing on your dining-table while wearing cloven high heels, or a brace of hammer-throwers competing in your living-room.

The trick of moving animals bigger and more stupid than oneself is to remain calm and move slowly so that you all gently amble together to the required spot. If that doesn't work you must imitate a sheep dog. The cattle had charged back towards the gate, so I duly ambled up, hoping to evoke an atmosphere of cud-chewing ease, but, with the assistance of the excited eight-month-old Newfoundland puppy, it provoked them to take off in the opposite direction. Things went from very bad to awful. I shouted a lot. Eventually I got the bastards out. Then I had to mend the fence where they had got in while they thought it amusing to see if the gap could be breached again.

When the gap was plugged I inspected the damage. Lots of divots, lots of cowpats, but only random grazing. The limes had been swiped at in passing but were not ruined, and a couple of newly planted standard apples had had branches

There are a lot of big, hungry animals eyeing my luscious garden. Yesterday they made their move.

bitten off rather in the way that a football crowd will snap the odd car aerial.

When let into a new field cattle will always march round it, snatching a mouthful here and there, thoroughly casing the joint. They treated my garden like a school visit to a chocolate factory, sampling bits as they went but never stopping to feast. The only real disaster was that the embryonic hornbeam tunnel, based rather grandly on the fabulous hornbeam treillage of Queen Mary's Garden at Het Loo, was sampled down to half its height. As each plant had been chosen for height rather than bushiness and this unplanned pruning would have the effect of making them bushier, it means that all will have to be replaced. The rest of the hornbeam hedges, equally young, will probably be the better for their present nibbled condition.

The farmer has no responsibility to keep his cattle in. The burden is entirely mine to keep them out, so fencing is a vital part of our gardening, and at about £4 a metre, not cheap, given that there are over 300 metres to defend. However, my despair had by now turned into incandescent rage, so I rang the farmer just to be rude to him. He was charming, straightaway offering the fruits of his insurance policy. But how do you value cattle damage? It is one's time and spirit that are lost. Anyway, it was my fault for not fixing the fence when I noticed it was dodgy a couple of weeks before. Having started out spluttering I ended up apologizing to him.

Then Ron and Fred turned up. There is always an element of pot luck about this. They are both retired bricklayers, both have lived locally all their lives, and both are helping us fix up a range of barns butting on to the house. They come when they feel like it. This is a form of gardening, as it involves the creation of a potting shed, tool shed, new area for compost, a new terrace, garden walls and paths. The making of these things contributes as much to the garden as any planting, weeding or sowing and I get as much pleasure from them as from all those things. Fred doesn't say much, has the face of a gnarled angel and is the boss of the two. Ron chats all day and calls Fred Boy and me Boss. At first I felt uneasy about this, not knowing if it marked undue respect or skittish irony on account of his superior age, skill and experience set against my supply of cash. But as the months have gone by I realize that it is only the cash bit that counts. I pay him and am therefore his boss. He calls my wife who, through a combination of beauty and natural reserve inspires much more polite deference than me, Babes. This could have been a trifle over-familiar, if not a Big Mistake, given that he is a bricklayer and she an architect with a violent antipathy to sexual patronization, but it works, coming across as gallant in a rather archaic way.

We spend a lot of time discussing bonds with Fred and Ron. Yesterday was crucial as we had two lots of bonds meeting, doubling the anxiety. Were

The trick of moving animals bigger and more stupid than oneself is to remain calm and move slowly so that you all gently amble together to the required spot. If that doesn't work you must imitate a sheep dog.

we to use Flemish bond for the new wall enclosing the yard like the wall across the brick path (Basket Weave bond) or match in with the Hop Kiln, which dominates this new bit of garden, which is English Garden Wall bond? In the wall's sunny lea there is to be a new sitting area paved with bricks in Stretcher bond but – and this is where we ran into all sorts of difficulties – a new path is to run parallel to this and in order to match the existing path had to be Basket Weave bond. This is on top of the long search not only for suitable bricks that matched the surprisingly orange colour of the Hop Kiln but also for the different bricks for the path that, unlike the wall bricks, were tough enough for walking on and would withstand frost. We wait on Fred's pondered advice. Ron is chirpy and doesn't give a toss. 'Whatever you likes, Boss. Anything you like.' All this makes every difference to the garden, and unlike planting arrangements, cannot be easily changed. It is gardening with a vengeance and a big financial stake.

Even our country weeds are different to your towny ones. Docks and nettles rule my gardening life. The two go hand-in-hand, the Yin and Yang of weeds. Because this garden was a field for at least 600 years before us, containing stock for most of that time, the ground is rich in nitrogen. In a country garden this means nettles by the thousand. I dig them out of the cultivated bits, extracting yards of yellow rubbery roots, and mow off the tops of the ones where I want grass. From April to October it is a constant battle, which, if you let up for a week, they win.

Docks are fantastically vigorous in this heavy soil. The roots go down like enormous carrots, usually coming up somewhere inaccessible like the prickliest centre of a rose. Still, I cannot complain too much. The garden belongs to the docks and nettles and they are merely struggling to regain the land that I have taken over to settle. It's a good clean fight, but what with the fencing and the construction work and the vainglorious constructions aping seventeenth-century palatial gardens, it doesn't leave a lot of time for most people's idea of 'gardening'.

■ When laying brick paths it is essential to chose a brick that is not too porous, otherwise it will crumble when the frost gets to it. There is no need to lay the bricks on cement. Put down a layer of hardcore topped with at least 3 inches of sand. Use a board to get the sand absolutely level and lay the bricks on this slightly higher than their intended finished height. When they are in position they can be gently tamped down firm with a board laid across them. Brush a dry mix of 6:1 sand and cement into the joints which will harden and secure the bricks while still allowing drainage.

■ Glysophate, the sole but indispensable spray I use, does no more than make nettles feel groggy and turn yellow. They always come back. But a combination of spraying every three or four months and topping with the mower will eventually weaken them fatally. Luckily docks are very easily killed by Glysophate although if any seed before spraying they will invariably produce hundreds of offspring. Like nettles, they can be weakened by regular cutting.

■ Glysophate is retailed under the trade names of 'Roundup', 'Tumbleweed', 'Zeneca Tough Weed Killer', 'B&Q Complete Weedkiller'. I always use 'Roundup', and a recent *Gardening Which?* survey showed this to be the best value for money. The larger the amount you buy, the cheaper it is. Glysophate only works on the growing green bit of the weed and is best for couch, thistle, dock and bindweed.

25.6.95 **Slugs and Snails**

Last year I visited the garden of Bramdean House in Hampshire and so admired the idea of using straw as paths in the kitchen garden that I rushed home, ordered some bales of barley straw from my neighbour and laid the straw in 3-inch-thick wads to make narrow walkways amongst the veg. The plan was to renew them completely every couple of months or so, carting the trodden, sodden old straw to the compost heap. It worked well. Cheap, good-looking paths were had by all. But it was a big mistake. I noticed that my new vegetable garden was infested with slugs and when I came to make my first spring-clean of the straw I saw that these slugs had laid their eggs along every inch of the warm, damp soil beneath. Below the surface of my cheap, good-looking paths there existed a sluggy netherworld.

Most slugs in fact live in the soil, coming out to pillage after dark. Try going out into the garden the next warm, damp evening and shine a torch around. The chances are that the garden will be slowly writhing with slimy bodies. In one experiment 27,500 slugs were taken from one small garden without making any noticeable difference to slug activity. Densities of 200 slugs per square yard are moderate.

When I gardened in London it was not so much slugs as snails that ruled the roost. Their taste extended more towards flowers than veg, with hostas their choicest delicacy. How snails do love a hosta! Unless one conducted a constant vendetta against them (which I did), the hostas were reduced almost overnight to stringy tatters. There is a school of horticultural thought that says the answer to hosta depredation is to choose your variety carefully. Avoid variegated ones and stick with the larger, thicker-leafed varieties like the *H. sieboldiana* family, 'Francis Williams' or 'Elegance', for example.

I asked Roger Bowden, who with his wife Ann runs a nursery dealing exclusively in hostas, whether he could recommend snail-proof varieties. He could not. In his experience no hosta was immune although at the beginning of the season snails would go for the thinnest leaves first, but when these had been eaten they moved resolutely on to the thicker, larger leaves. Hostas like damp, shady sites and so do slugs, so the two tend to go together, although snails, he agreed, were a bigger problem than slugs.

Whilst slugs are brazenly there most of the time, but even more so after rain and at night, snails have a habit of hiding during the day and oozing craftily out at night in numbers that belie all possible hiding places. The truth is that they love brick walls best of all, especially with crumbly or loose mortar. That applies to almost all London gardens and the average plot will house thousands of the things, reproducing constantly. It is a losing battle to try to stop them.

I saw that these slugs had laid their eggs along every inch of the warm, damp soil beneath. Below the surface of my cheap, good-looking paths there existed a sluggy netherworld.

But as long as the battle was there to be lost I fought it. My technique was to empty a packet of salt into the bottom of a bucket and add a pint or two of water. I would water the garden at dusk and wait until it grew properly dark. Then I crept out, ducking behind the cover of the bushes so that I was on them before they could make for cover. Each snail was picked up and popped into the saline bucket where they died a fizzy death. Like the Walrus and his oysters I deeply sympathize for their ugly deaths but sorted out those of the largest size none the less fast for my sorrow. Half an hour's work might account for a couple of hundred snails, which would be good going for a year's worth of slug pellets. However, collecting adult snails can lead to an increase in their population. Apparently snails regulate their population density and growth rate by the amount of slime trails left by the adult snails. Where the ground is thoroughly slimed the young stay small, mooching in an unpredatory fashion in the walls, waiting for a window in the slime quota so that they can grow and slime about themselves. So by collecting hundreds of adult snails in one night you are going to cause an explosion of snail growth and reproduction.

I rather like snails actually, and if they did not eat my hostas I should happily live peaceably alongside them. They are like rabbits, which I also like, but kill without compunction if they stray over the fence into my garden.

But slugs are horrid. Even though they are simply snails that have evolved away from their shells, they have none of the charm of *Helix aspersa*, the garden snail. One cannot imagine a pet slug in the way a pet snail might be endearing. The slug smears itself on lettuce and pops up in the best washed salad, bores holes into potatoes before they are ready to harvest, eats every bit of succulent greenery going, and, half-leech half-bogy, is disgusting to the touch.

Slug pellets are the usual method of control, and to a certain extent, they work. The chemical in them is metaldehyde, which is noxious to humans as well as slugs. The pellets look rather like sweeties and are therefore a bit dodgy if you have small children, as well as looking ugly in themselves. The main problem is that they only deal with surface attacks, whereas slugs live below ground. For every one you kill above ground there are dozens waiting to attack in subterranean sluggy bunkers. Applying a liquid solution of aluminium sulphate is designed to kill the eggs and soak in to do its stuff in the soil, but once again, only works up to a point. It is reckoned that even intensive use of slug pellets will account for only 10 per cent of any given slug population.

Last spring nematodes became available to the general public as a specific predator of slugs. So far the indications are that they work fairly well, but results are variable – like all methods of dealing with the beastly things. We have had a mild, wet winter which is ideal for slugs. A really cold spell would probably do more good than any pellet or nematode. For nematodes to work,

I rather like snails actually, and if they did not eat my hostas I should happily live peaceably alongside them. They are like rabbits, which I also like, but kill without compunction if they stray over the fence into my garden.

the ground must be warm and wet, and their efficacy cannot be judged unless the conditions are right for them. Nematodes are slug-specific and will ignore the most succulent of snails.

Beetles eat slugs, particularly the Rove beetles, including the scorpion-like Devil's Coach-horse (*Staphylinus caesareus*) and the Ground beetle (*Carabus auratus*) whose larvae also happily dine off slugs and snails. The trouble is that for their predations to be effective you have to create a beetle-friendly garden, and using slug pellets and chemical solutions will damage the beetles as well as the slugs.

Hedgehogs eat beetles but prefer a juicy slug. They are to be encouraged in the garden. Once again, this means no slug pellets. Toads eat young slugs, as do ducks, chickens and guinea fowl – particularly in winter when the ground is bare. Thrushes eat snails. The law of supply and demand says that in order to get these attractive additions to the garden there has to be a supply of food – so no snails, no thrushes. No slugs, no hedgehogs, toads or beetles.

The best way to deal with slugs or snails is physically to get between them and the object of their hunger. Any form of barrier will do, although probably gravel or grit is the most effective. Spread this as a mulch around hostas, delphiniums and all other susceptible plants, and the slugs and snails will avoid crawling over the abrasive surface. Holly leaves work well, as do the coarser bark chippings.

Slugs eat rotting vegetation, so if you are digging compost or manure into the soil, you will improve things by making sure that it is very well decayed before putting it into the ground, thereby providing less for the slugs to eat. Roger Bowden advocates using mushroom compost mainly because it has less foodstuff for the slugs.

Good husbandry will help. Keep the ground well dug so that it drains, and keep weeds well hoed between crops so that the surface of the soil dries fast after rain. Thin plants properly so that they are strong and the ground between them is bare. Gather up all fallen and dead leaves and compost them before returning their goodness to the soil..

Finally, I suspect that the greatest influence on the growing slug and snail problem is fashion. Ever since the wonderful Rosemary Verey unveiled her famous potager at Barnsley House, the trend has been towards growing vegetables in as decorative a manner as possible. Box – which harbours snails like nothing else – has become *de rigueur* around everything that can be edged. Kitchen gardens are crammed with plants, every spare inch supporting square yards of juicy leaves. Vegetables are eaten smaller and younger, so thinning is reduced and planting intensified. Digging has become less popular, partly through idleness, partly because there is so much growing in every bit of ground that there is no chance to dig and mainly because of the popularity of mulching. All this creates perfect conditions for slugs and snails. You may not like the unfashionable habits of decent spacing, thorough digging and bare soil between plants that can dry to a scratchy, abrasive surface, but then neither do slugs.

■ Hosta growers: Carroll Gardens, Inc., 444 East Main St., P.O. Box 310, Westminster, MD. 21158 (410) 848-5422.

■ Slugs like beer. Put an inch of beer into a jam jar and place it on its side. The slugs crawl in, drink and die. Remove the corpses every morning.

■ Water only once a week, ideally in the morning. Give the ground a really good soak but allow time for the soil to dry off. A daily drizzle keeps the surface moist and good for slithering.

■ Cultivate the ground with a rototiller in very cold or very hot weather. This will kill many slugs and expose the others to predators.

■ For the record, there are four main culprits in the slug world: the Grey field slug (*Derocas reticulatum*) which is beigeish grey; the Garden slug (*Arion hortensis*), shiny black with an orange belly; the Keeled slug (*Milax budapestensis*), black with a thin orange line down the centre of its back, and the Black slug (*Arion ater*), which is usually black, but can come in almost any colour, and is differentiated from all others by its size.

■ Grey field slugs eat anything and will reproduce three generations a year.

■ The Garden slug is also omnivorous; its party tricks are to eat off bean plants at ground level and riddle potatoes with holes.

■ The Keeled slug spends almost all its life underground, feeding off root crops.

■ The Black slug is the biggest of the lot and grows as long as 8 inches. Despite its size it is the least harmful of all garden slugs.

26.6.96 Garden Design

The moment has come for me to dip my hobnailed foot into the loamy waters of the garden design controversy. It is a perennial debate that whiles away the duller moments of a winter evening when sex, drugs or rock and roll momentarily lose their allure.

The standard view is that the world of horticulture is drawn up into two lines. On the one hand are the serried ranks of Plantsmen, focusing their considerable intelligence and energies on quietly growing plants as well as possible, and on the other are the Designers, a motley bunch who hide their lack of knowledge behind trendiness and a deal of flamboyant publicity. A plantsman's hands are engrained with honest soil and toil whereas the designer's hands carry only the stains of a leaky pen. Plantsmen are Roundheads and Designers Royalists. Plantsmen know the Latin names of almost everything and Designers know the plant well...it's on the tip of their tongue...oh, you know.

James Fenton – whose garden I have never seen, but whose poetry I admire – wrote a piece in the *Independent* after the Chelsea Flower Show, railing against the existence of garden designers. The edition in question has long been used to light the fire, but I seem to recall that his line was that garden designers were like the people who train politicians to wear certain clothes and speak in soundbites: not only not the thing itself but a corruption of the thing itself. By providing gardens like fitted kitchens they are destroying the essence and magic of gardening which is an idiosyncratic process of accretion.

By providing gardens like fitted kitchens they are destroying the essence and magic of gardening which is an idiosyncratic process of accretion.

The result might be frightful, but even the horridest gardens from this school are to be encouraged, otherwise gardening will continue even further up its own horticultural backside.

He is both right in an important way and absolutely wrong in another. Let's take the rightness first.

A garden can be ugly, brash, boring and shallow. Lots are. Just because it is filled with expensive topiary, trees moved at mind-boggling expense, all the colours of the plant spectrum, it does not mean that it will be a beautiful place. To take the kitchen analogy a little further, when you walk into the kitchen of an unmucked-about farmhouse lived in by the same family for generations you are immediately absorbing good meals, good company, as well as consoling cups of tea drunk silently at the table. A fitted kitchen relies on first appearances. It carries nothing within it other than function. For a garden to have meaning it must be personal. One of the side-effects of this is to put it beyond value-judgement. You either like it or not. But one of the fundamentals of any profession is that its practice can be good or bad. So professional garden designers have a vested interest in promoting the qualitative measurement of design in order that they may be clearly seen to be on the right side of the divide. Clearly this process denies the subtlety and richness that the 'best' (ones that I like most) gardens across the world all have. So much against the designers.

There seem to be three categories of people who employ professional garden designers. The first differ from the vast majority of the population only in their affluence. They like gardens but have not a clue about gardening. Because they are rich they tend to spend far too much money on the process and take delivery of a garden like a suite of furniture. I remember having dinner with a designer who worked for another very well-known designer and he had spent the day on site at a large garden they were creating for the cost of £1 million. The thing that really galled him was that he knew he could create every bit as good a garden for a tenth of that price. Beyond a certain (pretty high) point, money was the wrong creative fuel.

The second group have gardens already but want to bring them up to social scratch. They want the latest fad, be it a knot garden or pleached limes, and they want it now. In a year or two they will want it no longer.

The third group value the creativity and spark of design and are excited by talent in any field. They have to have to be rich to indulge this passion to any great extent, but will employ a garden designer in exactly the same spirit as they will use an architect or commission a piece of new furniture. They want the designer to create something original containing something of the personalities and vagaries of both creator and client. The result might be frightful, but even the horridest gardens from this school are to be encouraged, otherwise gardening will continue even further up its own horticultural backside.

I have made three gardens of my own. All three have been quite different and the process of designing each has been an essential, conscious creative act. It seems to me that garden design has two strands. The first is to do with all

the bits of gardening that are not dominated by horticulture such as paths, barriers, views, size and shape of lawns, borders or groups of trees. The second is the arrangement of colours, textures and forms. Above all one has to be aware of the surroundings and to make something from them. In the end this should amount to a kind of quirky inevitability. It is possible to achieve that complete state artlessly. James Fenton refers to gardens he saw and loved in Malaysia and I know a few cottage gardens in Herefordshire that are unimprovable although certainly not designed. But it is disingenuous to think that this has a purity transcending design. I bet the owners would love to change them – probably to something we would think hideous.

If we have to choose sides I know that I must join the Designers, for all their forces of mediocrity and bland uniformity. Do not reject garden design on the back of over-expensive, clichéd stage-sets that you see at Chelsea. There are honourable exceptions even there (Dan Pearson, Paul Cooper) and these should be applauded from the treetops, but garden design is essential on a humbler scale in every single garden. If we do not value it and take it seriously then we shall all be taken over by the Roundheads and lose that vital fire of creativity in the garden.

July

■ It is time for a second sowing of parsley. This will carry you through to Christmas and another sowing in late September should see you through to next May.
■ Roses are at their peak. Before they go over, collect the petals of old roses and carefully lay them out on newspaper in a dry, dark, but not too hot place. Centifolias, albas, damasks and gallicas all have perfumes that last well into autumn in a pot-pourri and will remind one of the best of these summer days.
■ Plant out leek seedlings now. They are better planted in blocks at about 6-inch intervals. Make a hole with a dibber [a pointed hand tool] and pop each leek in it without filling it back in. Fill the hole with water. Keep watered. The leek will grow to fill the hole and the water will wash soil down around the roots.
■ Treat patches of nettles as a beneficial crop. Even if you do not pick the young shoots for eating (more fool you), cut them and put them on to the compost heap. They break down fast and work as an activator for the rest of the heap.
■ Make a point of walking in the garden at dusk. It is the best moment at this the best time of the year. Colours shine out from the half-light and all scent is at its richest. These late evenings are on the wane – so make the most of them now.

14.7.96 **The Scented Garden**

A garden without scent is a two-dimensional place. Scent adds substance to every contact with a garden. Sometimes this is shockingly powerful, a falling in love with and through scent, as when for the first time each year you catch the fragrance of new-mown grass, or when one of a dozen heavenly roses is lifted tentatively to your nose and all expectations are surpassed. Sometimes it is part of our own internal map of the garden, a measure of our intimacy with it, just as the bitter tang of docks on the skin and nettle roots are part of my knowledge of my own garden. But mostly we take scent for granted and do not give it the focused enjoyment that it deserves.

The only way that we can judge or measure smell is on a scale from like to dislike. There is no objective standard to refer to. A smell I don't like is a stink or a stench. Roses are fragrant and herbs aromatic. This is probably an evolutionary device so that our initial preference for a smell warns us of possible harm: we only need to know if we dislike a smell to question its safety.

With colours we learn an absolute standard, and even though the application of those standards can be fairly arbitrary, we have a good idea of what is meant by the word red. On the whole, every colour describes itself, but we nearly always describe a smell in terms of something else. Surprisingly few things have an identifiable smell. In the garden pears do, as do box, tomatoes and freshly cut grass. But if we have to describe the smell to someone who has never experienced it we immediately start to fumble inadequately. It hardly ever occurs to us to analyse smells: and if we try it is incredibly difficult to use language to describe them. It is enough to recognize them, although no one knows how we create a memory bank of different fragrances.

It is certain that we dramatically underuse our ability to smell. Only when we lose the facility of another sense, like sight, do we call upon our olfactory reserves and find that we can smell inanimate objects as clearly as we could formerly see them. It seems probably that smelling danger, smelling trouble, smelling the air are all practical descriptive phrases.

Every day each one of us draws about 23,000 breaths, dipping into a deep well of smells, almost all of them confusing and unrecognizable. As the scent molecules go up our nose the messages go straight to the rear of the brain, to the part used for controlling libido, for feelings and emotions.

This means that no two people will react to smell in the same way. When I smell sunshine on *Buxus sempervirens* I am instantly suffused with pleasure induced by recollection of happy hours in my childhood swimming in my aunt's pool that was enclosed by a wobbly box hedge. When Queen Anne smelt it she felt ill and consequently had all box ripped up from the gardens at Hampton Court and Kensington Palace as soon as she succeeded William III, who had planted them.

When we experience a new scent all we can know is a measure of like or dislike. That is going to be markedly affected by the other conditions of pleasure or unhappiness. A certain perfume caught as you become intimately close to someone you feel attracted to will always smell good thereafter. A child smelling the same perfume as it is being reprimanded will dislike it for the rest of its life.

Whilst we all sort of know this and sort of enjoy it in the garden, it is possible to use scent proactively in any kind of garden. The first thing to do

Whilst we all sort of know this and sort of enjoy it in the garden, it is possible to use scent proactively in any kind of garden. The first thing to do is to work out what makes you feel good and go for these plants, regardless of received opinion about what smells good or not.

is to work out what makes you feel good and go for these plants, regardless of received opinion about what smells good or not.

Then you have to take stock of when and how you use the garden. If your custom is to stand outside drinking a final cup of tea before setting off for work in the morning, it makes sense to plant something that will smell at its best in the morning. However, if you hardly ever go into the garden until you come home in the evening, it is sensible to make the most of plants that release their scent at night.

My favourite time and place in my own garden is walking at night along a path between an avenue of clipped limes that are underplanted with *Nicotiana sylvestris*. During the day the curiously sticky, fleshy leaves dominate the slightly shrunken white flowers, but at dusk these seem to open out and give off the most delicious and evocative of all garden scents, rich, musky and utterly sensual. The confines of the avenue stop the scent being blown away, and it is worth creating pockets to hold scent. Many of the night-scented plants grow naturally in valley bottoms where their fragrance is more likely to be trapped.

Flowers that release their scent at night all tend to be white or pale-coloured, which obviously increases their visibility, and they release their scent as the air cools. This reduces the competition to find a pollinator as well as increasing the chances of the pollinating insect moving on to another plant from the same family, both devices designed to improve evolutionary success. Plants which smell best at night include *Nicotiana sylvestris*, night-scented stock (*Mathiola bicornis*), honeysuckles, night-blooming jasmine (*Cestrum nocturnum*), *Hoya carnosa*, datura, the Evening primrose (*Oenothera biennis*), verbena, and all the white flowering shrubs such as philadelphus, syringa, eleagnus, clethra and osmanthus that smell stronger at night than during the day. Of course, a midsummer's day is filled with an almost bewildering variety of scent, creating a mixture from which it is hard to extract individual aromas. But lilies will always stand out from the perfumed crowd. The Madonna lily (*Lilium candidum*), is perhaps the easiest to grow, performing well in a pot as long as the drainage is good. It has a distinctively honeyed fragrance. *L. regale* is also unfussy and smells fruitier. One of the best displays of lilies I ever saw was at a hotel in Yorkshire where they were grown in blocks surrounded by hedges of lavender. Stunning.

Here's a puzzle for you: if you came across Lady Archer sitting next to a pyracantha in full flower, which would smell the sweeter? Answers in the form of a junk novel, please. Huge advances will be paid. For all her apparent fragrance, I bet the pyracantha would win. It has one of the sweetest

The one smell that is more heart-racingly beautiful and impossible to capture or contain within a garden than the scent of any plant, is the smell of warm, dusty soil immediately after a light shower of rain.

(cloyingly so) smells in the garden and attracts bees like nothing else. The heavy odour of *Jasminum officionale* can also be so powerful as to be overwhelming, and it should not be grown in a contained area where the scent will be trapped and suffocating. It has strength enough to spare to withstand being blown about open spaces. But to be suffocated by the scent of sweet peas would be a wonderful end. Grow them where every ounce of perfume can be savoured. Modern versions such as the 'Spencer' varieties do not smell, which is as crazy as supermarket food that does not taste. Buy the 'Grandiflora' mixes or named varieties like 'Painted Lady'.

I particularly love foliage that is scented when touched. Scented-leaved pelargoniums have an astonishing range of smells, all mimicking other plants. *P. tormentosum* smells of peppermint, *P. odoratissimum* of apple, *P.* 'Mabel Grey' of lemon, *P. graveolens* of roses, and *P.* x *fragrans* of pine. Rosemary, mint, basil and lavender instantly smell when crushed, as do bay and citrus leaves. It is the combination of senses, touch and scent, that is so good, tying you into intimacy with your garden.

It is wrong to get hung up on the scent of flowers as if they were the prime source of garden smells. Think of the huge range of scents that belong to the garden: there is the smell of a bonfire and the richness of a handful of dirt in March, the wet tang of the wind as it flaps around the full greenness of the garden and the dry scent of frost. The greenhouse has an unforgettable musty sweetness, and an old potting shed smells of terracotta and potting compost. There is the incredible honey-sweetness of fallen fruit in an orchard and the damp, truffly blanket of smell that wet leaves cast. It is not just the new-mown grass that we recognize but also the mower that cut it, petrol, hot engine and all. Stones smell and gravel releases its own bony scent as it is raked.

But the one smell that is more heart-racingly beautiful and impossible to capture or contain within a garden than the scent of any plant is the smell of warm, dusty soil immediately after a light shower of rain. The water releases an aroma of such fecundity that you almost expect growth to start erupting around you like time-lapse photography. There are usually just a couple of such moments in each of my summers and every time I want to dance for pure sensuous joy.

■ Place plants with aromatic leaves on the border with a path so that you have to brush against them as you pass, releasing their scent. Plant the tiny *Mentha requienii* between paving stones so that your footsteps become minty. Chamomile never really makes a lawn but it can make aromatic stepping points in a grass path.

■ Many trees have wonderful scents. *Thuja plicata* has little visual attraction for me but the leaves smell lovely when crushed, giving off a strong whiff of peardrops. *T. standishii* smells of lemon. Junipers smell idiosyncratically resinous and if you are on acid soil the Oregon Douglas fir, *Pseudotsuga menziesii*, is equally pleasantly pungent. Most pines smell of, um… pine and in the right setting it makes them a superb garden tree. The buds of balsam poplar are filled with resin that carries its scent strong and far in spring. *Populus trichocarpa* is the best type to grow if you have reasonable space for it. Wind in the leaves of a walnut tree will provoke it to give off its distinctive fruity smell: a good, underplanted garden tree.

■ Plant now for winter smells. *Lonicera fragrantissima* [Zones 5-9], *Hamamelis mollis* [Zones 5-9], *Viburnum farreri* [Zones 6-8], *Mahonia japonica* [Zones 7-9], *Daphne mezereum* [Zones 5-8] and Wintersweet (*Chimonathus praecox*) [Zones 7-9] will all provide welcome fragrance on the bleakest winter day.

■There are a few plants with really unpleasant scents. Amongst these I would include the blossom of hawthorn, so exciting for the eye but too sickly for the nose, *Lysichiton americanum* that stinks of rotting cabbage in spring, and the Dragon arum, *Drancunculus vulgaris*.

21.7.96 **Touch**

It was spring. I was alone in the garden of my childhood. The trees had not yet come into leaf, but the sky was warm, gentle sun on my skin, peace glowing like light from every object around me. The soil was rilled like corduroy and worked to an umber tilth. I ran its silkiness through my fingers, rummaging my hands through the seedbed until they grew down into the earth, fingers spreading through the grainy particles of dirt, taking root deep in the garden. I awoke with a lasting sense of well-being.

Forget Jung, Freud and my addled psyche, the point is overwhelmingly tactile – once you have felt the first warm soil of spring in your hands it never goes from the memory, however soft and undextrous your hands become. It pops back up, even in your dreams.

The relationship between hand and garden is akin to that of lovers: It is never enough just to look on in admiration. People say disparagingly (tinged with jealousy) that two lovers were 'all over each other', and so are gardeners in love with their garden, irresistibly drawn to caress leaves, cradle flowers in their palm, trace the fissure on the bark of a tree, or fluff the new leaves of a hedge in passing. You touch garden and garden touches you, giving back pleasures entirely of the flesh.

Yet the gardener's hands are hardly the image of romantic glamour, invariably calloused and swollen with labour, engrained with soil lodged within the epidermis despite endless scrubbing. It is impossible to garden effectively with long or painted nails, and cuts and abrasions are inevitable. The gardener's hands have to be refined down to bluntness best to perform with the delicacy and strength that the job demands.

My own hands are so essential to my experience of the garden that I cannot imagine what would be left for me without them. Otherwise gardening would be a platonic relationship, one not consummated or made whole. I need to feel the soil, touch every leaf or flower, and love the feel of a well-balanced spade, rake or hoe in the hand. There is a 'rightness' to weight that is inexplicable in any other terms than 'feel'. This manifests

Forget Jung, Freud and my addled psyche, the point is overwhelmingly tactile – once you have felt the first warm soil of spring in your hands it never goes from the memory, however soft and undextrous your hands become. It pops back up, even in your dreams.

itself most noticeably with hand tools. Given the choice of ten identical spades, one will feel more 'right' than the other nine for every individual – even though it is possible for all ten to choose a different spade. When one has an ideal tool in one's hand and it is being used well, then the function itself becomes pure pleasure and it does not matter what is being dug or cut or hoed or what the conditions are. There is a Zen-like flow between man and inanimate object that is perfect harmony. This is gritty, practical reality experienced sooner or later by every gardener and is one of the less honoured and greatest pleasures of gardening.

Touch differs from other senses in that it has no specialized piece of equipment to measure and sense it. Hands are not the organ of touch any more than is the soft skin inside an elbow. The entire skin – all 20 square feet of it – is a sensate organ and we can simultaneously prick our finger while brushing a petal against our cheek, feel our shirt scratch at the neck and sun hot on our brow, aware of the cold dribble of sweat running down our flank. It is like having noses all over the body or ears on our legs.

Of course the skin feels everything but knows nothing. The brain alone makes sense out of feeling, and every type of tactile sensation, be it pleasure, pain, itch or measurement, has to travel to the brain via neural receptor elements in the skin that are at the end of axons connected with the spinal cord and brain stem.

But however cerebral or analytical you are about gardening, it is an extraordinarily tactile business. Think how often you are on your knees weeding, planting, looking. What else do you do that gets you grovelling down in the dirt so much? Think how much exercise there is in digging or planting, how every muscle gets used: it is all body. Yet everything is done to reduce the corporality of gardening, be it by machine, mulch, computer or tricks to save labour. Real gardening is a gutsy, physical affair and it is appropriate to relish the labour as much as the aesthetic pleasure that is created from all the effort.

For the blind or short-sighted, the hand develops depths of refinement untapped by the clear-sighted. The abilities are there, of course, but most of us merely skim the surface of our senses, lazy swallows picking flies of sensation of the water rather than diving deep. A friend who gardens one of our most famous and well-stocked gardens took a blind person round the garden this spring. She was astonished to find that of all the thousands of plants the one that was found to be the most pleasurable to touch was a tulip, fingertips drawing up the tapering flower in a way that the sighted person would scarcely think of doing. Nothing else had the exquisitely satiny sensuousness. I can't wait until

My own hands are so essential to my experience of the garden that I cannot imagine what would be left for me without them. Otherwise gardening would be a platonic relationship, one not consummated or made whole.

next spring to experience it for myself.

There is a wonderful passage in Richard Jefferies' novel, *Amaryllis at the Fair*, where the hero farmer, Iden, 'would often go out and sit under the russet apple till the dew filled the grass like a green sea. When the tide of the dew had risen he would take off his heavy boots and stockings, and so walk about in the cool shadows of the eve, paddling in the wet grass. He liked the refreshing coolness and touch of the sward... it was because he liked the grass.' How intimate it is to walk sensuously through the dew with bare feet because you like the grass! Gardeners tend to take a macho pride in their sturdy footwear, be it boots or wellingtons, and forgo the pleasures of bare feet, both on grass and warm soil, which both feels good and tells you something about your garden that no other sensation can: it is part of the sensory map that creates intimacy.

I have always admired the hardiness of those who garden in shorts, given the range of unwelcome intimacy that you are thereby exposed to, from nettles and thorns to allergic reactions and knees embossed with stones. I would rather deprive myself of the tactile delights twixt knee and ankle and keep my trousers on.

I had intended to furnish this piece with suggestions of plants for various tactile sensations, be they furry, soft, abrasive or whatever, but I was falling into the trap that so many would-be gardening gurus make for themselves. It would direct the garden towards plants and try to objectify sensation, whereas gardens are about gardeners and our perceptions subjective and changeable from day to day. People are always so much more interesting than plants. It does not matter what you touch but how you react to that sensation. The other day I read about women working in city business who felt that they still had to obey a formal dress code to meet the expectations of men. They tolerated this because beneath this outer layer they could wear the underwear that pleased them, often as sensuous and luxurious as their outer clothing was drab and conventional. Gardens should be like this. They are the underwear you choose to please yourself, not the formal attire imposed by other people's expectations. If your garden feels good to you – literally – then it follows that it will look good.

Plants not to touch

■ Neither rue (*Ruta graveolens*) nor Giant Hogweed (*Heracleum mantegazzianum*) seems to have apparent stings or barbs, but the slightest brush with the leaves of either plant on skin that is exposed to bright ultra-violet rays causes painful blisters that take a long time to heal. The skin of the hands is sufficiently tough to resist this, but never garden near either plant with your shirt off on a bright summer's day. Other plants will cause an unpleasant reaction when touched. Stinging nettles are the most common, although not often deliberately cultivated, despite the excellent soup to be enjoyed from young nettle tops.

■ You cannot buy a poinsettia nowadays without practically signing a disclaimer to potential health problems caused by its sap. Poinsettia is a member of the Euphorbia family and some people do find themselves irritated by the milky sap of a number of euphorbias, though simple contact with the plant will do no harm. But no one comes off better in a brush with any rose, bramble, cactus, holly, yucca, speargrass or prickly pear.

28.7.96 **Taste**

I have often sat down to a meal at someone's house to be told proudly that everything on my plate comes from the garden. It implies a commendable level of industry and horticultural skill but is no guarantee of the quality of taste. It is as though all culinary discretion is suspended and, to mangle Dr Johnson's observation on women preachers, one is to applaud that it is done at all rather than how well it is done. This attitude has long pervaded all fruit and vegetable growing in this country, with all instruction geared towards producing edible garden produce early, late, big, in vast quantity, in succession, indoors, in window boxes, in winter and in time, but very seldom deliciously or with the prime consideration being its tastiness. I suppose that there had to be some compensation for all the hours slogging away in the vegetable garden and that the rewards were unlikely to come from the kitchen, given that until recently in this country, you could expect all vegetables to be cooked to a neutral slush. But we all have cosmopolitan palates now. Spanning Cajun, Thai or Eastern European Peasant in an ordinary week, our meals are like a pick 'n' mix counter of cuisines. We know how many beans make fine food. It's only in Leominster that olive oil is still for earache and an avocado something that makes the custard taste bad.

But even with educated tastebuds, we are all very bad at describing tastes. We are too influenced by what tastes nice or nasty to be objective about what it tastes like. The best that we can do is to categorize a few universal tastes, although there is no scientific basis for this. It is generally agreed that there are four reliable taste stimuli: salt, sweet, bitter and sour. But such delineations are more labels of convenience than scientific definitions. Interestingly, 'tastelessness' is best defined as that which most closely tastes of our own saliva. That is why tap water – which has osmotic properties more akin to saliva than distilled water – has less taste than the purer distilled water. This is at the heart of how we instinctively choose to combine tastes. If the saliva is bathed in a sweet dessert, then an accompanying dry wine will taste much drier and the dessert much sweeter. If, however, we drink a sweet dessert wine with it, the balance of taste ensures that the combination modifies our sensation levels.

To my knowledge there is nothing you can grow in the garden that is identifiably salty. I have written about bitter and sour garden foods in these pages before – chicory is archetypally bitter and cooking apples sour – but by far the majority of fruits and vegetables are sweet, and the modern Western world is a culture obsessed by sweetness. Until the introduction of sugar cane from the Americas in the seventeenth-century, most people only had the natural sweetness in foods, with the precious addition of honey as and when it

We know how many beans make fine food. It's only in Leominster that olive oil is still for earache and an avocado something that makes the custard taste bad.

could be got to sweeten their tooth. Sweetmeats were a delicacy and Elizabeth I's famous black teeth are a testimony to the irresistible allure of sweetness to those who have access to it. In fact we need lots of it to taste it at all as we can only detect one part of sweetness in 200, whereas bitterness can be tasted in a mixture 10, 000 times more dilute.

The secret of combining subtle flavours with sweetness is warmth. Because of our expertise in food storage, we have lost the art of collecting food as and when we want it. Chilling food spreads its sweetness thin, masking taste with a cloying saccharine. The best place to store food for best taste is in the ground or on the plant that bears it, not in a chilling cabinet or fridge. Go to any Mediterranean market and you will find a finer selection of vegetables on display in the sun, picked straight from smallholdings and gardens, than in London's largest chilled foodstores. The fridge might make us less prone to food poisoning but it also blandifies all tastes. There is much to be said for a larder.

The garden holds a sunny, sensual sweetness that no supermarket can match. Anyone who has picked and eaten a ripe strawberry from the warm earth knows this as a defining moment. All other strawberries are measured by that first bite into its honey flesh. In the smallest garden this level of gourmet sensuality can be repeated daily. There are peaches to be eaten warm from the brick of the wall they are grown against, peas picked off the tendrilly plant and shucked straight from pod to mouth, baby carrots pulled from the warm soil, swished under a tap and crunched by the dozen, tomatoes waiting to release their own musty muskiness as teeth break their skin, herbs picked into a mingled sprig seconds before sprinkling into an omelette, plums so fat with their ripeness they demand to be gorged to be appreciated properly, and dusty figs that slowly turn inside out between the thumbs in almost unbearable voluptuousness. At such times plants exist solely for our pleasure.

The Tudor and Stuart gardeners concentrated their skills more on growing fruit than vegetables, revelling in the vast range of varieties and tastes that they provided. There are over 1000 varieties of apple alone, each with a definable flavour. If you devoted a lifetime to epicurean exploration of orchard fruits, from apricots to the almost rotting edge of 'bletted' [ripened and softened in storage] medlars, you would still be discovering new tastes in your fruity old age. In many ways growing 'top' fruit (i.e. fruit that grows on trees, such as apples, pears, plums, gages, cherries, figs, medlars and mulberries) is much more suitable for the modern gardener than vegetable gardening, these trees needing no cultivation other than a little pruning, being blossomy each spring, providing leafy shade in the summer and structure in the winter. But it is out of fashion at the moment, regarded as mere top-storey decoration for boringly trendy potagers.

If you devoted a lifetime to epicurean exploration of orchard fruits, from apricots to the almost rotting edge of 'bletted' medlars, you would still be discovering new tastes in your fruity old age.

The gulf in quality between what fruit and vegetables look and taste like is unnecessary for the modern gardener with little time or space to get into the full-scale machismo of conventional vegetable gardening, where biggest is always best. Luckily women are entering the field as authorities concentrating on tasty food rather than displays of maleness. It is time for men to adapt and learn to grow delicious rather than just big food. After all, creating a range of exquisite sensations is much more fun than comparing the size of your marrows.

■Smaller vegetables invariably taste more intense than their bigger counterparts. By growing plants closer together and harvesting them younger, you not only need less space but also get a quality of food that cannot be bought in any shop. You are also able to grow a surprising range of tastes in a limited space from the sweetness of carrots, parsnips, baby turnips and beetroot the size of golf balls to baby cauliflowers, every kind of bean and lettuce, as well as small but practical onions, shallots, leeks and garlic.

■Intensity of taste with a baby carrot or young broad bean can be matched directly by intensity of organization within available growing space. By growing your crops in blocks and grids rather than rows in small squares about 5 x 5 feet, you make everything accessible from the edges and every usable inch of ground productive.

■It is important to use catch-crops where size counts for less than taste and space is at a premium. This means sowing a fast-maturing crop like radish, lettuce or spinach amongst slow-growing ones like celery, onions or peas. The fast crop has grown, been harvested and eaten before it is crowded out by the maturing slow one. The principle of succession within one crop – typically lettuce – and between different types of vegetable ensures a steady supply of food that you have chosen, that most satisfies your tastebuds and for which absolute freshness is at a premium.

30.7.95 **Red!**

I went to lunch in a beautiful garden overlooking Hay-on-Wye. We sat surrounded by a mass of purply-grey roses – 'Cardinal Richelieu', 'William Lobb', 'Charles de Mills' – at the edge of one of the best 'white' gardens I have seen, a dry courtyard filled with 'Iceberg' roses, *Alchemilla mollis*, lilies. My friend is a tulip nut and we were idly chatting about suppliers and longevity of tulip type. She could identify longevity down to colours. Then she said something that flicked a switch in my head. Red, she said, you know, bright scarlet, goes on and on.

Precisely.

The impact of red spreads like huge ripples from a little stone. My hostess went on to say that as a rule she disliked bright red in a garden, I disagreed with her and we agreed to differ. One of the reasons I do like red – bright, strong vermilion through to scarlet, not a smoky, subtle, deeply trendy maroon – is that it is a hot shout saying, 'Look at me! I'm alive and strong and God, I relish it!' Red always leaps forward and can therefore be tricky if it has more retiring colours around it. It is like the bright, bouncy child in the class straining to answer each question: one longs for them sometimes to shut up and give the others a chance. So it has to be used judiciously. In practice this means not mixing it in a spotty way with pastel colours (the very word pastel

One of the reasons I do like red... is that it is a hot shout saying, 'Look at me! I'm alive and strong and God, I relish it!'

gives me the creeps, although I love lavenders, pinks and pale greens – it is redolent of too many years in the fashion business, I think).

The safest and truest companion to hot reds is its opposite, green. The perfect example of this is English holly, *Ilex aquifolium*, whose shiny green leaves and bright red berries so powerfully symbolize life in the dead core of winter. The berries of hawthorn, pyracantha, cotoneaster, rose hips and the edible fruits such as raspberry and redcurrants all work powerfully for this same reason of the contrast between red and green. Most plants with red flowers or fruit have green leaves which serve to make the red seem redder. If these plants are placed against a more general green background they stand out all the more, and at this time of year when there is a collective lull in the herbaceous border, the vermilion flowers of geum, poppy or Jerusalem Cross (*Lychnis chalcedonica*) blaze out from the collective green of the general border foliage. The red salvias such as *S. splendens* 'Blaze of Fire' or *S. elegans* need not be treated like a municipal bedding plant but grown as the shrubby perennial that salvia is, along with the bergamot *Monarda* 'Cambridge Scarlet', the chocolate *Cosmos C. atrosanguineus* and *Lobelia* x *speciosa* cultivars.

I have gained enormous pleasure in particular this year from my *Geum* x *borisii*. It is a commonplace plant, easily available, and has flowered from mid-May and is still going strong. I love the way that it splays out on strong, slender stems and scatters brightness against a more sombre background. It is funny how one falls in and out of love with plants that one might have known for years – rather like particular pieces of music.

Red roses are altogether trickier, almost entirely spoilt by the floral industry's perversion of scentless, characterless, mass-produced article. There are plenty of wonderful purply-reds and deep pinks, but they do not count. There must be no ambiguity. Red means bright red. However, there are some scorchers that I must have in my garden. 'Henri Martin' is one, a medium-sized moss rose that is particularly floriferous, The *moyesii* rose, 'Geranium', is another. 'Paul's Scarlet' climber is rightly named, and I planted one last year which is tentatively performing now. The gallica 'Sissinghurst Castle' is a good strong red, but I do not have it. Before anyone writes in with a list of scarlet Hybrid Teas as long as the ink in their pen, I acknowledge their existence but am too ignorant to write about them.

The place where red works most powerfully is in the vegetable garden. It is worth planting ruby chard for entertainment value alone, even if you never intend to eat it. The flowers of runner beans justify their cultivation, and strawberries, redcurrants and raspberries are as decorative as they are delicious. Radiccio is easy and provides late-summer ruddiness. I grow Worcester Pearmain apples both for eating off the tree in August (hardly ever worth buying as they are picked unripe and do not travel) and for marvelling at their red voluptuousness. Either plant a sole-coloured nasturtium like *Tropaeolum* 'Hermine Grasshof' or just pinch out all but the scarlet flowers in a mixed packet and the vegetable garden blazes with angry joy.

Red has to be used judiciously. In practice this means not mixing it in a spotty way with pastel colours (the very word pastel gives me the creeps... it is redolent of too many years in the fashion business, I think).

July

Annuals produce the brightest range of reds because they have most need to hustle for germination in their few months of flowering. This can lead to what I call estate-agent gardening ('The garden is planted in a riot of colour...') but can also make a fierce, almost pure display that can be lovely. Zinnias, petunias, cosmos, *Phlox drummondii*, *dianthus*, poppy (the annual reds in my garden) all focus colour into strong but unriotous display if used against a predominantly green backdrop.

The most famous exceptions to this rule – the most famous collection of red planting altogether – are the red double borders at Hidcote Manor. I had the good fortune to spend an entire day looking at them while filming them a couple of summers ago and went from suspicion (a private, unhorticultural neurosis) to untrammelled admiration. The scheme depends predominantly upon the combination of red and purple to achieve its effect, although there is unavoidably a lot of green there too. 'Purple' is extended to straight blues which, with straight reds, the eye combines. Orange heats up the scheme, working particularly well to lift the greens. In this age of a million white gardens, it is surprising that more people have not cottoned on to the effectiveness of this undervalued garden. Certain plants, like the dahlia 'Bishop of Llandaff', have become trendy, although 'Bloodstone' – same colour but with water-lily flower-heads – is used to just as good effect at Hidcote.

Because red can never be restful, and most people demand that their gardens should be a place of rest, mental if not physical, one should use a red area as a procession within a confined space. Even if you have a very small garden, there is likely to be a section that will lend itself to the sort of scarlet movement perfected at Hidcote. There are certain tricks that the National Trust have employed at Hidcote that are worth learning. The first is that red containing yellow should never be mixed with red containing blue. So the vermilion of *Lychnis chalcedonica* (red containing yellow) cannot rub shoulders with *Lobelia* 'Cherry Ripe'. I am inherently suspicious of hard-and-fast rules and enjoy seeing them broken, but it is certainly worth experimenting with this as a guide if not a binding piece of legislation. Likewise the use of purple foliage to add an overall depth and intensity to what otherwise might become a brazen rash of colour.

Red foliage is hard to come by. In autumn much depends upon the relationship between daytime heat and night-time cold in August and September, and this country rarely has sufficient of either to get a really good scarlet display. However, there are reliable exceptions. The Scarlet oak (*Quercus coccinea*), Sweet gum (*Liquidamber styraciflua*), *Cotinus coggygria* 'Flame', the acers, *rubrum*, *saccharinum*, *palmatum*, *japonicum* and *nikoense*, will all flame to order. Cotoneaster can be impressively scarlet of leaf in October,

and most vines blaze bright red for a week or so. But we know that this leafy red is a dying of the light – it is a final flurry rather than the vulgar insouciance of high-summer flowers. One of the best reds comes after all the leaves have long fallen, and that is on the stems of dogwood, *Cornus alba* 'Sibirica', whose red stems seem all the more vivid against a harsh frosty backdrop.

A final thought – why not bright red garden furniture strategically placed against a rich green yew hedge? I have never seen it. Anyway, don't be coy; keep the red flag flying.

■ Beware of magenta! I find it an extraordinarily difficult colour to work, because of its pinky blueness. It can jar terribly and is much overused, I think. If you are going to use it, keep it away from scarlet and try clashing it with yellow. Strong stuff!

■ Dull reds can be made to seem much richer if planted next to grey or glaucous foliage, which in turn will appear greener by contrast.

■ Hot reds are particularly good from mid-to end-summer because the foliage becomes duller and less yellow. Bear that in mind when planning your planting and look for red as a follow-up colour from mid-July onwards. Plant the hottest reds in a west-facing border, so that they spend most of the day in shade which will give them depth and liven up the weaker evening light.

■ Many thanks to the dozens of you who responded to my request for accounts of rosemary dying inexplicably. All the stories are remarkably similar. A branch browns off and dies back and then the whole bush follows. Some of the letters describe what is probably the effect of the unusually late and harsh frost this last Easter, but most point towards a virus of some sort.

4.8.96 **Sound**

As a child I slept in an attic room surrounded by the branches of a huge beech tree. There was something immensely comforting about lying snug in bed and listening to the leaves flap and patter against the house on a windy autumnal night. Nowadays the sound of wind in the night sets me gardening in my head, triggering a mental checklist of any trees that might not be supported properly, any windows left open in the greenhouse, or unstaked soft growth in midsummer liable to be damaged. Be it day or night, no garden is ever silent. Birds, insects, machines and wind all combine to make constant sound, if not noise. We all have our own definition of what is a desirable sound, and generally we will all agree that this is likely to be gentle and musical, but association is everything and it may include mechanical sounds – after all, the buzz of a distant mower can be pleasing.

Every gardener tiptoes along a thin line between absolute control and anarchy and this applies to every aspect of the garden, including sound. You can encourage birds and plants to catch the wind. Think how eerie a garden would be entirely devoid of birdsong! In its silence it would be a restless, uncomfortable place. In the main a garden provides the ideal habitat for many birds. Songbirds like the thrush, blackbird and robin dominate the airwaves in spring but the less conspicuous but constant chatterings, beeps, mewings, snatches of song and shrill alarms of other birds such as starlings, swallows, sparrows, wrens, finches and tits are just as important. It doesn't stop at dusk. Above my present garden the wheeling curlews call like lost souls all the spring nights long and I once heard an appalling commotion outside in my Hackney garden and discovered four owls screeching and sneezing at each other from sheds and rooftops within 50 yards of the garden, as noisy as the lads on a night out.

All the birds that one now finds commonly in a garden originate from woodland, and the nearer your garden approximates to this original habitat, the happier the birds will be. This means that one has to avoid too much tidiness, never use insecticides, slugbait or any form of pesticide, and allow sufficient cover to develop for the birds to nest in. The tidiness above all refers to seed-heads that should be left on plants until they have all fallen or been eaten. This is particularly important at the end of summer when birds are building up reserves for winter. It also means leaving dead branches and even trees to stand, as they provide ideal sites for grubs and insects to breed in.

Wind dominates most gardens. As well as being the single most influential element in how plants fare, it is the primary driver of sound, carrying and making it, everything having its own tune when brushed by the wind.

Spring leaves are silkily sibilant, like young girls rustling in new party dresses. As the same leaves dry out at the back end of the year their rustle becomes more brittle and rattles rather than whispers. Willows rustle like a grass skirt and birches shake the wind out of themselves. In a strong wind pines whoosh and roar like waves crashing on to a distant shore. Just occasionally leaves sound in perfect stillness. I have heard oak leaves clatter like plates dropping on a stone floor as they fall to the ground after a heavy frost on an absolutely still autumn day. It is the sound of a door closing finally on autumn.

It is worth planting grasses for their acoustic properties alone. The wind seems to shuffle through them. The range is large, from the gigantic bamboos (which are simply woody grasses), such as *Bambusa muliplex* growing to 50 feet down to the tiny Squirrel-tail grass (*Hordeum jubatum*) that grows only to a maximum of 2 feet tall. The family of Miscanthus has seventeen different species, all tall and stately. *Miscanthus sinensis* is the most commonly grown, with a number of good varieties, including the pink-feathered M. 'Kleine Fontäne' which is suitable for small gardens, reaching only 4 feet, to M. 'Silberfeder', which grows to 6 feet and has silvery plumes.

Many gardeners are familiar with what is rather loosely called 'pampas grass' (which is more often a species like *Cortaderia selloana* from New Zealand, nowhere near the South American pampas) growing in isolated clumps on the margins of lawns.

Grasses do not need to be planted as individual specimens but can be

The sound of wind in the night sets me gardening in my head, triggering a mental checklist of any trees that might not be supported properly, any windows left open in the greenhouse, or unstaked soft growth in midsummer liable to be damaged.

integrated into the mixed planting of a border, although some, like *Glyceria maxima* 'Variegata' will spread voraciously. I made the mistake of planting this in a herbaceous border where it tried to take over the entire plot. It now is relegated to the Wild Garden where it looks much better. In winter the 3-foot stems sway in the wind with a sound like rustling silk. Most grasses will tolerate dry conditions although they need sun to do well. However, the 2-foot-high Moor grass, *Molinia caerulea*, will grow in wet spots, and looks especially good against a dark background.

Never cut the stems and leaves of any grass back in autumn, as this deprives it of insulating protection over winter as well as depriving the gardener of its idiosyncratic wind-blown song. The old growth should be cut down to the ground in March to allow the vivid new grasses to take over.

A light breeze in the orange winter leaves of hornbeam hedges sounds exactly like rain pattering down. My garden is newly planted with miles of the stuff and all last winter I would find myself looking up to try to see the rain I could hear but not feel before realizing where the sound was coming from. In fact you almost always sense rain with your ears first. It is the one sound that every gardener curses and rejoices in according to season. Raindrops falling on parched soil at the end of the day is music to the gardener's ears, although the same rain falling on ground that has dried sufficiently to work on just as you are grabbing a precious hour in the garden is a dread sound.

Just as the Inuit have dozens of words to describe snow, so it is an indication of its importance in our society that there are so many words for the action of precipitation of rain: to drizzle, pour, shower, pelt, sheet, bucket, patter, spit, tip, beat – each description conjures up a different sound. Every gardener has lain in bed in the early hours listening to the rain and interpreting the effect on the garden purely by the sound on the tiles, window-panes or leaves outside.

The sound of rain on new leaves in early June is quite different to the sound of rain on the yellowing, dry leaves of October. In winter the rain slides through the leafless branches to the ground with a muffled patter unknown for half the year.

Rain on evergreens, however, is constant, although the variation between the brittle slap of raindrops on a shiny leaf like laurel or holly is quite different to the way that yew or box absorbs and muffles the rain, holding the water sponge-like and soaking your clothes as you brush against them after the rain has long stopped.

A light breeze in the orange winter leaves of hornbeam hedges sounds exactly like rain pattering down. My garden is newly planted with miles of the stuff and all last winter I would find myself looking up to try to see the rain I could hear but not feel before realizing where the sound was coming from.

Like wind and birdsong, water can be made to perform. You can get kits that will make fountains of all dimensions and forms according to your particular whim or delusion of grandeur, but sometimes small is best. I recall visiting Snowshill, the garden made by Charles Wade in the Cotswolds, and being entranced by a simple copper spout dribbling water into a tiny basin that overflowed into a cistern set in the ground, creating more music. Only a little sound, but it had a harmony to it that was captivating. This could easily be reproduced in the tiniest garden with a battery pump circulating the water to flow endlessly.

■ The human ear has great facility for choosing which sound to focus on – as anyone holding a conversation at a party will know – and you can use this as an aural screen. Blocking unwanted sound from your garden is almost impossible as sound insulation is a measure of density. You need 100 yards of solid planting to eliminate a sound, but you can provide noise that will distract you from the intrusion of a road or neighbours. This might be wind chimes, or running water, or an extra good environment for birds – all will be effective screens.
■ A few plants create their own sound effects. Cranesbills fling their seeds from the pod with a clearly defined ping and broom pods fire out seed-bullets with the crack of a pistol. When ripe seed-pods of wood sorrel are touched, they open explosively, scattering seeds widely. The reason for this is obvious: the plant disperses its seed as far as possible and thereby widens the opportunity for it to germinate and spread.
   The Squirting cucumber, *Ecballium elaterium*, when stroked, responds with a squelchy ejaculation of seed. Nature is never self-conscious.
■ Different surfaces make for different sounds when walked on, and it is worth considering this when choosing them. It is impossible to walk quietly on gravel which is useful as a burglar alarm when spread below windows. Concrete has a dead, flat sound whereas brick is mellower. Stone slabs make footsteps into a slap. Grass is muffled and wooden decking echoes pleasantly.

6.8.95 **Blue!**

Can a white gardener grow the blues? With difficulty. (How many non-white gardeners are there in this country? There's an interesting sociological study. Another time.) The problem is not that blue is inherently more difficult to tend than any other colour, but that there is such a limited range of plants in a true blue.

In medieval manuscripts blue was exclusively produced from lapis lazuli which came exclusively from the area around modern Afghanistan via Venice. Consequently it was rarer and more valuable than gold. Colourwise, that is certainly true in the garden. Absolute blue has to be hunted down and used as a floral jewel amidst a range spanning from the blue-green of *Hosta sieboldiana* leaves to the blue-purple of so many plants.

Blue is conventionally a cool, distancing colour, but as red is added to the pigment, it warms up considerably, until you reach purple which is overtly rich and hot. As you add yellow to blue it becomes less intense and dislocated until you reach the utter harmony of green. Clearly there comes a point when the eye differentiates and labels a colour lavender, mauve, lilac or purple rather than blue, but it is a subtle and imprecise thing to label.

Blue draws the eye out away from other colours rather than red's insistent tug into itself, so that too much blue together can have a rather fretful effect. On a large scale, in sea, sky or even a field of linseed (a recent and lovely agricultural addition to the countryside), this is restful and inspiring in equal measure, but in the more claustrophobic space of a garden it can be uncomfortable and unfocused.

Of course it is almost impossible to have an area dominated by blue. There is too much green to hand for that, and the sky is too often a shade of grey not to have a powerful leavening effect. Despite the 'Blue and green should never be seen' rule, they invariably are, with no noticeable collapse of moral order. Just the two colours together make a soft but inconclusive jangle. But put orange into the mix and things at once pull together. I have a corner of a border where the orange of day lilies (*Hemerocallis*), green foliage, cornflowers (*Centaurea cyanus*) at the back and the Californian bluebell (*Phacelia campanularia*) growing low in front of them was hardly designed as a colour scheme, but it seems to work.

Blue is made by the short-wave movements of the electrons in the blue pigment molecules absorbing short light-waves and at the same time reflects its opposite – yellow. The combination of these opposites has a particularly vibrant freshness. One thinks of daffodils growing with scillas, bright yellow tulips with blue hyacinths, or lavender growing alongside senecio. Some plants, like the Swan river daisy (*Brachyscome iberidifolia*), have the two colours inbuilt, with blue petals and yellow centres. Like yellow sun in a blue sky, the combination is distinctly cheering.

Blue and white has the effect of making the white seem whiter. All the purveyors of washing powder cottoned on to this and have long been flogging us 'blue whiteness', even though this is clearly a nonsense. Thankfully the antiseptic, Habitat catalogue wholesomeness of the combination is invariably leavened by a strong dose of green foliage. But every gardener post Vita Sackville-West has learnt to make their white garden wash whiter with the judicious use of blue – in particular with glaucous foliage like rue, hosta, cardoon or stachys. It is much rarer to find a garden (by which I mean a designed area of planting, be it only a small section of a larger garden) deliberately planted as Blue and White, and I have never seen one. However, Tony Lord writes about the blue and white garden at Le Pontracart near Dieppe in his consistently wonderful book *Best Borders*. The effect is, apparently, gentle and tranquil. Most of the blues are pure, insofar as very few plants that verge towards purple are allowed entrance. Cosmos, phlox and *Achillea* 'The Pearl' are all dazzlingly pure white.

As I mentioned earlier, true blue flowers are few and far between. Perhaps

On a large scale, in sea, sky or even a field of linseed, blue is restful and inspiring in equal measure, but in the more claustrophobic space of a garden it can be uncomfortable and unfocused.

the flower with the most blue pigment to be saturated with the most light is *Anchusa azurea* 'Loddon Royalist'. This flower is a yardstick by which to measure blueness. It flowers from the end of May into July, and needs a well-drained, not-too-rich soil to get the best colour and performance. Other than that, it is easy and should be grown in every garden. The Himalayan poppy, *Meconopsis betonicifolia*, is an almost legendary plant, always referred to as the plant with the 'cleanest' or 'purest' blue, which is an interesting insight into the psychological effect of colour. Unfortunately it is very unhappy on lime and needs a cool, damp, humus-rich position in light shade to do best. But if you can grow rhododendrons there is no conceivable reason not to grow it. Although I have no experience of it, Christopher Brickell in his book *Garden Plants* recommends *M. x sheldonii* as the best variety, which is a cross between *M. betonificolia* and *M. grandis*. The clumps should be divided every two or three years in autumn or early spring.

Another shockingly difficult plant to grow is the Chatham Island forget-me-not, *Myosotidium hortensia*. I first saw this in the Dublin garden of Helen Dillon, whereupon, after I had admired its electric blueness, she gave me a small plant. I did as I was instructed and have planted it in warm shade, with rich soil and daily watering. It looks miserable. It needs plenty of water but must have free drainage, loves heat but hates sun and is hardly frost-hardy. I shall persevere because its flowering in May is a celebration worth eleven months' effort.

However, you do not have to suffer to play the blues. Bung some bulbs in the ground this month and scillas, muscari, bluebells, *Anemone blanda* and *Iris reticulata* should all come up unassisted in spring. The Chilean blue crocus (*Tecophilaea cyanocrocus*) is much less common but fantastic if you can get hold of it. Grazing has made it all but extinct in its native Chile, but it is successfully grown here. It is best treated as an alpine and grown in pots in rich compost mixed half and half with sharpsand.

Clematis alpina 'Francis Rivis' has reliably blue flowers in April, and ceanothus, in all its various forms, will flower profusely if sheltered from cold winds or too harsh frosts. *Pulmonaria* 'Blue Ensign', common or garden forget-me-not (*Myosotis*) and *Brunnera macrophylla* are all steady plants, which will grow in shade and are suitably blue. On the whole I prefer English names to the Latin, but navelwort sounds too much like an unpleasant excretion, perhaps the abdominal equivalent of earwax, to be used instead of *Omphalodes*. Still, whatever you call it, (and *O. verna* is called Blue-eyed Mary), it is a fine plant. *O. verna* comes first, followed by *O. cappadocica*. Both are woodland

All the purveyors of washing powder cottoned on to this and have long been flogging us 'blue whiteness', even though this is clearly a nonsense... every gardener post Vita Sackville-West has learnt to make their white garden wash whiter with the judicious use of blue.

plants and like a rich, moisture-retentive soil. *Vinca minor* can be overlooked, both literally, as they creep along the ground among other plants (herbs, in my garden) and in value, because of the smallness of the flowers. But they are of a lovely, lovely blue intensity. *Nigella damascena*, cornflowers (*Centaurea cyanus*), violas, petunias, lobelias and borage are all easy-to-grow blue annuals and biennials. There are a number of blue cranesbills, of which *Geranium pratense* is pale, *G.* 'Johnson's Blue' rather deeper, *G. himalayense* perhaps deeper still, and *G.* x *magnificum* the deepest.

The most obvious blue in the garden at any season glares out from delphiniums. Much work has gone into growing shorter varieties that will not blow over. This is a piece of horticultural nonsense. It wholly misses the point of the plant. Delphiniums are interesting because they are big, not despite it. Try 'Loch Maree' or 'Loch Leven' for blueness, but stick to some shade of blue or other even though one can now get delphiniums in almost any hue.

In Portugal last summer agapanthus were growing in the hedgerows with the abandon of bluebells in an English wood in May. They are likely to be a little less free with their favours over here, as they really like hot sun along with a very well-drained (but not dry) soil. Nevertheless, a superb plant. *Agapanthus africanus* is a wonderful blue but a bit delicate and may not cope with winter in harsher areas. *A. campanulatus* is pretty much fully hardy and *A.* 'Headbourne Hybrids' are reliably hardy.

Salvia patens is a favourite of mine, which has curved, intensely blue flowers in late summer. Apparently there is a giant form, 'Guanajuato', introduced from its native Mexico, which has large flowers in plants over 5 feet tall. I can't wait to see one. As its Mexican origin suggests, it is not entirely hardy and is best grown as a half-hardy annual unless one lifts the tubers and stores them like dahlias. The last blue on my (incomplete) list is the Michaelmas daisy. *Aster amellus* 'King George' or *A.a.* 'Moorheim Gem' are violet-blue with yellow stamens. *A.* x *frickartii* 'Monch' is a gentler blue, and *A. thomsonii* 'Nanus' a smaller version which would fit in a small garden.

■ It is hedge-cutting time. Yew, in particular, is best cut in August. Electric hedge-trimmers are best for a long stretch, although shears are perfectly good for the average-sized garden. To get a true level, drive a post in at both ends (or every 10 yards or so if it is a long hedge) and run a string between them. Cut to this guide. The lower the hedge, the harder it is to cut straight by eye. Always clip the top of a hedge first and then the sides. Most hedges should be cut with a batter, that is, a gentle slope, so that it is wider at the base than the top. The Garden Art Press has republished Nathaniel Lloyd's classic *Garden Craftsmanship In Yew And Box*. It covers every aspect of topiary and hedging in these two plants.

■ Rhododendrons and azaleas can now be layered. Take a healthy lower shoot and bend it down to the ground. Nick the underside where it touches the surface and peg it down, first creating a pocket of fibrous compost for the roots to grow in. It will take at least a year to take.

■ Strawberries are faster to reproduce from layering. Each strawberry plant throws out long runners with plantlets along its length. Choose three or four nearest the parent plant and peg them down, giving the soil a good dressing of compost if it is a bit thin. They should be ready to separate from the parent plant after about six weeks, when they can be moved to their permanent position. Strawberry plants lose vigour fast – including runners – so you will need to buy fresh stock every five years or so.

■ Plan your bulb-planting programming, sorting out what new stock you need ready for planting at the end of the month.

■ Angelica should be sown now so that the young plants can be planted out in their final position in the autumn.

■ Earwigs are the biggest potential enemies of dahlias and chrysanthemums. Stuff a small flower with hay or straw and place it upside down on the plant's supporting cane. The earwigs will spend the day in its cosy darkness, unaware that you will remove them while they snooze.

■ If you have not done so already, pinch out the tops of your tomatoes so that their remaining energy goes into developing fruit. Gradually remove lower leaves, especially in a greenhouse, so that the fruit can ripen and the air move around, reducing the chance of disease. If you grow pumpkins, remove excessive leaf from these too, exposing the pumpkins to the sun so that they can ripen.

11.8.96 Glaucous Plants

I read the other day how a pop star, now in his pony-tailed middle age, had taken to the newly discovered pleasures of the garden. He was of the habit of walking round with a large spliff and admiring his laurels (each to his own) 'An' I think, they're just so green!' I empathized closely with this particular philosophy, because I have found myself recently wandering round my garden, large cup of tea in hand, looking at the poppies and thinking that they are just so bluish-greyish green.

In his brilliant book *The Primary Colours* (Picador), Alexander Theroux points out that many languages, including ancient Greek and until recently Japanese, lack a distinctive word for blue and that the majority of existing world languages have the same word for blue and green. He explains that as language develops and acquires names for colour, the colours always enter in the same order. First black and white, then red, then yellow or green, followed by green or yellow. But green always includes what we think of as blue, and the next colour added to a language is the distinction between green and blue. So the radiant blue of the Aegean was always referred to as green or 'dark' by the ancient Greeks. So, in Chinese T'ang poetry, the same character is used for grass-colour and sky-colour. Blue, then, is always a linguistic device rather than an absolute colour. When we gaze upon a piece of lapis lazuli, a delphinium or meconopsis, awash with their blueness, it is easy to regard this merely as a piece of academic quaintness. But there is a whole range of plants in the garden that exist along this descriptive frontier that are botanically described as glaucous, which the *OED* defines as being 'of a dull green passing into greyish blue'. (I think the 'passing into' is superb.) Unlike sea, sky, spring leaves or grasses, these are not plants whose foliage can at times drift between dull green and bluish-grey, but are fixed permanently at that moment of linguistic crisis.

I have found myself recently wandering around my garden, large cup of tea in hand, looking at the poppies and thinking that they are just so bluish-greyish green.

The word glaucous incorporates the ambiguity of the colour, halfway between glory and raucous, halfway between grey and green and blue, so chalky it almost becomes a shade of white and yet strong and distinctive and always very beautiful. I have been struck by it this year more than ever before – the curry plants and hostas and poppies. Not the poppy flowers, of course, but the leaves and the seed-heads. Especially the poppy-heads. The poppies have been as good this year as I have known them and the flowers have left behind sculpted seed-heads dusty with greyish blue-green, a by-product of the flower but worth planting for this alone. If you strip the leaves and put the stalks and seed-heads in water, they will retain their mysterious, indeterminate colour for a surprisingly long time, whereas out of doors they dry into the rattle-bags we more commonly think of them as.

In my herb garden, now that the roses are a memory stored like logs to warm the winter with, the needle-grey blueness of the foliage of curry plants, (*Helichrysum italicum*) with their dots of egg-yolk flowers seem exceptionally strong this year too. Maybe I have not noticed them properly before, but it might be to do with the dryness of our weather over the past few years. Many glaucous plants are well adapted to dry conditions and will thrive where their more conventionally chlorophyllic neighbours look droopy. They have a pale bloom of colour that implies health. Their blueness is encouraged by direct sunlight, so even in wet seasons, with the exception of hostas, they need to be out of the shade as much as possible.

Their bloom is often created by a fine coating of hairs on the leaf surface, reflecting light, deflecting wind and reducing transpiration. Plants like rue (*Ruta graveolens*), which is as near to blue without being blue as a plant can reasonably be, have a waxy coat over their leaves to protect themselves from heat and drying winds, and it is this coating that gives the green its bluish cast. Eucalypts are another well-developed example of this. Onopordums, those lovely giant thistles, have seeded themselves all over my garden, the leaves coated with white hairs taking them to the paler end of the glaucal scale. The Sea holly (*Eryngium giganteum*) is another prickly self-seeder that copes well with drought and is a ghostly blue-grey. It is often known as 'Miss Willmott's Ghost' because Ellen Willmott, a celebrated Edwardian gardener, used surreptitiously to scatter its seeds around friends' gardens.

The Giant mullein (*Verbascum olympicum*) seeds like mad, the rosettes growing in their second year to great spires blobbed with yellow flowers like paint. Glaucous leaves and yellow are always a happy combination.

Despite being a vegetable and reacting well to rich soil, the cardoons (*Cynara cardunculus*) in my garden seem unaffected by drought and grow massively at the back of the border. Another big border plant, *Macleaya*

Unlike sea, sky, spring leaves or grasses, these are not plants whose foliage can at times drift between dull green and bluish-grey, but are fixed permanently at that moment of linguistic crisis.

microcarpa 'Coral Plume', is also flourishing, the pink of the feathery flowers running into the stems and looking good against the subtlety of the leaves. The underside of the macleaya leaves is very chalky and the topside, as it becomes increasingly exposed to sun, loses this and becomes almost conventionally green. Sage is like this too, with new leaves pointing up, their bellies green passing to blue, but as they mature they settle into a more stolid greenness.

I said that the roses were over, but *Rosa glauca* has flowers that are a pink sideshow. It is grown mainly for its wonderful leaves, a haze of smoky green just hinting at pinkness, lasting till October. It works well in a wilder piece of the garden or at the back of a border, left unpruned, where its lower branches can be hidden. The weeping pear (*Pyrus salicifolia*) is less ambiguous, veering clearly to the grey end of the glaucous range, its Latin name giving away its similarity to willow, whose leaves across the huge family of Salix tend towards blue. *Eleaagnus angustifolia* is also willow-like of leaf and remarkably similar to the weeping pear. It is a good shrub and has the added virtue of producing very sweet-scented yellowish flowers in early summer.

I am becoming a belated fan of euphorbias and shall write of this new enthusiasm more fully at a later date, but it is worth celebrating *Euphorbia nicaeensis* here. The leaves are a lovely pale greyish-blue without any of the chalkiness that can make the no-man's land between green and blue even more vague.

The plant that most people think of when the word glaucous is bandied about is *Hosta sieboldiana*. In principle hostas do not like dry conditions, although in practice they are remarkably tolerant of a wide range of conditions. However, if they are dry all summer they do need a good soak in winter. Bearing this in mind, I have planted hostas on a piece of ground that floods in winter but is dry all summer. It seems to be working. The potentially huge *H.* 'Snowden' is already big and will grow a lot more, lighting up the dappled shade of that corner. Water glaucous hostas directly at the roots, and do not sprinkle the leaves as this washes off the glaucous bloom.

Finally, matt 'dull green passing into greyish blue' makes the ideal colour for painted surfaces in the garden, strong enough to be good to look at standing alone and also balancing all other colours that might be around it.

■ August is an underrated month in the garden. Not only can it look very good, but it is also a good time to start next year's planting. Almost anything can be planted or moved now, as long as it is watered well a day before lifting and kept well watered until autumn. Cut back the foliage and flowers of any large plants to reduce the demands on the root system, which will go on growing well into autumn and be established by next spring.

■ If you have not yet ordered your spring bulbs, now is the time to do so. I am as disorganized as anyone, but each year I vow I will start my bulb planting in August, although a steady dribble of planting through to October will reward you with a steady flowering throughout next spring.

■ Almost all hedges will be improved with a cut now, especially yew. Burn yew clippings as they are poisonous, especially when they have dried out a little.

■ Sow lettuce now for autumnal eating. Lettuce does not germinate in heat, so if the weather is very hot, water the seedbed and cover it with a carpet or cardboard for a day. Sow in the evening after the sun has gone down.

13. 8. 95 **Yellow!**

Relative to humans, most mammals are bad at differentiating colour, although a surprisingly high percentage of men are colour-blind (up to 5% of men fail to differentiate pale purple from grey although less than half of 1 per cent of women have the same crippling disability). But very, very few people, male or female, have trouble identifying yellow. We know that one does not 'see' with the eye, for that is merely a tool for collecting visual information. It is the brain that organizes and uses that information to have meaning. Therefore there is some reason why yellow matters to us. The eye sees it and bang! we all yellow it up greedily. Mind you, there are an inordinate number of gardeners who do their best to deny this. My wife was one such until she saw the (yellow) light, banning all yellows from our London garden after the end of April, as though there was a kind of Xanthic closing time.

The other gardener of my age that I most admire – Sarah Raven – also has a thing about yellow. Both are barmy to be so pigmentally incorrect. A garden without great splashes of yellow is as dull as a grey November afternoon.

One of the confusions about yellow is that we associate it primarily with spring. It is the colour of the sun and just when we have least sun in the sky little stars of colour start popping up out of the ground. Aconites, crocus, daffodils, primrose, yellow tulips, troilus, winter jasmine, forsythia, stachyurus, mahonia, yellow flags (*Iris pseudocorus*) – all are yellow against green foliage or bare branches. There is a purity and strength about it that is utterly heartening, feeding one with the strength to battle through to spring proper.

But that is just phase one. As April opens out into May, the range of colours increases dramatically and with it the possible colour permutations. Most people know that yellow and blue work well as near opposites (the opposite of yellow is actually violet), with bluebells and daffodils, *Anemone blanda* and daffodils, muscari and daffodils, anything bluish with daffodils, all clicking into an appointed coloured place. Yellow and red are a less common mix, making traditionally 'hot' colours, although it is the orange that is hot, not the separate components. The first sighting of them together is usually done with tulips and wallflowers (although wallflowers are more often orange than red). In spring this is garish, vulgar and lovely. The same combinations by mid-summer become rich and musky, mainly because there are more purple and deep alizarin colours to add depth. I have heard excited reports of Christopher Lloyd's new planting of the Old Rose Garden with vibrant, tropical colours, and I see in this month's edition of *The Garden* that he uses the dahlia 'David Howard' which has exactly this contrast of purplish, alizarin leaves and yellow (well, yellowish-orange). As Ian Dury commented so aptly about Sex 'n' Drugs 'n' Rock and Roll, the combination is Very Good Indeed.

Yellow matters to us. The eye sees it and bang! we all yellow it up greedily. Mind you, there are an inordinate number of gardeners who do their best to deny this.

High and late summer come armed with big plants, wearing their yellow on their sleeves. I am thinking of rudbeckia, solidago, ligularia, sunflowers, dahlias, gladioli, hemerocallis, inula, oenethera, phlomis *et al*. To try to combine these bruisers with blue is likely to end in failure because that combination is essentially one of delicacy and freshness. These plants are extroverts all and need to rub shoulders with less sensitive souls. Purple is as rumbustious as the most brazen of them and is usually the best late-summer foil. Green is also surprisingly good – surprising because it is, of course, already there in foliage and stem and does not have to be planned. A purely yellow border works well against a mass of deep green foliage.

Sometimes this effect can be achieved with radical simplicity. I planted tansy (*Tanacetum vulgare*) in our herb garden, as well I might, given its extensive culinary and medicinal properties ranging from the flavouring of Irish sausages to the restoration of menstrual flow, where it rapidly became an invasive weed. This year we have dug up the creeping roots as best we could and transplanted them to the Wild Garden where they are romping unfettered, yellow heads against both green leaves and green fields behind them. It is a fine sight.

Even better are the yellow and green of early spring that you get from euphorbias. I love them more and more as each year passes. *Euphorbia polychroma* looks as though it has been dipped into yellow paint, and *E. characias* is as yellow, but a more subtle blend from glaucous green to its bright tips. The plants seem to be lit from inside their skins, glowing like an electric light and yet subtle and mysterious. I think that a lot of that comes from the glaucousness of the green.

Later in the year there are plants that have this combination more markedly. As I write, the curry plant (*Helichrysum angustifolium*) is at its best, the flowers a strong yellow above and a paler, shiny tone on the undersides, with very pale grey-green stems and leaves. It is an utterly calm combination, without any of the shouting of the big border yellows. Mulleins (*Verbascum thapsus*) have the same silver and lemon combination, although you would be pushed to find two plants more dissimilar than this and the curry plant. The Great mullein grows to a towering 7 feet and is made grey by a whitish bloom that covers the foliage. The flowers appear by degrees, so it is the overall effect rather than a perfect moment that is valuable, but all in all it is a treasure.

A less spectacular plant, but one that is infinitely useful, is Lady's Mantle (*Alchemilla mollis*), perhaps made contemptible by over-familiarity, but always good in a number of different situations. Alchemilla is the billowing plant *par excellence*, lasting through the whole of summer, spilling over the edge of a million borders on to a million paths and lawns countrywide. Like euphorbia, the effect of the tiny yellow flowers and hairy green foliage is more a shade of

One of the confusions about yellow is that we associate it primarily with spring. It is the colour of the sun and just when we have least sun in the sky little stars of colour start popping up out of the ground.

yellowish-green than greenish-yellow, if one feels that those hairs are worth splitting. The hairs make the green seem silvery, adding gentleness to gentility. Apparently Gertrude Jekyll prepared the eye for an area of grey with pools of yellow plants. The glaucous foliage is somehow made purer by the afterglow in the mind of the yellow one has just seen.

An afterglow the eye should never have to recall is the combination of yellow and bright pink, or, equally horrid, bright yellow and soft pink. I confess that I have such a combination as a result of carelessly chucking plants in together without proper attention to detail. *Ligularia* x *palmatiloba* (pushing yellow as far to orange as yellow can rightfully go) is cheek by jowl with *Rosa rugosa* 'Roseraie de l'Hay'. Ugh! One of them has to go. As the site inclines to flood, I think the moisture-loving ligularia will stay and a new home be found for the rose.

I love the yellowness of September, with leaves sliding towards autumn, the grass bleached straw-colour, and the straw itself – where the farmers refrain from madly ploughing the minute the combine has left the field – a tawny ochre. *Clematis orientalis* 'Bill Mackenzie' will keep its yellow flowers right into Christmas if the weather stays vaguely mild and the holly *Ilex aquifolium* 'Bacciflava' has yellow berries like clusters of tiny lemons. *Sternbergia lutea* is as bright as any spring bulb and Golden Rod (another plant people tend to be snooty about) and rudbeckia keep all their guns blazing well into the end of the month. And then the light dims, the leaves flush red, the earth dominates and there is enough sodden brownness to make me long for the first yellow of spring again.

■ We are approaching the time when dew becomes a feature of even the driest spell of weather. This makes August a good time for seeding or turfing a new lawn. The soil is warm enough to ensure quick germination and the dew supplies the bare minimum of moisture. Keep the soil moist with a hose as necessary. If sown now the grass should be established enough to weather the winter and fully operational as a lawn by next spring.

■ Avoid the temptation to prune back your lavender now, even though it may have finished flowering, because if you do so it will stimulate new growth and this is unlikely to survive any hard frosts. Leave it till next spring and see your analyst about learning to cope with the resultant untidiness.

■ Plant perennials that will flower in spring and early summer, such as peonies. They will then establish strong roots before they go dormant and wake up with that extra growing power next spring.

■ Plant Madonna lilies over the next three weeks or so, while they are dormant. If they are to flower next year they have to overwinter with a flat rosette of leaves, so must have a chance to develop this in autumn. Do not plant too deep, keeping the tips no more than 2 inches below the surface. Unless you have very light soil, add some grit beneath them as you plant, to keep them well drained.

■ It is a good time of year to give the borders a general feed of a slow-release fertilizer such as bonemeal or hoof and horn. This will encourage good root growth during the early autumn before dormancy.

■ There is a tendency to leave paving, wall building and all other kinds of 'hard' gardening to winter, but late summer is an excellent time for this as it is dry, the days are longer, and in truth there is not that much to do in the garden. Make a start on a piece of hard landscaping and get it done before winter and the business of autumn.

1.9.96 **Children**

The most esteemed gardens tend to be made by women whose children have grown up, or by spinsters or homosexuals. Aside from their love of gardens, the three groups have one thing in common: no children. Children and serious gardening are wholly incompatible. Grown-ups want an ordered peace where children need sheltered anarchy. Gardens and gardeners are fragile things, poor dears, and children are tough, boisterous, irreverent and noisy. They care nothing for plants other than their immediate sensation at any given moment and have no idea of the central concept in the gardener's life, which is transience and change. Only the shining now has any meaning to the child playing in a sunny garden. Remember that greatest poet of childhood innocence, Thomas Traherne, in his *Centuries of Meditation*: 'All appeared New, and Strange at the first, inexpressibly rare, and Delightful, and Beautiful...all things abided Eternaly as they were in their Proper Places.... The Skies were mine, and so were the Sun and Moon and Stars, and all the World was mine, and I the onlie Spectator and Enjoyer of it. I knew no Churlish Proprieties, nor Bounds nor Divisions.' Conventional gardening is only about churlish proprieties, bounds and divisions.

This makes a dynamic between absolute control of a domestic space and the ensuing reaction to the way that plants express their unruly independence of this. At best it makes great art. At worst it is a neurotic desert. The better the gardener, the more confident they can be about playing and letting go the reins of control. Really great gardens seem to teeter on the edge of anarchy yet have a balance and poise that seem inevitable. But this sort of 'play' is miles away from any child's idea of play. For this piece I conducted a wide-ranging survey and asked my three children what they most wanted from a garden. The answers were immediate: tree house, tree house, mountain bike course. Anything else? Their own piece of garden? Wildlife pond perhaps? Nope. A tree house. With a swing thing and a cooker. The mountain bike course had to have really steep hills and a muddy bit. Oh, and a wood.

We have been making our garden from scratch over the past three years and I immodestly think it's getting quite good, with fourteen individual areas, interlocking but each with its own character. But a tree house and mountain bike course are not among them. For a tree house you need trees, and the only ones here have been planted by me and none is yet capable of containing a house. There is a football pitch with a proper goal and three sections of cultivated ground devoted to the children's plants, but after the initial burst of enthusiasm (one magical afternoon) their gardens ceased to be very entertaining, and Adam has gone right off football at the moment.

In the further interests of investigative journalism, at 7.13 this morning I

I conducted a wide-ranging survey and asked my three children what they most wanted from a garden. The answers were immediate: tree house, tree house, mountain bike course.

have just done a spot-check round the garden. I discovered: one bike wedged in a yew cone; one bike blocking the path to the leeks; one bike upside-down in the potting shed tied up with baler twine (why?); one pair knickers (pink) hanging from light in porch; one cassette case (empty) and an expensive glass (empty) among the carrots; one pair of handcuffs attached to a skipping-rope and a blindfolded teddy strung across the entrance to the herb garden; my socket set, a club hammer and three tent pegs hammered into the lawn; a squeaky Father Christmas (punctured by the dogs), a football (punctured by the dogs), and a new toy that blows bubbles when you crank a handle, all underneath a large *Lonicera purpussii*; a battery-operated Power Ranger's sword (battery flat), yellow tennis ball and a ball of modelling clay (gone rock-hard) on garden table, which was smeared with streaks of dried clay; puckered lumps of clay stuck where they had been thrown on to a new brick wall opposite.

That is a pretty average cross-section of the children's contribution to the garden. I guess that none of these things could be found in any of the National Trust or the more solemnly 'good' private gardens I have visited. But then neither could the other major contribution to the garden that my children provide, which is laughter, noisy shrieks of it, peppered with screams and tears. Children add laughter and tripping, racing, tumbling movement rather than the bovine trudge of the grown-up visitor.

You see how this is shaping up? How can the child-loving parent be a garden-loving gardener? You want and need that sensuous escape from what Traherne calls the Dirty Devices of this World, and they want an adventure playground. It seems an insuperable problem. But a book written by the garden designer Bunny Guinness called *Family Gardens* (David & Charles, £20), has given me inspiration and hope for a compromise between these two conflicting demands. Her thesis is that if you plan to integrate children into the garden from the start and design the garden around this assumption, then you will find space for them to play and you to garden, regardless of the size of your patch. The important thing is to give children their own space. Not necessarily space on the scale of a mountain bike course, but most definitely tree-house space (oh, the guilt!). The garden has to be shared in the same way that the house is. If they have their own bit that is unequivocally theirs and geared towards their own needs, then they will accommodate your needs in your bit. Their own 'garden' is not going to do the trick. It is too much a mini-version of the grown-up garden. When space is limited some sort of building is ideal, and a tree house best of all. If you have no trees, then a house constructed on stilts will do. There is something about being up in the air that is magical, and earthbound adults ignore this at their children's peril. Failing that, an old garden shed or a building constructed like an allotment shed of doors, sash

How can the child-loving parent be a garden-loving gardener? You want and need that sensuous escape from what Traherne calls the Dirty Devices of this World, and they want an adventure playground.

windows, corrugated iron and polythene is fine. But make that space.

Once that space is created, they might want a garden attached. Don't be precious about this. Remember this is a game, playing at gardening, not an apprenticeship for your horticultural world. Plant sunflowers, marigolds, beans, peas, nasturtiums and poppies. Keep your finer sensibilities out of it and the planting bright, vulgar, big and brash. Bunny Guinness is very good about the unavoidable intrusions of games into the grown-up garden. However great the tree house, any child will want space for ball games of all kinds, and a lawn, however small, is the only answer for this. See the lawn as a play area skilfully designed as garden rather than the other way round. Plant around it with tough shrubs like cotoneaster, kerria or buddleia that will withstand being trampled over as balls are being retrieved. If you must have a border at the edge of the lawn, protect it with a low box hedge that will act as a crash barrier and is resilient enough to recover from a spot of childish GBH.

Sandpits and ponds do not have to be alien impositions on to the garden. Bunny Guinness shows how she made a paddling pool and sandpit to look like a natural sandy-shored brook with pebbles laid on concrete forming a drainable waterproof base and soft planting around the fringes. This is very simple but genuinely inspired.

She is also a fan of a technique that I have been playing with (mainly for my own childish pleasure) in my own garden: living structures. By using cuttings from a vigorous willow such as 'Bowles Hybrid', which grows at a rate of about 8 feet a year, you can make enclosed spaces in an astonishingly short time. She illustrates examples of willow tunnels and labyrinths that I know from personal experience are fun and terribly easy to make. Best of all, they are places where adult and child come together with a common purpose – to play.

■Some plants are beautiful but poisonous or can irritate tender young skin, so be very wary of growing rue (*Ruta graveolens*), and Giant Hogweed (*Heracleum mantegazzianum*) as both can burn skin badly if the sap from the leaves is touched at a time of strong sunlight.

Lots of plants are more or less toxic if eaten, but this is not a problem if a degree of common sense is used. The following however, should be watched:

Laburnum is really toxic, especially the seeds, which look to a child like peas in a pod. In my opinion it should never be grown in a garden frequented by young children.

Monkshood (*Aconitum*) is severely toxic, especially the roots.

Not just the berries of Deadly Nightshade (*Atropa belladonna*) are poisonous, but the whole plant, as is yew, although the berries are likely to be most attractive to a child.

■Many gardening books advise against planting weeping willows (*Salix* x *chrysocoma*) because they are too big, but they are the perfect tree for children. The curtain of ground-sweeping branches makes a natural private 'house' and the tree is eminently climbable. When the children outgrow it and it outgrows the garden, cut it down.

■ I am sure that our high regard for strawberries is based mainly on childhood memories because they are wildly overrated and children adore them. They grow very well in pots as long as they get a lot of watering. The big juicy maincrop ones like 'Cambridge Vigour' satisfy the demand for size, whilst the much smaller Alpine strawberries such as 'Alexandria' will go on fruiting all summer.

■ September is the ideal month for taking box cuttings. It is so expensive to buy and such a useful plant that you can never have too many cuttings. Take them in batches throughout this month from a vigorous parent plant, cutting just below this year's growth. Strip the stem of most of the leaves and plant a couple of inches deep in a sheltered, gritty seedbed. A cloche will help if you have it, but is not essential. Keep them watered and weeded. They will be rooted by spring and ready to plant out next September.

8.9.96 Tomatoes

OK. No pussy-footing about, straight in at the deep end and tackle the tough question first: is a tomato a fruit or a vegetable? Er, sort of both. The round red things you eat are the fruits of the tomato plant. Which seems to make it a fruit. But... in the fourteen books that I referred to for this piece, only one classed tomatoes as fruit and the other thirteen unambiguously called it a vegetable. Well, that's sorted then. Live dangerously. A fruit that you look up in vegetable books. A vegetable that produces fruit. A tomato is a round, red, juicy, free spirit, defying classification. It is not necessarily red either, or round. When they were first introduced from Mexico to Europe by the Spaniards, tomatoes were predominantly yellow, hence the name *pomodoro* given by the Italian botanist Matthiolus in 1544.

In fact ripe tomatoes come in a range of colours from green through yellow and orange to bright red, vary from pure hue to stripes and subtle blotches and range in size from the tiny 'Yellow Currant' that is about ½-inch in diameter to the enormous sub-pumpkin-sized 'Brandywine', and can alter shape through a variety of manifestations of tomatoeyness from the delicate roundness of 'Gardener's Delight', via elongated plum tomatoes, to the swollen ribbiness of 'Ruffled Yellow' that looks like the segments of an orange on steroids.

Yet most people happily buy from supermarkets tomatoes that are predictable in every way including the almost total absence of taste. The test of a good vegetable is always the same: would you relish it as a dish on its own, with no accompaniment other than a little salt, pepper and good olive oil? Supermarket tomatoes are the television presenters of the culinary world, and there can be no circle of hell lower than that. They are hardly intended as food. Like TV presenters, they are packaged as glossy 'garnish' and lack taste or substance. Tinned ones are nearly always nicer.

We have always had a slightly ambiguous relationship with the fruit in a way that seems never to have troubled Mediterranean countries. Although the Mexican name of *tomatl* is clearly the source of the modern name, the tomato was known as the 'Love Apple' partly because of its supposedly aphrodisiac

Supermarket tomatoes are the television presenters of the culinary world, and there can be no circle of hell lower than that. They are hardly intended as food. Like TV presenters, they are packaged as glossy 'garnish' and lack taste or substance. Tinned ones are nearly always nicer.

qualities and partly, I suspect, as a corruption of the Italian *pomodoro*, which became *pomme d'amour*. Its magical properties underline the suspicion with which it was regarded: it was quickly seen as a solanum and a close relative of the potato and Deadly Nightshade (*Solanum nigrum*). The suspicion is not entirely unfounded, as the leaves will do you no good at all if chomped.

Commercial tomatoes are often grown hydroponically (i.e. in water rather than soil) so that they attain optimum size as quickly as possible and are green when picked (i.e. unripe), then prematurely ripened by carefully controlled exposure to ethylene gas and stored in coolers at precisely 38°F. Often dipped in wax to make them shine, they arrive on the shelf a mummified corpse of a fresh tomato, a mere representation of what is terribly easily grown in a gro-bag or pot in any sunny spot. But a generation that has grown up having never experienced biting through the tough skin of a freshly picked tomato to the slightly acidic flesh, viscous seeds dribbling down the chin, literally knows no better.

It is a pity that many people have the idea that you need a greenhouse to grow tomatoes. Outdoor ones nearly always have more taste and are just as easy to grow, although the fruits will be slower to develop and ripen. If we have hot summers like we did last year, tomatoes are actually much easier to grow outside. They do not need staking and tying either. Bush varieties can be planted and more or less ignored other than for weeding. The secret of getting tasty rather than just good-looking fruit is to water moderately before the fruits develop and then keep them pretty dry as they ripen. Too much water makes them bland. They need ordinary garden soil, well-dug and prepared, but not as manured as, say, their cousin the potato. I see little point in adding any commercial feed to a tomato plant unless your soil is deficient in the first place. But they must have sun, as much as possible, to develop flavour. If you only have a shaded back-yard then you can still grow good tomatoes, but they will have to be picked green and used for chutney – which is a perfectly life-enhancing thing to do.

For the last couple of years I have grown tomatoes in deeply dug and manured beds inside the greenhouse, alongside identical plants growing in gro-bags sitting on concrete slabs. Although my analysis is empirical and unmeasured, I reckon that there has been no difference in crop, health of plant or taste. Yet these bags allow a tiny root-run and are nothing like the work to prepare. The only real drawback to them is that it is hard sticking a cane in to stake the plants as they grow. And the tall varieties must be staked. In this country we tend to put an individual cane per plant but I saw tomatoes in Spain the other day growing up wigwams, like runner beans. It seemed a good idea. Without support they get top-heavy and break and the fruits lie on the

For years I was bothered with constant reference to 'trusses'. Why did tomatoes have trusses and nothing else (other than ruptured gardeners)? No book ever explained exactly what a truss was.

ground where they will rot or get eaten by slugs. The thing to do is to put the cane in when the 6-inch plant is put into the ground and tie it in as it grows.

You have to pinch out the stems that sprout from the junction of the main stem and the horizontal 'branches'. This is because these diagonal growths are too vigorous and rarely bear fruit. By removing them, the energy goes into fruit production rather than the plant itself.

For years I was bothered with constant reference to 'trusses'. Why did tomatoes have trusses and nothing else (other than ruptured gardeners)? No book ever explained exactly what a truss was. The dictionary says that it is a 'compact cluster of flowers growing on one stalk', which helps, but it is a piece of gardening jargon of the sort beloved by those who know and so alienating to those who do not. Anyway, the same books will all say something along the lines of letting four or five trusses 'set' (more confusion – how do you know when they have set or not?) and then instructing you to pinch out the top growth. My innate bolshiness has made me ignore and experiment with this for a number of years but the principle behind it is reasonable. A tall or non-bush tomato plant wants to grow on and on up and can easily make 10 feet if left to do so. In this country the first frosts will kill all tomato plants and only genuinely hot days will ripen the fruit. So you reduce the number of fruit produced to the maximum that can be reasonably ripened, which is achieved by pinching out the top of the plant, which stops it growing and producing more fruit as it does so. Once stopped, all horticultural attention can be lavished on the fruits that exist rather than producing any more. Also the pruned plants – for you are training the tomato plant just as surely as you train an espalier – are neater, take up far less space, can consequently be planted much closer together (which, as we have seen from the gro-bag example, does not seem to restrict fruit production) and are easier to manage.

Now, why hasn't any gardening book ever said that? So many gardening books are like computer manuals used to be, full of indecipherable jargon and a kind of dreary, trainspottery clubbiness, and written on the assumption that you already know the thing that drove you to read it in the first place.

The truth is that there is a type of gardener who just loves fiddling about in the greenhouse with tomatoes. The growing of them is much more interesting to them than the end-product, so the more arcane and mysterious the process, the better they feel about themselves. Bush tomatoes are the opposite of this. Wait until the first week of June, buy a tray of a dozen plants of a variety like 'Tornado', 'Amateur', 'Red Alert', or best of all the Italian variety 'Roma', plant them in as sunny a site as you have and let them get on with it. The fruit should ripen about eighty days after planting.

■ If you have any tall-growing outdoor tomatoes with green fruits that do not look as though they will ripen before the warm weather runs out at the end of this month, you can untie them from their support and carefully lay them on the ground before putting a cloche over them. This will tease out extra ripeness from some of them. The rest will do for chutney.

■ At this time of year it is very common for fully grown tomatoes to split before ripening. This is because they have been overwatered, and in early autumn unsummery rain will do that naturally. Protect fruit from too much water by mulching heavily when the ground is dry.

■ Every year I throw my tomato plants and any rotten or badly split fruits on the compost heap and every subsequent spring there are thousands of tiny tomato plants in my borders. Don't be alarmed if this happens to you. I like them. They are easy to pull up and can be transplanted to a more controlled site for cropping.

■ If you grow tomatoes in a greenhouse it is a good idea to change the soil every two or three years. The best new topsoil is made from turves stored upside-down for a year, so if you are lifting any turf, keep it in a stack for future use as clean topsoil. When you use it, cut through it with a spade rather than trying to separate the long-welded turves.

11. 9. 94 **Sexiness**

'I imagine being swept away amongst the flowers in my garden, particularly when the *regale lilies* are in full bloom, because the scent is intoxicating, and they come out at a time when the roses and the honeysuckle are out. It's a scented garden, a garden for all the senses.' This does not come from the RHS monthly magazine but from that well-known horticultural volume, *Englishwomen's Sexual Fantasies*, by Rachel Silver (Century). At this point I have to resist the temptation to make some clever(ish) remark about the title, because that would go against the essence of what I am about to say.

There are gardeners who have sublimated their sexuality into the fecundity of growing things – one thinks of middle-aged women whose children have grown up and whose husbands are fat and busy or limp and dried-up – but for most of us the relationship between sex and gardening flows happily from the subconscious to consciousness with an easy ebb. It is hardly a decision to enjoy the association. In fact, it has to be a conscious decision to suppress it.

But because it does not have glamour, that sexiness is somehow bypassed and remains hidden under a heap of dry botanizing and anorak-clad worthiness. Yet anyone who has gardened in any creative way at all will know about the sensuality of creating and tending a garden. That sensuality is there to be experienced in all weathers and in every season, be it the excitement of running rich, crumbly soil through one's fingers in spring and knowing that the time is exactly right to sow, or the scent of honeysuckle or tobacco plants on a summer's night, or the shining frost sheathing the naked branches of the hazel just beyond the back door, or any other of a thousand moments when the senses are seduced.

But talking about these things is preaching to the converted. You do not need words to experience them. So gardening words tend to be restricted to advice rather than description. I know about the wonderful excitement of gardening. Any description is only likely to reduce the intensity of the experience. It is like the annoyingly cryptic and oblique descriptions of mystical experience which edge towards the banal or smug and usually boil down to saying 'If you knew, then you would know what there is to know.' Right on.

Nevertheless, other equally domestic subjects have managed to become glamorous. Cooking is now sexy, yet in my childhood it was the province of Fanny Craddock, WI worthiness and patronizing advice. A few exalted cooks were admired, yet for the most part expectations were dismally low and the standard of public food was pretty dire, even though every household cooked every day and had a member who was technically competent. It is a situation very similar to gardening today. We are remarkably undemanding and uncritical horticulturally. It is thought to be rude to criticize a garden, just as my mother would have waded through a disgusting meal rather than complain.

Why is this? Why is the earthy sensuality of gardening not celebrated with the same fervour as the joys of eating? I think it has something to do with gender. Gardening got hijacked by men wanting to give it scientific credibility. Its virtues had to be measurable to be properly worthy. Therefore the mechanics of gardening came to be valued above the aesthetics by the gardening hierarchy. This was partly due to professional gardeners (invariably male) only being allowed to exercise mechanical skills, with the means therefore elevated above any end, and partly due to the male obsession with classifying and compartmentalizing everything. Thus the obsession with techniques of digging, compost heaps and the botany of plants reduces gardening to an absurdly prosaic level – it is as though the relative merits of Marilyn Monroe and Brigitte Bardot were judged within the limitations of their genealogy, hair-washing technique and bowel movements. Fascinating as this might be to some people, it completely misses the point.

There is also the male predilection for converting gardening into Jobs and Projects. I have to admit guilt on this score. The garden is the perfect playground for the game of getting things done. There are times when this is necessary, but it carries with it the implication that it is what and when you do it that matter rather than how it is done. Jobs get ticked off on a permanently revolving calendar, awfully like trains jotted down at the end of Crewe station. Satisfying, but definitely not sexy.

With this trainspotter mentality comes a restricting – not to say constricting – attitude to time that men seem to have towards gardening. I would like a pound for every time someone has told me that they don't have time to garden, as though there was a statutory minimum number of hours needed to qualify. You have the time that you have. Everything is flexible. You can prepare a delicious and beautiful meal in ten minutes if you take care choosing the ingredients. So it is with gardening.

Gardening is slow and sensuous and subtle with some obvious and uncomplicated moments that need no analysis or explanation. To make gardening into a series of jobs that can only be appreciated by being mastered is to misunderstand the point of it. You do it because it is good to do it. Not because there are prizes to be won. Making a beautiful place is a side benefit – rather like happiness being a side benefit of living well. But making an erotic place is an essential ingredient of any good garden. Bowers, arbours, small spaces crammed with flowers, austere spaces perfectly proportioned – these are all sexy. They are carefully created and controlled yet they also pulse with an innate anarchy. By gardening in this spirit you tap into the vein we all have

Anyone who has gardened in any creative way at all will know about the sensuality of creating and tending a garden. That sensuality is there to be experienced in all weathers and in every season.

Why is the earthy sensuality of gardening not celebrated with the same fervour as the joys of eating? I think it has something to do with gender. Gardening got hijacked by men wanting to give it scientific credibility.

inside us where the terms are dictated not by quantifiable techniques but by the subtle and fecund forces of poetry, change and fantasy.

■ I dislike sprays and hardly ever use them, yet I am a great fan of 'Roundup', the glysophate weedkiller, which is particularly effective in killing grasses, docks, thistles and annual weeds. But there are very few times in a year when I am there to spray and I have spray to hand when the weather and growth conditions are right. I have just made a resolution always to have a supply in the shed. I don't suppose I use it more than twice a year, but it is invaluable and relatively safe to use, becoming inert on hitting the ground. It kills plants by translocation and it is safe to plant or sow in the soil within forty-eight hours of spraying. But never, ever spray when there is a hint of a breeze, let alone a wind, and make sure that the area you spray is free from children and pets for at least three hours. As I say, this restricts the opportunities to spray to a handful of times a year, so it is doubly important to be ready for them.
■ Always clean out the sprayer or watering can after using a weedkiller and leave it filled with clean water. Then if some spills or a child plays with it, any residual mixture will be safely dilute.
■ It is best to spray weeds when they are beginning to grow vigorously. It is sometimes better to cut them back and let them regrow before spraying, rather than wasting expensive spray on mature weeds.
■ 'Roundup' is never very effective against nettles. They are best cut and added to the compost heap at this time of year, where they make a good activator.

22.9.96 Medlars and Quinces

Stand in the garden and sniff the air; you can smell autumn coming in like the tide drawing across summer's beach. There is an aroma of apples, pears, plums and damsons, mingled, in these parts, with the tang of hops. A bit of mist and a touch of mellow fruitfulness and it must be autumn again. That's as it should be. Everything is in its place and most of us are glad to be driven by that rhythm, even though it takes us away from seasons where we want to linger. It is good for garden writers because, just between you and me, summer goes on for a bit. Come the end of August and one is scratching about for something new to say. But you turn the corner into autumn and yippee, there's all that fruit to be written about before it rots and winter sets in.

But some fruit doesn't get much of a look-in. Apples and pears are far more interesting than the pathetic range available in shops, but, like oranges, they are not the only fruit. For instance, when was the last time you saw a medlar for sale, or bought a few pounds of mulberries? All these fruits are old and quirky and deserve to be grown more widely than they are.

A hundred years ago you might well have rounded off your dinner with a glass of port, hazelnuts and a few bletted medlars, although now they are thoroughly out of fashion. Bob Flowerdew in his very good *Bob Flowerdew's Complete Fruit Book* (Kyle Cathie, £19.99) says that 'The taste is somewhat like that of rotten pear and they are now disdained.' Not by me, Bob. Distinctive, yes, but disdainful, no. Although this disdain is not just modern squeamishness. That least squeamish of men, William Cobbett, describes a medlar tree as 'A very poor thing, indeed... It is hardly worth notice, being, at best, only one degree better than a rotten apple.' Geoffrey Grigson opens his entry on medlars in his *The Englishman's Flora* with the incredulous 'Have you ever met anyone who enjoys eating a ripe and rotten medlar?' Yes, I have. My friend Henry's mother. Henry's father planted the tree, *Mespilus germanica* 'Royal', in 1931, and every year it produces hundreds of nut brown, leathery fruits which Mrs Humphreys used to store until properly bletted and eat rather as one does a pomegranate. Bletting is an odd word, only used, as far as I am aware, in association with medlars. It sounds as though it ought to be a piece of ancient dialect but it turns out to be more prosaic, lifted straight from the French, *blettir*, to make soft.

The Humphreys' tree is large and lovely with a gnarled and cantankerous trunk. 'Royal' has small fruits, as does 'Nottingham', and both are supposed to be the most tasty. I have planted a couple of 'Nottingham' in my garden, and I notice that they are grafted on to a craetageus rootstock rather than the quince that you expect for an apple. There is a visual affinity between medlar and hawthorn, and the 'Bronvaux' medlar (*Crataegomepilus dardarii*) has been bred to make a cross between the two.

Despite these cultivated varieties, medlars are ancient and pretty much unimproved over the last millennium, which seems to add to their virtues to me. They can still be found growing wild in hedgerows and woodland, with their large white flowers as fine as any fruit blossom in spring. Grigson tells us that in Aelfric's Glossary of AD 1000 it is given its Anglo-Saxon name of *openaers*, which refers to the, um, curious anatomical likeness of the fruit rather than the effect of eating it, which if anything apparently has a tendency to 'bind'. The only time I have seen an open arse was in a film by John Waters where an anonymous individual proceeded to give a remarkable display of the exceptional control of his sphincter in time to music. I regret to say that I did not have a medlar to hand to make the direct comparison. Nevertheless, in this age of coy euphemism, how can one fail to love such a rude fruit?

If, after this last snippet of information you really cannot bring yourself to eat the fruit raw, try medlar jelly, which is universally admired. It is hard to set and the addition of pectin robs it of the idiosyncratic flavour, but lemon

Stand in the garden and sniff the air; you can smell autumn coming in like the tide drawing across summer's beach...A bit of mist and a touch of mellow fruitfulness and it must be autumn again.

juice should do the trick. For jelly, use the medlars before bletting, collecting them from the ground when they are still hard.

If you plant a mulberry in your garden you should plant a quince as its neighbour. Fail to plant the two together and you are inviting ill-luck upon the house. To get the detail of the spell spot on, the mulberry should be planted to the south of the house and the quince to the north (which begs the question of how far you stretch the term 'neighbour'. But we will leave that nit unpicked.) Edible quinces will grow from a decorative chaenomeles, but much better are the quinces from the much rarer quince tree, *Cydonia oblonga*, grown purely for the fruit. Quinces grow slowly into a compact but proper tree and like wet ground, so are ideal for the banks of a pond or stream. Mulberries grow quite fast and like well-drained soil. On the face of it they do not make natural bedfellows.

Quince is a lovely fruit, of a beautifully warm yellow and a wonderful fragrance. Quince immeasurably improves apple in any form, makes wonderful jelly and custard and was the original marmalade, the Portuguese preserve made from quinces being called *marmelada*.

Even if you never eat quinces it is worth growing them for use as a pomander in a bowl, scenting the room as sweetly as any flower. Jewish mythology has it that the forbidden fruit in the garden of Eden was not an apple, but a quince, the quintessential fruit of good and evil. With its broad-hipped shape it is a sexy fruit (which not even the most fervent admirer could claim for a medlar) and was considered an emblem of love. In Mediterranean countries brides would eat a quince before retiring to the bridal bed, properly fortified for the nuptial rites.

In this country the bride would need to cook quinces for quite a long time before they became edible, which probably says as much about our amorous temperament and habits as it does about quinces. However, once cooked, the flesh is as delicious as that of any fruit.

■ The elder, *Sambucus nigra*, grows like a weed on any wasteland, but its berries are beautiful and delicious and should be harvested like any fruit. They are ripe when the tassels droop down. They cannot be eaten raw but are lovely in pies and preserves and make excellent wine as well as a syrup rich in vitamin C that is delicious as the base for a hot drink. Cultivated elder will take radical pruning every spring to keep it small and yet still bear lots of fruit.

■ If you have a fruit tree – particularly an apple – with mildew, it is important to rake up the leaves as they fall and burn them. Make sure that the ground around the tree is clear of grass and weeds and lightly forked over. This stops the fungus living on the ground and so re-infecting the tree.

In this country the bride would need to cook quinces for quite a long time before they became edible, which probably says as much about our amorous temperament and habits as it does about quinces.

■ Start digging now. Double-digging is hard work but will do more than almost anything else to improve the cultivation of a border, be it for flowers, fruit or veg. Plan to do just half an hour a week for the next few months, concentrating on getting one area done really well in preparation for planting next spring. The whole point is to loosen and enrich the soil to two spits' (or spade-head's) depth. Treat it as exercise and a commitment to the garden rather than a chore.

20.10.96 **Nuts**

When we moved into our present house there was a solitary tree set in 2 acres of overgrown paddock. The tree was perhaps 15 feet high and set awkwardly close to the back door. This was the sum of our 'garden'. Yet I realized at once that the tree was a treasure. It was (and still preciously is) a hazel, and a wonderfully old one at that. It produces a mass of hazelnuts every autumn and judging from the hollow, uncoppiced trunk at the centre of its stool, has done so for a couple of hundred years. Growing nuts for deliberate harvest is rare in modern gardens, but until this century they were a much valued crop, and a nuttery is the garden version of a hazel coppice, a kind of nutty orchard and a lovely notion, with its own botany of plants adapted to the cycle of coppicing. I am planning to plant one myself in an odd section of my garden, using hazel, walnut and sweet chestnut, although the latter do not readily grow in this part of the world.

Even if hazel produced no nuts at all it would still have been just as carefully cultivated, as it is the most readily coppiced element of managed woodland, providing wood in eight-to-ten-year cycles for fencing, tools, bean sticks, thatching spars and fuel for cooking. There are few plants that have been so entirely integrated into daily life in this country over the centuries. An indication of its close relationship to human life is the degree of lore that surrounds it. It is magical in all Western countries but in Ireland it is no less than the Tree of Knowledge, and it protected against fairies, was the most suitable source of the water-diviner's rod, and a double nut (two nuts on one stem) would cure toothache and could be usefully thrown at witches. It has a magic within my own private mythology, being the tree of my childhood, the tree I escaped to, hiding within its thickets, the tree that provided material for my bows and arrows and sticks and staves of all kinds. Yellow pollen brushed on to clothes from its February catkins, the smell of its crushed leaves and the feel of slightly springy autumn nutshell between my teeth are still troubled magic to me and I would never knowingly destroy a hazel.

But a hazel within a garden is essentially a fruit tree. The nuts are not the fruit but the seeds of the tree. These are rich in oil so have a high nutritional and calorific value and are deliciously sweet. They were one of the staples of prehistoric people, especially the Celts, and were an emblem of wisdom. The expressions 'in a nutshell' and 'sweet as a nut' surely emanated originally from hazels. It is not only humans that value them for food. For most of early autumn our terrier sits beneath the nut tree gazing wistfully at the branches above her in the hope of not a nut but a squirrel falling off the tree into her mouth.

Growing nuts for deliberate harvest is rare in modern gardens, but until this century they were a much valued crop, and a nuttery is the garden version of a hazel coppice, a kind of nutty orchard and a lovely notion.

The wild hazel of woodland is *Corylus avellana*, or the cob. As Geoffrey Grigson points out in *The Englishman's Flora*, 'it is decidedly pagan'. To make it Christian it was given the name of St Philibert, a seventh-century Benedictine. This has become filbert. Confusingly, we now classify *C. maxima* as a filbert and differentiate it from a cob by the way that the husk completely envelops the nut, which in turn is rather longer than the more rounded cob. Even more confusingly, one variety of filbert, the Lambert filbert, which was introduced in about 1830, is also called the Kentish cob. Other varieties included the Frizzled filbert and the Cosford nut. The Victorians evidently took their hazels seriously, and regarded the slow luxury of cracking the shells and extracting the kernels to the accompaniment of a glass of port as a rich pleasure. So do I.

The nuts should be allowed to ripen on the tree and be gathered as soon as they fall, but the temptation to collect them from the branches is usually too great. The village I live in has what in less politically correct times would be called a village idiot. He is a gentle, middle-aged man who spends most of his days helping his elderly mum do the housework and smoking his pipe while he leans on their front gate. I nearly ran him down yesterday as he was trying to swipe nuts off a tree overhanging the road. He stuffed the stick he was using inside his jacket, looking guilty as I went by. I am sorry to have startled him.

If the hazel is the most common of nuts, then the walnut is certainly the most majestic. Unlike the hazel, it makes a distinctive and regal tree up to 150 feet high. *Juglans regia*, the common walnut, was introduced to Britain by the Romans, and Thomas Tusser, in his *Five Hundred Good Points of Husbandry,* published in 1557, mentions the need to gather walnuts dry, lest they spoil, so they were clearly a useful and established crop by then. There was a burst of walnut planting at the end of the eighteenth century in this part of Herefordshire, with the idea of making walnut 'orchards', but too many trees failed for the idea to materialize. However, there is the happy residue of lines of walnuts in fields of cattle across the county.

Walnuts are the richest of all nuts and provide the richest of all timbers. Perhaps this is why we value them so for the tree, though pretty drab, is always prized in any garden. The American walnut, *Juglans nigra*, grows much bigger than the English version, although the latter has that wonderfully silvery-grey cast to the bark. The fruit appears like a small, white-flecked apple, which splits as it ripens to reveal the kernel inside. The kernel is what we call the walnut. Walnuts like heavy, moist ground and grow slowly and intensely resent being transplanted, so they need careful positioning. They need to be either put in the ground very small, or grown in a pot for the first few years and then moved into their final position. Either way, they cannot be expected to produce any fruit for at least ten years. They pollinate erratically, so it is best always to plant two together.

The Horse chestnut is a native of northern Greece and was introduced to Britain in 1615. It has been a hit ever since, making the largest flowering tree, the best sticky buds in spring, the best shade from which to consider a summer's day and, most wonderful of all, conkers. This is the nut that is perhaps the most ubiquitous symbol of autumn. It has no peer for glossy beauty. That roan sheen only lasts for a matter of hours so is doubly precious for the eyes. The tree will grow anywhere, grow fast and keep growing for a long time. There is an avenue near Godalming in Surrey that was planted in 1664 and is still going strong and the mile-long chestnut avenue in Bushy Park, north of Hampton Court, was planted by Sir Christopher Wren in 1699. Do not be tempted to plant the Red chestnut (which is in fact a cross between a Horse chestnut and the American Red buckeye) because it is an ugly tree and should not be encouraged. Stick to the unpretentious loveliness of the white candelabras of the white version in May.

Here's an interesting aside: the game of conkers only began as late as about 1850, yet a similar game has been around for centuries using hazelnuts or snail shells. Horse chestnuts were an ideal replacement; why the delay in taking them up? The answer seems to be that most chestnuts were planted on private estates, guarded zealously by tyrannical gamekeepers. 'Stealing' nuts of any sort meant big trouble. It was not until the beginning of the nineteenth-century that Horse chestnuts began to be planted in towns, and not until the middle of the century did it become a public tree providing a free supply of conkers for children to play with.

But I am straying from my brief. Horse chestnuts are inedible and there's an end to it. I, like most children, have munched them as a display of bravado, but they are terribly bitter. The Sweet chestnut (*Castanea sativa*), however, is not only edible but historically an important source of nutrition. It is a tree that identifies the geology of an area as surely as a rhododendron.

It likes a light, well-drained, acidic soil, and where it will grow it does so with exuberance, and where it feels uncomfortable it simply refuses to take up residence. It is extremely fast-growing and responsive to hard pruning, so tends to interchange with hazel as the primary coppice tree; large swathes of Kent are covered with chestnut coppices producing powerful straight poles for fencing. Although we used to feast off the raw nuts to the point of sickness when I was at school, they are best roasted. The casings of the kernels are as

The hazel has a magic within my own private mythology, being the tree of my childhood, the tree I escaped to, hiding within its thickets, the tree that provided material for my bows and arrows and sticks and staves of all kinds.

prickly as hedgehogs and they decorate the autumnal tree like lime-green Christmas baubles. The nuts become edible after the first frosts.

Sweet chestnuts are fantastically long-lived, growing into majestically gnarled and twisted trees (literally, as the trunk begins to spiral after a few hundred years). None in this country is older than the arrival of the Romans, but apparently there was one on Mount Etna that was still producing nuts after 3000 years. The fruit kept a number of Sicilian families going but they eventually killed it by lopping off branches for fuel to roast the nuts.

■ Richard Mabey has just published his eagerly awaited *Flora Britannica* (Sinclair Stevenson, £30). I plundered it for material for this column and lost hours in doing so as I was quite unable to put it down. It is a wonderful work of entertainment and scholarship and I cannot recommend it too highly to anyone who has any interest in the countryside or plants of any description. A masterpiece.

■ It is a good season for new books. There is a new edition of Hugh Johnson's *The Principles of Gardening* under the title *Hugh Johnson's Gardening Companion – The Principles And Practice of the Gardener's Art* (Mitchell Beazley, £25). The first edition was produced fifteen years ago and I use it a lot. It is a rare example of a highly illustrated book whose text is worth reading in its own right. I hope this new edition will draw more people's attention to it.

■ Hazel can, of course, be planted entirely decoratively. *Corylus maxima* 'Purpurea' is one of the very best purple-leafed shrubs in a border, *C. avellana 'contorta'* has twisted stems that have the attraction of natural bonsai, and *C. colurna*, or the Turkish hazel, makes a fine, single-stemmed tree.

■ Hazelnuts will store until Christmas if kept in their husk, which stops them from drying out too fast. If collected while still green, they should be left in a dry place and they will ripen by about November.

■ The American walnut exudes a kind of self-protective poison from its roots and this particularly affects apples, so keep the two trees well apart.

22.10.95 **A Bluffer's Guide to Gardening**

It's a funny old game. I have spent the last week touring round the country promoting my new book (*The Weekend Gardener*, Bloomsbury, £16.99), talking to groups of people in bookshops. The idea is that I waffle for about twenty minutes and then field questions. Most of the questions are predictable and therefore researchable, but there are always a couple that I haven't the foggiest about. The trouble is that people won't take 'I don't know' for an answer. They need you to know in order to justify having had sufficient faith to come all the way to listen to you. So there are times, I am afraid to admit, when I bluff my way through ignorance.

I have always felt very uncomfortable at being introduced as a gardening 'expert'. There is no coy modesty at work here – I just do not have sufficient horticultural expertise to warrant the label. And there is always the sour-lipped type with a homicidal gleam in their eye edging forward to test me, to find a chink in this chainmail of omniscience that others require. At least it gives them easy pleasure because there is more chink than chain. But there are a number of ploys that the ordinary person could use to win friends (in the local garden club at least). So here is a brief bluffer's guide to gardening:

The trouble is that people won't take 'I don't know' for an answer. They need you to know in order to justify having had sufficient faith to come all the way to listen to you.

1. Join the RHS and visit the Chelsea Flower Show each year. Go on a Members' Day and cover enough ground to ensure you are seen by at least one acquaintance. Concentrate on the outdoor gardens and of a couple of them vaguely memorize the theme. This will buy you a surprising amount of garden cred for the year.

2. Learn the names of the current gurus and sages. Christopher Lloyd is Always Right. Rosemary Verey, Beth Chatto and Penelope Hobhouse are respected and very respectable. Dan Pearson is groovy but *Gardener's World*, *Gardeners' Question Time* and all garden magazines are nice but naff.

3. Become knowledgeable about a detail. People are always impressed with specific knowledge and gardening is an area where there is scope for endless specialization. The chances of being found out are relatively small and one can test the waters before setting sail on one's own exotic barge of arcane knowledge.

Excellent areas are large-leafed tropical plants; alpines; ferns (with a special fondness for antipodean tree ferns – easy to check out in botanical gardens), grasses, orchids or cacti. Observe how all politicians brazenly turn any question to their chosen channel of knowledge or propaganda and likewise amaze and awe your friends with the incisive application of fungal diseases of ferns to any question.

A less intensive way of focusing limited knowledge is to express a loathing for certain plant groups or types. By banning foliage plants, annuals, yellow, pink or variegated plants from your garden, you are strategically cutting down the areas of learning required.

4. Get a smattering of garden history. This instantly confers a spurious horticultural validity. You might not be able to grow anything successfully yourself but if you can archly refer to the Reptonesque playfulness of some circular flowerbeds or the almost Robinsonian abandon of a friend's uncut orchard, then you can look down at all you survey. To get the most from this vantage-point it is always good to be able to bring a certain amount of internationalism into the debate. Particularly pointworthy are Asian references, juggling the intricacies of Confucian and Zen garden design. If you find yourself in the unhappy position of talking to someone who really knows about this, there is always the escape route of 'Of course the Western mind can never really deal with the subtleties of Eastern thought without a really thorough linguistic grounding.' Then you smile apologetically, as if to say that is lax but, you know, charmingly human...

5. Keep your hands dirty. A true gardener has engrained dirt, resistant to the most vigorous scrubbing. There is a whole breed of county ladies in tweeds, pearls and sensible shoes who go through their lives with exquisite manners and horny hands enseamed with grime from a lifetime in the garden.

Rub earth liberally into the hands and acquire a callus or two if possible. I used to have a thick pad of skin on the outer edge of my forefinger from endless chafing with spade, rake and hoe and entertained my children by using it as a pin cushion. Now the calluses are on my bottom and tongue from sitting and talking too much.

6. Tend the edges of your garden. It is extraordinary what a little time spent on the marginal areas of the garden can achieve. Where the edges are supposed to be cut, cut them neatly. Weed between paving. Trim hedges, even if all around the hedge is wilderness. Use strategically spaced topiary, keeping it to balls or cones which are much easier to clip than anything involving flat planes. Cut paths in long grass the width of your mower (so it takes only one pass to cut) and keep them mown. The eye will admire the crisp balance of the path rather than the disorder of the flanking unmown grass.If you have the money, pave or brick all paths. Flank all of them with box, lavender, santolina or hyssop. All need clipping just once a year and cut the right kind of confident garden dash.

7. Invest in mulch. Most people fail to mulch thickly enough, but a 4-inch layer of mushroom compost or bark applied every spring/and autumn will keep the weeds down, improve the soil and make the place look as though someone knows what they are about.

■ You can prepare a pond for winter by drastically thinning out underwater oxygenating plants and removing old waterlily leaves. This reduces the decaying vegetation on the bottom of the pool which will produce toxic gases when the top frosts over.
■ If you have a greenhouse, line it with bubblewrap now, before the weather gets too cold. This can be bought in rolls and taped on to the glass or frame.
■ I remember all the chrysanths being dug up and stored in boxes of soil in the greenhouse at about this time of year when I was a child, but there is no need to do this if you live in a reasonably mild area. However, if you leave them in the ground do not cut them back. Leave the dead stalks on over winter.
■ You can begin to plant deciduous hedging now, giving it a real chance to develop new roots before the worst of winter.

There is always the sour-lipped type with a homicidal gleam in their eye edging forward to test me, to find a chink in this chainmail of omniscience that others require.

27.10.96 **New Age Gardening**

Given gardening's comfortably middle-aged, bourgeois image, it is surprising how many wackos it attracts. For such an earthy business there are an awful lot of heads floating about in the clouds. Now, I personally find the clouds a good place for the head to be, especially when feet are on the ground and hands in it. Gardens are dreams made real and, as the songwriter so perceptively noticed, if you haven't got a dream, how you gonna make a dream come true? Whilst the outward faces of gardens are inventions, made up by men and women dreaming, the workings of them are, according to your persuasion, either science or magic. These things seem to go in cycles, with so-called primitive societies happy to buy the magic and rational cultures applying science. The magical school of gardening is having something of a resurgence, what with astro-gardening, sheng-fui, ley-lines, lunar cycles, Gaia, aromatherapy and homoeopathy. Science says that this is the result of these specific things interrelating.

Think how inexplicable plants must have seemed before the age of science. They appeared from nothing, lived and died by the calendar and had a huge range of effects on humans, healing, feeding, poisoning and altering the mind. Magic was the only possible explanation for this, and astrology, numerology, the scriptures and classical myths were all pressed into service at one time or another to provide explanation. In a time when religious belief of one type or another was absolute, no explanation or comprehension was necessary: it was simply necessary to believe. Faith was an absolute virtue.

This blind faith manifested itself throughout the garden and the hedgerow. Flowers that bloomed out of season were ominous. White, sweet-smelling and drooping plants such as hawthorn, elder or snowdrop signified death and were unlucky in the house. It is no coincidence that white is the colour of mourning in the East. Red flowers, the colour of blood, signified life and warded off witches. Red and white flowers put together were bad news all round, presumably because the message was thoroughly confusing.

Any plants with thorns or serrated leaves such as holly, hawthorn again, elder, houseleek or rowan were 'lightening plants that warded off evil spirits, and their destruction invariably brought bad luck. Why? How? Magic. And in a world where nature in every manifestation was miraculous, who could not believe in magic ? Anyone stung by nettles still reaches for dock leaf to ease the sting. Foxgloves provide digoxin for heart disease, willow aspirin and mint menthol. Science does not change the facts, just explains them away.

It is confusing. I love magic and badly want it to happen. I want cabbage to 'head up' better when planted under the sign of Aries and lawns to grow lusher when sown while the moon is waxing in exactly the way that I want to believe that I could win the lottery. Anyone who tells me that there is more chance of being hit by an asteroid on my way to buy the ticket is a puritanical dullard. But a rational one.

The truth is that we all hate scientists for their smugness. They are the swots at the back of the class who quietly get everything right. They are the gardeners who carefully redress the pH balance of their soil and prefer the powdered chemical feed to the muck heap. We love poets and artists for their

Given gardening's comfortably middle-aged, bourgeois image, it is surprising how many wackos it attracts.

wrongness and bluster. The poetic gardener makes it all up as he goes along. The scientist executes a carefully conceived plan. Science explains everything and makes nothing. Poetry does nothing for anybody but justifies everything. Superstition, folklore, mythology and ritual rely upon magic bolstered by ignorance and innocence, whilst ignorance has a shadowy glamour that knowledge shines an unkind light on. It is no coincidence that television is flooded with X-files, sci-fi, paranormal and 'magical' technology, because science is most attractive to the lay person when it is inexplicable.

New Age gardening, therefore, is a reversion to long-standing magic rather than any 'new' attitudes towards growing things.

But one of the New Age patterns of understanding that combines scientific explanation and magic is the theory of Gaia. The name is chosen from the Greek goddess who was the mythological personification of the earth, and significantly, the first being that sprang from Chaos. Gaia encapsulates the notion of the earth as a self-sustaining, self-nurturing entity. The idea is that the earth, in all its natural manifestations, from ocean to mountain and with all living things on it, is alive and interrelated. Scientific research shows increasing evidence of this: that, for example, humans share many more similarities than differences with a frog or a wombat. Leave the planet alone and these similarities will act to sort it out via its inherent self-regulating system. Meddle with the inbuilt balance of things and you interfere with the functioning of the entire planet. Everything is connected to everything because everything is just a unit in a single living organism that is the planet. Rushing on past all the questions that inevitably arise from this thesis (such as how much can man tamper with this balance? If the planet is intrinsically self-healable and if man is just one small component of the planet, surely it can heal anything we do to harm it?), you can see the attraction this has for the hippier side of gardening. It is magic and science rolled into one satisfactorily vague concept that can be worshipped in the garden. Let me hasten to say that I'm not sceptical – just ignorant. But the message is clear: the planet is a living body. Thus any garden is both part of that body and a symbol of its wholeness. You must therefore garden in harmony with the planet.

This is easy. It happens. The biosphere has interlocking cycles of energy, organic matter and inorganic nutrients. These cycles are driven by the sun and regulated by living organisms. Your garden plants dominate the garden's own bio-mass and replenish the oxygen supply. Every organism that dies contributes to the general store of organic matter which decomposers such as bacteria and fungi then transform into nutrients. The soil, enriched by these nutrients and supplied with air and water, provides the ideal growing medium for plants. And so it goes round.

A garden is therefore potentially a process towards a fully sustainable balance, harmoniously existing from single cell to great oak, as long as the gardener can resist the temptation to be constantly halting this natural progression by imposing a horticultural dictatorship rather than a benign communism.

Systems such as biodynamics as propounded by Rudolf Steiner, bio-intensive gardening and permaculture are all an attempt to harness the natural symbiosis of nature with man's need to grow food and make dream gardens. Biodynamics seems to work, but is loony. Steiner said that terrestrial forces are influenced by the moon, Mercury and Venus via the 'limestone element'. Cosmic forces come from Jupiter, Saturn and Mars as well as the sun and express themselves as light and warmth. Special 'preparations' are used on the soil and compost heap to dynamize them to optimize growing conditions. Wacky or what? Nevertheless, it is taken seriously, used extensively and seems to work. Especially in Australia.

Bio-intensive gardening is widely practised under the guise of the raised-bed, no-dig system. It depends upon never treading on the soil once the beds are prepared and, if you are prepared to suffer that tyranny, allows for very intensive production of vegetables within strictly organic methods.

Permaculture is altogether more radical and it takes a leap of the imagination to interpret it in gardening as we know it. But it is a fascinating, if slightly self-conscious, exercise in honouring Gaia. Instead of imposing the dream on the landscape, it blends into it. Trees are not cut down and scrub not cleared. Annuals are grown in temporary clearings created by fallen trees, where light can reach them, shrubs in the semi-shade, and shelter of trees, and climbers are encouraged to use the surrounding vegetation as support. It involves no digging, no pruning, no fertilizer, no weeding and no pesticides.

Mankind needs superstition, ritual and magic just as we need poetry, religion and magic. Remember the enduring image from *Edge of Darkness*, the BBC's superlative television drama based upon Gaia, where the planet, conquering all, produces flowers out of the nuclear winter? The real power of the image was not just that there were flowers growing from an actual and metaphorical wasteland, but that the colour of these flowers was a deep and utterly mysterious black.

■ Tidiness is the greatest enemy of garden harmony. 'Clean' bare soil is an environmental disaster. Give it a covering of plants or mulch. Whilst it is a good idea to gather leaves from paths and grass in order to redistribute them on bare soil when rotted, leave leaves on borders, leave rotting wood to provide food for insects, and leave dried flower-heads as an insulation layer over winter. Make a pile of your dead wood to enrich your own ecosystem. Gardening in the last 200 years has set increasing store on the variety and rarity of plants. Fight this pernicious trend and use only native trees and shrubs that fit readily into your ecosystem. A banana plant may give you a frisson of one-upmanship but will not do much for the local population of insects or birds.

■ Without necessarily embracing permaculture, it makes sense to go with prevailing conditions rather than struggling to transform them to some ideal. If your soil is wet and

I love magic and badly want it to happen...Anyone who tells me that there is more chance of being hit by an asteroid on my way to buy the ticket is a puritanical dullard. But a rational one.

heavy, grow plants that like wet and heavy soil. If you are on chalk, forget all ericaceous plants. Use your common sense.

■ Plant by the light of the moon for maximum horticultural effectiveness. The moon waxes and wanes on a four-week cycle, which can be broken into the following horticultural timetable, beginning with the new moon:

- ■ Week 1 is good for general balanced growth.
- ■ Week 2 is excellent for producing foliage.
- ■ Week 3 is best for root growth.
- ■ Week 4 is bad.

While you are about it, take heed of the astrological as well as the lunar cycle. So plant root crops when the moon is in an earth sign, leaf crops when in a water sign, flowers during an air sign and fruit in a fire sign.

30.10.94 **Pumpkins**

I sowed some pumpkin seeds this year, partly because I thought their great orange footballs would look jolly, partly because mine is a new garden and I have loads of space, so anything that grows dramatically is needed to add substance to the place, but mainly so that I could earn brownie points as a good father come Hallowe'en. The idea was that there would be at least a pumpkin per child, preferably two pumpkins each – a fleet of pumpkins – which we could cut and carve into toothy candle-lit grins. General delighted spookiness all round. Well, here we are, almost, and I do not have a single pumpkin to my name. I have lots of marrows {zucchini}, great whopping jobs, but everybody has marrows. Marrows are one of those crops that, if they grow at all, inevitably produce a glut, and a little marrow goes a long way. Or is treated as a courgette. But all the pumpkins failed to germinate. I sowed them in April in an unheated greenhouse and then again in May outside, directly into an old compost heap. I now know that both procedures were doomed.

Pumpkins need heat of at least 16°C/60°F to germinate and must be kept in the dark. Make sure that the compost is not cold, then sow them ½-inch deep on their edge – the seeds are flat like melon seeds. If you sow them in individual pots or modules (trays of polystyrene with a grid of square spaces) filled with a general-purpose compost and then cover until they have germinated, they can stay in them until planted out. If you sow into a seed tray, like I did, they will need pricking out into pots once they have come through. As with all pricking out, the smaller the plant is when you do this, the better. William Cobbett, writing 175 years ago, says that 'about the middle of May, the pots should be taken out and sunk in the natural ground, and a frame set over them, or they should have a covering of hoops and mats for the night time, just to keep off the frosts.' This sounds

The idea was that there would be at least a pumpkin per child, preferably two pumpkins each – a fleet of pumpkins – which we could cut and carve into toothy candle-lit grins.

It is odd that such a robust thing as a pumpkin should need mollycoddling but they are not natives and have not got used to our climate. It is easier to understand if one thinks of them as close relatives of cucumber.

elaborate but contains the essential wisdom of hardening off plants grown in indoor sheltered conditions before putting them out in their final position. Otherwise, however healthy, the culture shock is too great and they give up the ghost.

It is odd that such a robust thing as a pumpkin should need mollycoddling but they are not natives and have not got used to our climate. It is easier to understand if one thinks of them as close relatives of cucumber. However, once the sun comes out you can plant them outside – usually about the beginning of June. They are not fussy about soil but like a well-drained, rich root-run, so the technique used for marrows of digging a shallow pit filled with compost and planting them in that is a good one. My ploy of using a 'slow' compost heap (one with lots of weeds in that I am letting rot down for at least a year before using) worked well with marrows so should be ideal for pumpkins. They will then romp away with no assistance at all other than regular and plentiful watering, or so I am assured. I have told my children this – weeping in the corner and throwing me recriminating looks – and promised them pumpkins the size of coaches next year. In order that pumpkins may romp unfettered, you need to allow a spread of at least 6 feet per plant, which limits the amount you might grow in the average garden.

I know that when growing marrows the critical time to water them is as they are growing rather than after they have produced fruit, and it is better to give them a good bath once or twice a week than a daily shower. Until the leaves develop fully and act as a mulch to stop weeds, it is important that, to quote Cobbett again, 'a very nice hoeing be given to the ground' to keep them clear of weeds so that the pumpkins get all the water and nutrients available.

It seems that the American Indians first cultivated pumpkins 10,000 years ago and did so for the seeds only at first, which they ate, discovering the flesh tasted good as a by-product. By the time pumpkins reached Europe, in the seventeenth century, they were quickly adopted as a more wholesome alternative to cucumber and were used, mashed up, to bulk out bread or were eaten boiled and buttered or roasted, stuffed with sliced apples. Like cucumbers, they were also regarded with a degree of superstition and magic, thus: 'To make pompions [pumpkins] keep long, and not spoiled or rotted, you must sprinkle them with the juice of a houseleek...a woman having her termes and walking by the border of pompions, gourds and cucumbers, causeth them to dry and die, or to be bitter.'

Whilst I am sure that there are still gardeners down on allotments all over England who would merely question the wisdom of the houseleek bit, it seems that a more reliable way to make pumpkins keep is to let the skin get really hard, which it will do in response to sunshine. So uncovering them and putting them out in a dry sunny spot after harvesting will aid this. As with marrows, they must all be gathered in (with a section of stem attached to the fruit) as soon as the leaves begin to die, whether fully ripened or not. If left on the damp ground they will be attacked by slugs and will rot.

As a rule, pumpkins in this country take about 100 days to ripen, which stretches the normal season as far into autumn as it will go before the danger of frost is there. A ripe pumpkin will sound hollow when tapped and will go on ripening after picking, but must be stored in a frost-free place.

Gourds are part of the same family and I had a kind of failure with these too this year. They were sown – and failed – at the same time as my pumpkins because they were too cold, I suppose. About the beginning of June I threw away the contents of their seed tray in disgust, chucking them into the bag I keep in the greenhouse for used seed compost. Whereupon they recognized the place as home, germinated and grew like vine up round the roof. I now have a dozen mixed gourds sitting shinily in a bowl on the kitchen window-sill like the shrunken heads of vanquished pumpkins. Gourds of course are not edible, but I suppose I could hollow them out, cut faces into them, put a night-light inside and tell the children less is more...

■ A method of encouraging individual pumpkins to grow as large as possible is to heap soil over the axis of fruit-bearing laterals (the point where they emerge from the main stem), which makes the plant send out extra roots to obtain more food and moisture.

■ The planting season is upon us. All herbaceous plants, climbers and deciduous shrubs, trees and hedges are best planted between now and Christmas if possible. Take trouble with this, giving everything the best start possible. It is really important to firm everything in properly, staking it if need be, otherwise the inevitable winds that we will get between now and spring will rock and damage the delicate growing roots.

■ A lot of books encourage one to cut herbaceous plants back now, tidying the garden for the winter. I think that this is a pity. Leave all seed-heads for the birds and enjoy their starkness, especially in frosty weather. Nothing will be harmed if the job is done in March.

■ A sowing of lamb's lettuce can still be made, especially if you can put a cloche over it.

■ When digging the ground, resist the temptation to break it down into a neat and tidy appearance. Leave it in spade-sized clods and let the weather work it down. By spring it will not be compacted and should be friable and easy to work into a fine tilth.

5.11.95 **Bonfire of the Vanities**

Guy Fawkes Night is part of the gardening calendar, an orange hole burnt into the dark, with the smell of brown earth and worm casts on the lawn before cordite buries it, and the sudden silhouettes of fading vegetation as a backdrop to pyrotechnical wonder. We all feel a pang of pagan wonder despite our cynical grown-up souls. But Bonfire Night is also a pyre, burning the light, and exploding the easy softness of spring, summer and autumn, and marks the descent into the grey dampness that hangs like a depressive smog until winter proper arrives.

To carry me through this I need more than the remembered delicacy of high days. I need fire to burn a hole in my own darkness and as I get older and madder, the glow, both actual and remembered, from blazing orange flowers.

This is both tricky and trendy. The two are linked, because the trickiness lies in the extreme distaste that many (most) gardeners have felt for the brash garishness of orange in their gardens, and the trendiness is dependent upon the fact that bright, rich colours have not been popular until very recently. By definition something can only be trendy if it is unlike that which has preceded it.

Those who shudder at the splashes of orange I crave tend to be those who have a lot of pink in the garden. Orange and pink make uncomfortable flowerbed-fellows. Orange makes pink sacchariney and coy, and pink brings out the slut in orange. Both do very well with the deep crimsons and purples that are still lingering around the more protected parts of my garden – swathes of self-seeded *Verbena bonariensis*, a few late flowers of the rose 'Souvenir du Dr Jamain', some late snapdragons the colour of arterial blood, and the startling purple of one particular clump of Michaelmas daisy in quite the wrong place. But pick a patch of purple and it is curiously insipid in the jar. The greens of autumn are not up to the inspiration it needs, whereas the same colours in May or June would glow. However, put just one orange marigold in the purple mix and the whole thing takes off.

This association of strong colours runs against conventional horticultural wisdom. The hobnail-booted Surrey guru, Gertrude Jekyll, advocated making an orange garden followed by the balm of soothing greys. In fact the orange was there mainly to make the greys seem the more luminous and refreshing. This is because orange is dark despite being bright. I suppose that this is the consistent thread with the oranges, purples and velvety crimsons that I like so much. They are all rich jewel-colours, ruby, amethyst and topaz, throwing out intense colour but little light.

As any four-year-old knows, orange is a mixture of red and yellow, but as it darkens orange tends towards brown rather than red, becoming almost sienna. The wonderful sunflower 'Velvet Queen' is a rich bronzy brown and yet has clearly come via orange. Some of the rudbeckias, such as 'Marmalade' or the mixed 'Rustic' dwarves, have this same orangey-bronze colouring that is fantastically invigorating.

There is a temptation to get all subtle and sophisticated with bronzes, marmalades and topazes, whereas orange – plain, brash orange – is vulgar and gutsy and should be enjoyed as such. That is why I love the remnants of nasturtiums at this time of year and the African and French marigolds, *Tagetes erecta* and *patula* respectively. I sow them late in the vegetable garden where they blaze as common as muck until hammered into submission by a really hard succession of frosts. They are two fingers stuck up against the encircling gloom and any sophistication would dim their light. This is why orange looks very good low down in a border, the light dimmed over by surrounding

To carry me through this I need more than the remembered delicacy of high days. I need fire to burn a hole in my own darkness and as I get older and madder, the glow, both actual and remembered, from blazing orange flowers.

There is a temptation to get all subtle and sophisticated with bronzes, marmalades and topazes, whereas orange - plain, brash orange - is vulgar and gutsy and should be enjoyed as such.

plants. Sticking out over the top of other plants it will look merely madly gay, but hunkered down by the ground it shines with pure colour rather than light. One of the best autumnal examples of this is orange pumpkins sitting on the ground like a colony of garish, hugely overgrown chicks about to leave the nest. Pumpkins should be lifted off the ground around September time so that they dry properly, but I cannot resist leaving some until their foliage has completely died back so that I can fully enjoy their fat orange gutsiness.

In the full glare of the bright summer sun orange is best dotted in among the restrained blues, greys and yellows, and as long as they are kept apart from pinks, like rival fans at a local derby, they will invigorate rather than clash. *Geum* x *borisii*, seemingly held from on high and floating above its foliage rather than on the end of its long stems, is wonderfully effective in this role. As summer edges into autumn the oranges can mass slightly, chrysanthemums, dahlias, gladioli and red-hot pokers rudely milling in amongst the effete garden party.

Spring is more awkward. I have never liked the orangey strains of daffodils that are so popular as cut flowers, finding them without the freshness or innocence of pure yellow. There are orange tulips that would look good dotted amongst a blue and yellow May border or rising up from the glaucous leaves of *Hosta sieboldiana*, but you would have to be brave to plant them *en masse*. It is better, I think, to let the seasons dictate the colours rather than allocate colour schemes to certain areas and rigorously stick to that regardless of light, weather or seasonal mood.

Orange climbers almost always look odd, like a guest at the wrong party or a zany traffic light. This is, again, because they are too exposed to the light, too 'up there' to be taken seriously in our northern light. It is no coincidence that almost all truly orange-flowered climbers are tender and are uncomfortable lunatic escapees from the tropics.

■ This is the peak planting month. Get all deciduous trees, shrubs, climbers and perennials in the ground this month if at all possible. This gives them the chance to develop new roots before the growing demands of next spring.

■ Plant tulips throughout this month. Put them in deeper than most bulbs (for which the rule of thumb is a planting depth of twice the depth of the bulb itself) and give them as much drainage as possible.

■ Sow broad beans for an early spring crop. 'Aquadulce' or 'The Sutton' are two varieties suited to overwintering, although any variety of bean in the ground over winter is a sore temptation to mice.

■ If you are tidying your borders, avoid the temptation to mulch them with manure now. This would encourage soft growth that would be particularly susceptible to frost damage. Use a less nutritious mulch like bark, leafmould or straw and save the compost and manure for your spring mulch.

■ Wisteria can now be pruned back to a couple of inches on each spur, leaving three buds from which next year's flowers will grow. Tie all remaining growth securely.

10.11.96 **Capability Bob**

Our gardens have been hijacked by plants. The two are now inseparable to many gardeners, as though the defining elements of a house were the colour and fabric of the curtains or the types of kitchen utensils used. I have looked at lots of gardens in quite a few countries and have come to the conclusion that an obsession with plants is the ruination of a garden. These waters are muddied by the unclear distinction between what plants are and what plants do. Most plant spotters (sometimes known as plantsmen or, rather tricksily, plant lovers) are primarily interested in what a plant is. If it is unusual or difficult to grow, it is by definition good. Garden lovers are interested in what a plant does. Does it do blue/ yellow/ burgundy/ big/small flowers? Do scent? Grow like a weed?... terrific. Let's have loads of it.

But gardening as it has evolved regards the ability to grow a wide range of rare and curious plants as a higher form of horticulture. This is fascinating for the grower and can be exquisitely beautiful for the visitor, but can also be a crashing bore.

The root of this distinction centres on the conflicting notion of the garden as an integral place and the garden as a habitat for a collection of plants. If you junk the plant obsession and concentrate on the garden as a space within which to express yourself, then the range of creative opportunities immediately increases. It might seem far-fetched, but I think that there is a direct link here with the eighteenth-century tradition of landscape gardeners. Every garden is a piece of landscape waiting to be manipulated according to the gardener's fancy. Never has it been so easy to do as it is now. Mini-diggers have brought the earth-mover to the back door. All you need is 1-metre access, £50 a day hire fee and imagination. Plants come later, but the first step is making the earth move.

In my last garden I blithely undertook to make a sequence of four terraces on a steep hillside, each 40 yards long and 4 yards deep. A JCB driver called Ginger (never knew him by any other name) and myself at the wheel of a 3-ton dumper truck shifted some 5000 tons of rock and soil from the hillside from behind the house to the front. It took weeks and was fraught with all sorts of complications, but boy, what uncomplicated, heart-churning fun! Before you give your heart to 'hand-crafted' trug or dibber, let me put you straight: a JCB is the most exciting, sexy piece of garden equipment ever devised.

Of course, you do not need to have hillsides available to make your mark. Canals can be inches deep, mounds just a few feet high to transform your

I have looked at lots of gardens in quite a few countries and have come to the conclusion that an obsession with plants is the ruination of a garden.

space from dull back-garden to landscape. The trouble is that we have surrendered this territory to conventional artists. A gardener is coy about calling himself an artist. It's a bit too Californian, too embarrassingly pretentious. We garden in the spirit in which we wash up or paint the spare bedroom. Creative it isn't. But it could be. It is all there if you want it. What artists such as Andy Goldsworthy, David Nash, James Turrell or Richard Long do is there to be done by you in your garden. David Nash in particular has applied the skills of the gardener in training trees to grow into dancing shapes in the landscape. He uses pleaching, plashing, grafting and pruning just as other sculptors use skills such as woodcarving or moulding clay.

Topiary, in all its forms, is simply sculpture with living material. Some of the best topiary gardens, especially those of the modern designer Jaques Wirtz, are artistic masterpieces to equal anything in the sculptural canon. The fact that they grow and change appearance with a single season and yet can live to be hundreds of years old or die within months adds a dimension that has only recently been exploited by conventional artists.

However, the original landscape designers were artists who became gardeners by default. Perhaps the most influential of them all was William Kent whose work can still be seen at Rousham and Stowe. His sole aim was to create a series of dramatic pictures that you walked through. What he made was cold, logical architecture set in a loose yet entirely mannered landscape. Kent was no gardener, but he radically altered the notion of gardening. From that first step came the transformation of the landscape. He used gardens as a medium to express himself and cared for plants only in so far as they could help towards that end. He made a series of theatrical tableaux such as the Elysian fields at Stowe or the Vale of Venus at Rousham where earth-moving, planting and architecture all worked towards one theatrical end. Is it gardening? Who cares! It is wonderful.

Lancelot 'Capability' Brown was exceptional in that he was trained as a gardener, reaching the position of head gardener at Stowe before setting up on his own as a designer. Brown was above all a fixer. He made life easy for his patrons, treating their outdoors exactly as the modern interior designer does the indoors of the very rich. They 'do' houses. He 'did' parks. People knew the sort of thing that they were going to get, knew that it was extremely fashionable and knew that he would provide it with the minimum of hassle. What is interesting is that within these prosaically commercial parameters he changed a nation's attitude to landscape. If Kent was the first 'naturalistic' garden designer, Brown made the landscape user-friendly. From being hostile territory that could be cultivated and perhaps admired from a distance, Brown embraced it and brought it into the garden. Of course these 'gardens' were bloody great parks belonging to, by modern values, multi-millionaires. But they set the tone for what all Englishmen have since aspired to: a lottery winner's fantasy of a manicured park set about a whopping great mansion. The real difference is that now we want the finished product. We demand our landscapes and houses to be old. In Brown's day people had the confidence to make new landscapes and new houses. It is interesting to think that neither Brown nor his patrons ever saw any of his work except in its bare infancy. All the millions of trees that he planted would have looked more like a modern golf-course than rolling parkland. He planted for the future and his patrons willingly paid for later generations to reap that harvest. Millionaires now want their gardens delivered mature, preferably yesterday.

Humphrey Repton stepped neatly into Brown's shoes after his death in 1783, becoming favoured Exterior Designer. His skill was to domesticate the landscape further, to make it cosier and generally more fluffy. Like Brown, his landscapes blended into the countryside seamlessly because he used indigenous plants, save for the cedar of Lebanon, strategically placed. The Victorians carried this 'gardenizing' of the landscape to absurd extremes, incorporating faux landscapes within utterly domestic gardens. The best example is at Biddulph Grange in Staffordshire. Here all attempts at naturalization have been abandoned and wildly contrasting dreamscapes evolve into each other surreally, so that you walk from China to Egyptian temple to cottage garden to rocky glade. It has been beautifully restored by the National Trust and is one of the most deliciously eccentric gardens open to the public.

What made the hysterical extremes of Biddulph possible to execute was the huge influx of plants from all over the world that followed in the wake of British colonial expansion. Rich men commissioned private plant hunters to track down new species for their own private collections, just as a previous age collected antique statuary. What is the modern equivalent? Goldsmith collecting votes? Aspinall's Zoo? The point is that it was above all an expression of power and wealth. The plants became a fetish and the concept of a garden where plants were 'collected' became honourable instead of risible.

The next stage on this slippery slope towards philistinism was that gardens became tasteful and dominated by upper-class women with firm chins, cut-crystal voices and heavy boots. For the past 100 years these ladies remain as the icons of all aspirational gardeners. They occasionally wear out and replace themselves with clones, but to all intents and purposes they are one and the same model. Occasionally they are a man, but this is a minor modification on the type. Their only qualifications are that they are old, married to a rich husband, and live in the country in converted rectories. They have 'help' (a team of gardeners) to do the dirty work while they immerse themselves in the behaviour of plants. They are usually funny, fantastically knowledgeable and surprisingly irreverent. But their influence is baleful. People pathetically copy them and their gardens in the hope of being as rich and socially admired as them, and the results are bad pastiches based upon snobbery and a mishmash of garden-centre plants.

So, what's to do? We have lost the perception that a garden is a landscape

The next stage on this slippery slope towards philistinism was that gardens became tasteful and dominated by upper-class women with firm chins, cut-crystal voices and heavy boots. For the past 100 years these ladies remain as the icons of all aspirational gardeners.

that is ours to manipulate. In practice any planting, any construction does that. We are all landscape designers, whether we like it or not. We have got to value this and relish it for what it is rather than as a side-show to the cultivation of plants. Plants are a means to a creative end. If the intention is to create a series of living shapes in your landscape that please you then it makes sense to choose the best materials for that and to look after them in such a way that they grow as healthily and as fast as possible. In this way you learn about gardening without becoming a victim of the terrible plant-spotting disease. If you dig a canal or pond, make it with bricks, concrete or whatever, and then plant water-lilies because that is what your eye tells you the composition needs, you are by default a water-gardener and almost certainly will become knowledgeable in the process. Gardening is wonderfully practical and plants endlessly interesting: but context is everything and less botany and more landscaping would make better gardeners of us all.

If you are moved to try landscaping your garden, bear the following in mind:
■ Earth-moving makes a fantastic amount of mess. All of this can be cleared and tidied very quickly, but be prepared for a lot of mud.
■ Always use machinery when the ground is dry and going to remain dry. Frosty weather is ideal, but rapidly thaws to slimy mud, so always start work at first light.
■ Any heavy machinery will compact the soil, so cultivate deeply any ground that has been driven over.
■ Always keep topsoil and subsoil separate. This is harder to do than might be imagined, but very important.
■ If you are building any retaining walls, always allow gaps for water to drain. This is both to allow the soil to drain and to protect the wall as a build-up of water will knock down any construction.
■ If you are digging out ponds, ditches or paths, think of the extra material you are creating with which to go up: the spoil makes mounds, slopes and banks and should be part of your planning.
■ If planting for sculptural effect, resist the temptation of using big plants for immediate results. Small plants grow faster and more healthily and respond much better to training of any kind.

24.11.96 **Neighbours**

For a while we were good neighbours. He was a taxi driver who boasted of having been a driver for the Kray brothers ('Lovely boys') and of keeping a wide range of pets. We had just moved in. He had lived there for years. It was the pets that came between us. The ferret's cage left uncleaned for weeks parked a yard from our back-door was hard to stomach (literally) but the final straw was the decomposing body of an 8-foot python on the compost heap, attracting a swarm of flies around our baby's pram and creating an overwhelming stench of rotting flesh. We complained and he hated us for it. End of friendship.

Neighbours, eh! Who'd have them? Me and you and just about everyone with a garden. You can draw your curtains and block out the rest of the world once indoors but gardens are not so easily screened. A friend

recently told me that he had had an irate phone-call from a neighbour complaining about a 10-foot ash tree that he had planted close to their mutual boundary. Although her voice was shrill with rage, she professed her admiration for trees in general and ash trees in particular, nevertheless, this one was a blot on her landscape. It would grow monstrously big, it would one day shade her garden, it would look better elsewhere. When at last he cornered her on what exactly was the problem with his tree she apparently burst out with 'It's planted in the wrong place!' He had to admit that he had chosen the spot so that it was in exactly the right place to block out her house, which, as far as he was concerned, loomed uncomfortably large over his garden. But of course, blocking his unwanted view of her also blocked her scape beyond. There was no compromise, so they parted agreeing to hate each other.

There lies the nub of all neighbourly problems. One neighbour's counsel of domestic heaven is another's recipe for hell. Whilst it is essential that we all contract to a communal code of public behaviour, we cannot be expected to absorb and tolerate each other's private tastes and actions. It is hard enough with those we love, but impossible with neighbours. Yet it is curious how some people seem to feel that the garden is a halfway point between private and public territory. Can you complain about the colour of curtains, or underpants on the washing line? Is it reasonable to comment on the design of a window or the colour clash between the rose growing around it and the paint on the frame? The buffer-zone between the utterly personal and private and communal compromise seems to fall heavily across the garden fence.

The law does arbitrate to a certain extent, but a surprising amount is expected of neighbourly tolerance and common sense. You cannot build anything, including a fence, more than 2 yards high without planning permission. You have a right to cut back overhanging branches from a neighbour's tree in a line with your mutual boundary, but you do not have the right to the fruit or flowers that may be on those branches. They must be gathered and politely handed back over the fence.

You have no absolute right of light over your garden and you can no more ask a neighbour to remove a tree shading your vegetable plot than you can ask him to knock down his house. We accept the status quo when we move into a house and most people see that the vegetation causing unwanted shade is also providing privacy, shelter from the wind and a habitat for birds. But the mass introduction of Leyland cypress as screen hedging has meant that you can create a new, 20-30-foot-high solid, year-round visual barrier within the average occupancy of a household. Although this has led to well-publicized legal cases, the truth is that it is very difficult to get the law to resolve the matter and it is much cheaper to move house than take the matter to a court. Even if you do win your case, you cannot remove a screen, only have it lowered from ridiculously high to very high.

Just as you have no legal right to your view, even if that was the prime mover in making you choose to live in that house, by the same token you have no right not to be overviewed and it can be a gross intrusion into one's privacy to have a neighbour stare into your space. For the first five years in our London garden there was an unoccupied house at the far end. We grew accustomed to this and gravitated towards that sphere of privacy. Then a

For a while we were good neighbours. He was a taxi driver who boasted of having been a driver for the Kray brothers ('Lovely boys') and of keeping a wide range of pets.

family moved in and every weekend a teenaged boy spent hour after hour staring out of the window overlooking us in our garden. He jiggled as he looked, an intense, introverted motion halfway between dance and masturbation. I tried hostile stares, waving, smiling, ignoring him. Nothing worked. It was as intrusive as a face pressed against a window of our own house. It got to the point where my wife would not go into the garden if and when he was there.

We are too tightly packed into these islands to take such friction. Privacy is everything in a garden and I feel that it is one of the first things that needs to be established if you are to enjoy it fully.

The first thing to do is to decide exactly where your boundaries are. Photograph them, then put a fence or wall up on your own land and plant a hedge inside that. The mistake is to put a hedge up along the line of the boundary. Forgo a foot of territory for peace with your neighbours. If it is on your land then it is your hedge and there is nothing anyone can complain about. Putting a fence up means that you do not need to plant an 'instant' screen of Leyland cypress: 6-8 feet is usually high enough to establish a real sense of privacy. If there are buildings that you want to screen from your sight because they offend you, a few trees planted well inside the hedge will break up their line very effectively.

Once the boundaries are dealt with, you have to create zones of privacy within the garden. Front gardens are public. They are part of the frontage of the house and any attempt at privacy in a front garden is absurd, like a starlet hiding her face from paparazzi as she backs into the limelight. I have recently returned from Canada where as you drive around the suburbs you cannot fail to wonder at the lack of boundaries that people seem to need between houses. They dissolve from road to front door in such a confident, easy progression that you hardly notice it happen. Clearly there is no need to possess space in the way that there is in this country, no need to measure to the inch what we feel is rightfully ours.

But back gardens are different. They are part of the privacy of the household, in exactly the same way that the sitting-room or kitchen is. This is not the locked-off anonymity of an hotel room measured by the turn of a key, but the privacy of wearing what you like, saying what you like or growing what you like.

You have to consider what you use the garden for, and when. If you want to have a quiet drink outside with friends at the weekend or in the evening, then neighbours are more likely to be around, so the outdoor eating area needs to be more conventionally private. In practice this often means taking it away from the convenience of the house to the far end of the garden rather than blindly following the assumption that the sitting bit of the garden will be nearest to the house itself. If you want to be outside on weekdays or

It is curious how some people seem to feel that the garden is a halfway point between private and public territory. Can you complain about the colour of curtains, or underpants on the washing line?

at five in the morning, you are less likely to be overlooked and can tailor your garden accordingly. You also have to bear in mind that it is not so much where you do things in the garden as what you do. So mowing the lawn can take an audience but a meal on the same (newly cut) grass needs to be less of a shared experience.

In any case, lawns and paths are usually only semi-private. It is acceptable that they are visible from the upstairs windows of neighbouring houses. But there must be spaces that are hidden even from your own house. This can just be a seat big enough for two people or a whole garden within a garden, but there has to be a real sense of seclusion for it to work. I like gardens that resemble Russian dolls, a series of spaces within spaces, each revealing new pleasures and each containing realms of privacy. This has to be achieved in two rather than three dimensions, so it is best to use a combination of secret places leading off semi-public entrances such as paths or lawns like side-chapels from a nave, as well as using the sense of entering deeper into the core of the garden by plotting a progression through a sequence of enclosures. But however you achieve it, every garden should try to create at least one place entirely free from the neighbours' gaze.

■ Do not think that large plants will make a large hedge any quicker than small ones. By the time that they have recovered from the shock of being transplanted, much smaller specimens will have caught them up and will be healthier. Spend time and trouble on preparing the ground really well and save money by planting small, healthy plants, and your hedge will establish astonishingly quickly, be it yew, beech, hornbeam, holly or hawthorn.

■ I am a great fan of hornbeam (*Carpinus betulus*), which is used a lot on the Continent but plays second fiddle to beech in this country. It is a rich, lustrous green in summer, holds its leaves as torn russet flags all winter, and grows fast and strong although only needing cutting once a year. It should be planted much more than it is. Hornbeam and beech should not be pruned hard back at planting but allowed to establish for a full season before reducing by a third. This will thicken them up sufficiently.

■ I have been reading *Paradise Transformed: the Private Garden for the Twenty-first Century* by Guy Cooper and Gordon Taylor (The Monacelli Press). This is a beautifully put together and rare example of looking at entirely modern garden design in an intelligent and grown-up fashion. I heartily recommend it.

27.11.94 **Bonfires**

Today would have been my mother's seventy-fourth birthday. She has been dead these five years, but birthdays stick with us long after deathdays are forgotten. She gardened frantically but was no gardener. Hated it in fact, treating the garden as an enemy to be tamed and bowed into submission and all her children as foot-soldiers in that campaign. Despite long hours in the garden from the age of eight onwards, I have no memory of anyone ever planting anything. The whole business was a process of reduction, grass and hedges cut, weeds weeded, and wherever possible more cultivated yardage grassed over.

The only creative area was the kitchen garden which had to produce new growth to fulfil its role in her scheme of things. Brought into grim adulthood by the war, she never lost the urgent frugality that over a decade of rationing induced, despite relative affluence. Before the deep-freeze changed the pattern of eating and growing food for ever, the kitchen garden was an essential and obvious part of domesticity, and had to be run within the rhythm of the kitchen rather than that of the garden. In this role it escaped the full tyranny of her horticultural blitzkrieg. Being a natural skiver, I quickly learnt that it was better to volunteer for a job one liked than to wait and be allotted something on rota. Having got myself allocated to the vegetables, I would spin out an afternoon among the carrots or brassicas, usually left to my own devices as long as I could produce evidence that I had been 'working'. It was among the essential vegetables that I had my gardening epiphany, twenty years ago, surprised by horticultural joy. It would be nice to glamorize my mother's role in this, making her to be like an abbot(tess) of a Zen monastery, leading her filial disciples through earthy rigours to satori, but completely false. She did not believe in enlightenment.

But she did believe in a good bonfire. It was the only time that she was really happy in the garden. She had the knack of keeping one smouldering away for days, even weeks. Bonfires are environmentally incorrect now, but a quarter of a century ago we burnt everything – long grass, cabbage stalks, leaves, twigs, anything that could be cajoled into burning, but in our household we mainly burnt couch grass. This made ideal fuel for my mother's bonfires, being present in limitless supply and burning satisfyingly slowly. Weeds were tipped from the barrow into a heap to one side and fluffed on to the fire by the forkful. The trick was to put enough on to stop the wind from fanning the flames so that it would burn too fast but not to heap it on so lumpenly as to snuff it out. My mother used to take great therapeutic pleasure from setting it up exactly so, catching the heap on the cusp of fuel and famine so that it would secretly burn for twelve hours or more unattended, a thin string of smoke twining up from the top or leaking surreptitiously from the edges.

Being a natural skiver, I quickly learnt that it was better to volunteer for a job one liked than to wait and be allotted something on rota.

My mother used to take great therapeutic pleasure from setting it up exactly so, catching the heap on the cusp of fuel and famine so that it would secretly burn for twelve hours or more unattended, a thin string of smoke twining up from the top or leaking surreptitiously from the edges.

The Bonfire Heap was a place both geographical and increasingly physical, a tump beaten into grey earth that had stayed where it was for decades. Occasionally it would be excavated and the ashy soil spread, and within the strata of spoil were the charred relics of dropped penknives, busted hoes and the occasional coin – the archaeology of a thousand hours digging hundreds of barrowloads of couch. But it soon callused over and grew by layers into its carbuncled self.

The fresh ash from bonfires is an abundant source of potash – or potassium carbonate. Potash speeds up the production of sugars in leaves, quickening the ripening process and improving the production of fruit and flowers. Certain plants, like gooseberries, have a high demand for potash and will improve with annual dressing, whilst all plants will benefit from a balanced amount in the soil. Plants suffering from potassium deficiency will display the lack in their leaves first of all, turning yellow, blue or even purple, with brown margins. Fruit will be insipidly coloured and lack flavour. Most spectacularly of all, potatoes grown in potassium-deficient soil will turn black and soapy when cooked. Plants grown on very chalky or peaty soils – exact opposites – are particularly prone to potassium shortage and need constant topping up. Very light, sandy soils will lose nutrients very fast and will also need a regular dose of potash along with all other nutrients.

Although the bonfire burned the year round, becoming incandescent when the hay was burned and struggling against constant rain in a sodden winter, it became the focus of the garden at about this time of year. One would be sent, in the middle of a wholly unconnected activity, to 'check the bonfire'. You were expected to react like a fireman answering a call. The alarm was always prompted by flames seen from a window. Flames meant that the fire was taking matters too liberally into its own hands and had to be damped down with more weeds, turning the wayward flames into a lazy ooze of smoke. This is the starkest time of year in the garden, with the 'thin smoke without flame/ From the heaps of couch-grass'; and the cling of bonfire smell to clothes and hair as the true evocation of the season. Thomas Hardy's verse goes on: 'Yet this will go onward the same/ Though Dynasties pass.' But he was wrong. There comes the day when the bonfire must burn out and the ashes grow cold.

■ Seaweed is a very rich source of potassium. The farmers and market gardeners of the south-west coast and islands have used thousands of tons of seaweed every year on their fields for centuries, using it as a mulch, as a soil conditioner and as a feed. Liquid

Seaweed is the best feed for trees of all kinds and I use it for all containerized plants.

■ If you have not ordered your seed catalogues, do so now. Seeds are always sent out on a first-come, first-served basis, so to be sure to get everything you want it is necessary not to leave it till the last minute.

■ If we have a very dry, cold spell, you may have to water evergreens, which continue to respire – and therefore lose water – for the whole year. Much of so-called 'frost damage' to evergreens is caused by drought. Just as in summer, wind is the great enemy, drying everything off.

4.12.94 Gardening Magazines

Strewth! Pass the Prozac. I started out the day perfectly cheery, and sat down to go through some gardening magazines as research for this week's column. I normally never touch the things but went into the local newsagent yesterday and asked the proprietor for a selection of his finest horticultural periodicals. They came in a bag and stayed there until an hour ago. I had no idea! Are they regularly this awful?

It is not fair to name them and who knows, they might offer me good money to write for them one day. The dreadful ones are probably catering exactly and expertly for a specific market and sell by the 100,000 to that satisfied readership. If true, this is even more depressing. The image of gardening that they cold-bloodedly dispense is of a banal, philistine world where the cliché rules, press releases (I get them all too, so I know) are regurgitated word for word, and all aesthetic discrimination and judgement are ignored. To apply Orwell's dictum about language ('It becomes ugly and inaccurate because our thoughts are foolish, but the slovenliness of our language makes it easier to have foolish thoughts,') to the aesthetic standards of gardening journalism, it means that if you publish a journal for the 'ordinary', uneducated, aesthetically challenged masses, you will produce an equally restricted magazine which will in turn promote and spread dreary, ugly gardens.

It is almost impossible to talk about this sort of thing in England without Class taking over. You either sound like a snotty bastard looking down his nose at ordinary people in homes that they like, thank you very much, doing

I went into the local newsagent yesterday and asked the proprietor for a selection of his finest horticultural periodicals. They came in a bag and stayed there until an hour ago. I had no idea! Are they regularly this awful?

what gives them private pleasure, or as though you have an enormous chip on your shoulder. I heard a well-known garden person on the radio the other day speaking in drawling disdain about 'most people's' gardens and instantly hated him for it. It was clear that he knew nothing about 'most people' (or anything much at all for that matter) and that I knew there was a certain honesty about ordinariness that mattered which he had illustrated for me in the glare of his contempt.

But this is not a class issue. It is to do with the way that gardening is presented and perceived and it makes me angry and sad in equal measure. It must be possible to criticize something for being badly done without the subtext that the people who have done it or the people that it is done for are divided from oneself primarily by social class.

It is clear that the magazines at the lower end of the market make no attempt to sell themselves to the uninitiated. It is all about market share and brand loyalty. If you are not the sort of person that buys a gardening magazine regularly, the thinking goes, then hey! you're not going to be the sort of person that wants to buy a gardening magazine. The problem with this approach is that it disappears rapidly up its own backside. You end up with a publication for us, by us and as boring as hell.

If you compare gardening magazines to ones about interior decoration and design, there is a huge jump in standards. The latter try to look good. They have plenty of factual detail but are not obsessed with the technicalities of achieving effect. They understand that it matters a lot less how you do something than how it appears once it is done. Gardening magazines usually use an 'expert' (I put it in inverted commas because for five years I have been described by a television programme as their Gardening Expert, and I'm not, so I mistrust the label when applied in any part of the media) to write about his or her area of expertise. Sometimes this is jolly good but often it results in poor journalism coupled with an almost wilful absence of aesthetic discrimination. You would not expect to find an article on choosing wallpaper written by a brilliant paper-hanger, nor would you choose your wallpaper on its ease of hanging.

In short, magazines about houses take it as axiomatic that readers are more concerned about making their houses look good than the details of achieving any kind of look at all. Likewise you would not expect the fashion pages of publications to concentrate on how clothes are made. Gardening magazines work on the lowest common denominator: if it is done at all then it is done well enough.

Maybe I'm wrong. Perhaps it *is* to do with class. Perhaps gardening is still stuck with a class-consciousness that slipped out of the rest of life about thirty

I heard a well-known garden person on the radio the other day speaking in drawling disdain about 'most people's' gardens and instantly hated him for it. It was clear that he knew nothing about 'most people' (or anything much at all for that matter).

years ago. After all, most of the grand gardens people visit and magazines show are those belonging to nobs. People poke around their gardens more out of aspiration than for inspiration. Magazines that feature rooms and houses tend to include a greater cross-section of humanity, although I concede that there is a bias towards the rich.

I think that there is a lesson to be learnt here. If people would consider their gardens as spaces that they control and inhabit – exactly like their houses – they would loosen up sufficiently to make something of them. The chances are that the something would be horrid, but who cares, what matters is that it is an expression of individuality and creativity. Magazine editors have a responsibility to promote this – at the expense of badly designed pages of ugliness that are either patronizing to the reader or appallingly sycophantic and hagiographic.

There is an honourable exception and that is *Gardens Illustrated*. Until today I had rather mixed feelings about it, thinking it was too exclusive and introverted, but compared to the rest it stands as a beacon of enlightened gardening and publishing.

I had bought these magazines to prepare a piece on Christmas presents. It was going to be gently mocking. But then I got carried away. Here are a few (serious) suggestions for presents for gardeners.

Christmas present suggestions

■ A stainless steel spade. The single most useful piece of garden kit. It will last indefinitely, so worth every penny.

■ Good strong leather gloves. Most gardening gloves are too short on the cuff and too flimsy. On the whole gloves are a nuisance, so when you do need them they need to be really tough and fully protective.

■ Propagator. An electrically heated propagator for the window-sill makes a huge difference to one's garden life. If you have a greenhouse with power to put it in, so much the better. There are a number of different brands on the market, but go for the biggest you can accommodate, and the sturdiest. I have one that has three trays, each with four quarter-trays that can be inserted – very useful when you only want to propagate small quantities of seeds or cuttings . Individual covers are probably more useful than one big cover.

■ A decent watering can.

■ A citrus in a pot. One really healthy plant, orange or lemon, is a sure-fire winner.

11.12.94 **Mistletoe and Holly**

Tenbury Wells is a little town pitched in the angle where Shropshire, Worcestershire and Herefordshire meet. It has a high proportion of timbered houses jutting at impossible pitches and more solemn Georgian fronts on the High Street, but it is not in any way smart – too far from anywhere for that. It is surrounded by the kind of countryside that is becoming rare in Britain, land rich enough to support a family that works hard but too poor to make many rich. Those that do make a go of it often farm land that has been in the family for centuries. There are few quick bucks to be made and change is viewed with a suspicious eye.

It is a countryside of orchards, hop yards, hedges and red, heavy earth. (Hop gardens belong in the South-East only, although the etymologies of garden and yard – and garth – are inextricably linked. Which is why the British shouldn't be stuffy about Americans talking about their luxuriant green 'yards'.) The hops take the best soil but on the hillsides there are still some ancient orchards left, grazed by sheep and uncontaminated by spray, exhaust fumes or anything other than clean air.

This remoteness and purity of air provide the ideal conditions for the mistletoe that is the winter harvest of these orchards after all the apples have fallen and been gathered. Down in Tenbury cattle market there is an auction of holly, mistletoe, wreaths and Christmas trees for the four Tuesdays prior to Christmas Week. The only auction of its kind in the country, this is aimed at the wholesale market, with mistletoe and holly sold by the hundredweight, Christmas trees in lots of twenty, and 'wreaths and chaplets' by the dozen. The Christmas trees stand in the cattle stalls, the wreaths are laid out on the floor of sheep stalls, and the holly and mistletoe – up to 1000 lots at a time or fifty prickly tons – tied in a great bundle in the space where the cattle trucks normally park.

The mistletoe is cut by farmers as a perk. It grows as freely in the apple branches as the thistles on the ground below. No one has ever tried to grow it as a crop, which cannot be for commercial reasons, when you think of the seriousness that goes into the far more boring Christmas tree market.

The truth is that no one really knows how to grow mistletoe. It must have clean air – which cuts out most of the country anyway – and might well have to pass through the intestines of a bird to germinate successfully. The best way to grow your own mistletoe is to squidge the fruit – the milky-white berries – into the crack of a suitable tree, or into a flap made with your knife, between March and May. Mistletoe is a parasite and is picky about its host. It loves apple, likes poplar and hawthorn and will grow on oak. It is more likely to grow on rough bark than smooth, where the berries can get wedged into a crevice. Its normal process of germination is for the berry to be eaten by a bird (including the Mistle thrush – hence the name) which will then fly off to a branch nearby and either wipe its beak clean of the sticky flesh, accidentally depositing the little black seed, or excrete the seed in some digestionary future. This will be parcelled in its own manure heap. The rain will wash the seed down the bark until it gets caught in a crack, still with an amount of

Hop gardens belong in the South-East only, although the etymologies of garden and yard – and garth – are inextricably linked. Which is why the British shouldn't be stuffy about Americans talking about their luxuriant green 'yards'.

nourishment to see it on its way. The roots of the seedling grow inwards to the heartwood of the branch, eventually growing right round it, the roots radiating inwards like the spokes of a bicycle wheel.

At Tenbury market the mistletoe is always sold in lots together with holly. Other than the obvious Christmas association, the reason seems to be that holly grows particularly profusely along these Welsh Marches. It has always been considered magical and is thought to bring bad luck to anyone who fells a holly tree. Consequently there is plenty of holly about.

This is *Ilex aquifolium* or what Americans call English holly. There are – amazingly – over 400 species of holly and at least as many varieties again, but none beats the intensity of green and red of a hedgerow holly. One of the reasons for this is that holly in a hedge is either clipped or shaped by the wind, making the branches denser and thicker. Holly left to grow in a wood or in complete shelter will become lean and hungry-looking. Despite this aesthetic point, holly will actually be perfectly happy in the dry shade of other trees and will cast such a shade beneath its own skirts that nothing will grow in its lee.

The range of different hollies is staggering, from the weird *Ilex aquifolium* 'Crispa' whose whole being – trunk, branches and smooth leaves – twists crazily, to the Hedgehog holly, *Ilex aquifolium* 'Ferox', which not only has prickly edges to its leaves, but spikes all over each surface. There are the 'Highclere' hybrids (*Ilex* x *alterclerensis*) which are on the whole unprickly and more vigorous than *Ilex aquifolium* and its hybrids. You can get hollies that are practically all yellow with a touch of green, or hollies that are almost blue; milky hollies, hollies in every shade of green under the sun.

The holly at Tenbury is mainly brought in by travellers. These are not New Age anything, but gypsies and proud of it. If you attend a sale you will notice bands of small, dark men with lined, wise faces, accompanied by beautiful women. The holly is their harvest and they watch the prices as anxiously as any farmer at market. They either come to an agreement with a farmer to cut the holly from his hedges or just nick it. No one seems to mind.

The very best holly – dense with plenty of bright berries – is reaching £50–75 per hundredweight this year, with the poorer stuff making £10–40. Mistletoe makes £40–50 per hundredweight for the best quality and £10–25 for the dross. Apparently there is a shortage of good holly this year. This will have a serious effect on the quality of a lot of the travellers' Christmas. Market forces, some will say. But, as ever, it is more complicated than that. Hedges are being trimmed by flail indiscriminately and holly is being left berryless and uniform rather than being allowed to grow up above the hedgerow. Here, as everywhere, hedges are grubbed. Although many hedges are being replanted, holly is slow to grow and seldom planted now.

If you attend a sale you will notice bands of small, dark men with lined, wise faces, accompanied by beautiful women. The holly is their harvest and they watch the prices as anxiously as any farmer at market.

Mistletoe depends on mature orchards, which are being bulldozed by the week. New orchards have neither the space nor the neglect that mistletoe needs. Most of the mistletoe sold in our shops comes from France, where the air is less polluted and the orchards left alone. And in the past few years there has been an influx of cheap mistletoe from Eastern Europe, where mature oak woods are being felled for cash, their attendant balls of mistletoe falling with them.

■ Spring is the best time to plant holly, or failing that, early autumn. But once established, it hates to be moved. Do not worry if some of the older leaves fall in the spring or summer after planting: it is often a sign that the plant is rooting healthily.
■ Despite being such a feature of the English landscape, holly is not fully hardy in this country. In a very cold winter it will lose all its leaves and every now and then a really cold spell will kill it. If you have a treasured tree that is exposed to cold winds, wrap it in burlap when the weather gets really arctic.
■ The practice of hanging mistletoe and kissing beneath it stems from the time when it was hung above a door as a sign of peace and any visitor was greeted with a kiss of welcome. But each kiss should properly be paid for – with a berry plucked from the sprig. When the berries are all gone, the kissing has to stop.

22.12.96 **Christmas Trees**

A Christmas tree is a pretty kitsch thing, be it a glowing fibreglass affair adorned with a dancing fairy miming to Sir Heathcliff Richard singing carols, or a 10-foot monster shedding needles on a baronial floor. Christmas trees are not there because we think that they are the ideal decoration for that particular part of the house but just because that is what we ritually do.

Most people have an inkling about the mythology and folklore behind this Germanic custom, reintroduced by Prince Albert in 1840 after the initial introduction by St Boniface in 718 had apparently failed to catch on. We might even have heard of Yggdrasil, the World Tree of Norse mythology, whose branches and roots joined together Heaven, Earth and Hell, tree of life, knowledge, time and space. Yggdrasil is usually portrayed as an ash, but occasionally as an evergreen, which no ash is (although it is extraordinary how some young ashes this year have held their leaves right into this time of the solstice, which possibly accounts for the contradiction of identity). We sort of know about the winter solstice, the Green Man and the symbolism of life that evergreen branches such as holly, ivy and *Picea abies* (Christmas tree to you, squire) have at a time of year when even the sun seems to be dying. It is a defiant finger thrust up against all the natural evidence of decay around us. But by far the most fantastic aspect of a Christmas tree – and the reason that I loathe man-made imitations – is that you are bringing a living tree inside the house. What an amazing, mind-blowing concept! Forget your itsy-bitsy bonsai or pot-plants, this is a bit of wildwood uprooted into the living-room. Talk about taming nature!

People have always worshipped trees. Of all the things to bow down to, an impressive tree is as likely a candidate as anything. No one tree has cornered

A Christmas tree is a pretty kitsch thing, be it a glowing fibreglass affair adorned with a dancing fairy miming to Sir Heathcliff Richard singing carols, or a 10-foot monster shedding needles on a baronial floor.

the market in idolatry, but almost every culture has its revered variety, from the ash of the Norse to the mulberry of the Chinese via the banyan of India, the olive tree of the Arabs and the silver birch of the Siberians. The transubstantiation of flesh to wood figures in various mythologies, although the Greeks seemed to be particularly keen on the notion. It is not a surprising metamorphosis when one thinks of human life as being the most vividly living thing that man can conceive, as well as the most fragile, whereas a great tree is the most permanent and biggest living thing a human will ever come across.

It is never enough simply to bring the Christmas tree indoors and set it upright. It has to be decorated. We dress it in light and garlands so that this mysterious, magical object shines like a winter sky. In the daylight a Christmas tree is an overdressed partygoer tottering home along disapproving sober streets, but at night she is the belle of the ball.

Tree dressing is a long established folk-custom that spans cultures. Rags, gifts, items of clothing, jewellery are attached to significant trees as an offering against ills and to promote good fortune. In Barnes, the tree that Marc Bolan crashed into is festooned with ribbons and pictures. If it had been a lamp-post there might have been a wreath or two, but trees evoke this deep, atavistic response. It is seen as a symbol of magic rather than the magic itself – just like a Christmas tree, which becomes Yggdrasil, Merlin, Tinkerbell and fireworks, the terrifying forces of magic and forest all brought within doors and made safe for us to gather round and worship, carrying all the hopes and fears for the New Year ahead.

This is only primitive inasmuch as it strikes at the essence of human awareness. In the age of the Internet, trees still hold their mystery, and every time a little sapling is planted in the garden connections beyond comprehension are made across cultures and millennia.

Certain quantitative facts remain as awesome today as they would have seemed to our low-tech hunting fathers. The largest living thing in the world is a sequoia in California and in Britain alone there are living ash, oak, lime and yew trees all over 1000 years old. Over 500 churchyards have yews older than the church and the yew in the churchyard at Fortingall, Perthshire is reckoned to be between 2000 and 9000 years old. There are three trees in Powys believed to be 4500 years old.

Leave this country, and the venerability of some trees gets even more incredible. In 1955 a 'forest' of gnarled, squat (the biggest one was no more than 40 feet high) and seemingly half-dead trees was discovered growing at 10,000 feet in the White Mountains on the border between California and Nevada. These are Bristlecone pines (*Pinus aristata*) growing microscopically slowly in desert conditions of chronic drought, and there are some now 5000

years old, which makes them the oldest living things in the world.

Most of us buy a lottery ticket in real hope, but the chances of a yew in your garden lasting at least 1000 years must be much more realistic. Even after the tree dies, the wood endures and will apparently last longer than iron. The world's oldest known wooden artefact, a 250,000-year-old spear found at Clacton in Essex, is made of yew. In this light, gardening becomes as mind-boggling as star-gazing, and tree-worship mere common sense.

Gardeners rarely plant yews now as trees and have not done so for perhaps 300 years. Any mature trees are escapees from the confines of a former hedge or topiary, released by neglect. Churchyards are the commonest place to see the yew as a tree, and its connection with worship is apposite enough at this time of year as it has the densest and most consistent green of any tree in the middle of winter. The branches were used in spring too, to decorate the church at Easter and at Whitsun.

As every schoolchild knows, yew is the wood used for the longbow. I made one myself once, and although I made it from a branch, whereas it should properly come from the trunk, the orange wood made a sinuously beautiful object and fired the arrows far and true.

Recently gardeners have been collecting yew clippings, and an alkaloid named Taxol is extracted from them and used against ovarian cancer. More magic.

Holly is another native tree adopted for gardens that is duly celebrated at this time of year for its midwinter emerald gleam and, of course, its berries. Christmas is not complete without a few sprigs of berried holly. But no one in their right mind would substitute a holly tree for a conventional Christmas tree. Cutting down an entire tree is still taboo in most parts of the country. Trimming branches for Christmas decoration seems to be a trouble-free activity and is clearly worth doing simply for the decorative effect, without any overtones of magic. Holly was seen as a pagan fertility symbol, as well as a charm against witchcraft. Christianity borrowed its magic, and the thorns and berries symbolized the crown of thorns and Christ's blood. When you consider the startling brilliance of the berries that are at their best well before 25 December, it is surely the residual strength of pagan superstition that stops most people decorating the house before Christmas.

That decoration comes in hundreds of different variations for there are 400 species of holly with more than double that number of cultivars and hybrids. You can get dozens of different variegations – yellow berries, bright yellow leaves, smooth leaves, leaves with bristles all over the surface as well as the edges, leaves that curl and leaves that do not look like holly at all.

Holly grows richly here in Herefordshire, and the association with

People have always worshipped trees. Of all the things to bow down to, an impressive tree is as likely a candidate as anything. No one tree has cornered the market in idolatry, but almost every culture has its revered variety.

witchcraft is still common, with hollies left to grow freely along an otherwise trimmed hedge to avoid the retribution of bad luck that cutting them down would bring. This superstition has – as is so often the case – been allied to a practical modern purpose, and hollies often mark the site of land drains as they pass under a hedge. Across the country a holly will often mark a boundary, footpath or gateway.

Left to its own devices and given time, holly will reach 75 feet with a girth of over 10 feet, although it will be a spindly affair with none of the density of texture that makes holly such a good hedge when clipped by man or by cold wind. Holly will suffer dry conditions and grows in deep shade, although it looks best and is densest in sunlight.

Although the thought of munching a holly leaf brings tears to the eyes, it has long been used as winter fodder and stock will tug at any leaves that they can reach. Apparently it has exceptionally high calorific value. I have chewed linden leaves with pleasure but I think a sheep's jaws are needed to appreciate the full richness of a holly leaf. I'll stick to high-calorific Christmas pud.

■ Holly hates being disturbed once it is established. My experience is that it seems fine for up to six months but starts to show signs of distress, and the plant then teeters on the brink of life and death for a full year, losing most of its leaves and dying back at the tips. If you must move holly, it is best to do so in early spring or autumn with as large a rootball as possible so that the roots can get established before great demands are made of them. If the tree seems to be suffering, remove some or even all of the leaves. The good news is that holly can recover from what seems to be a terminal condition, so do not abandon it for at least a year after it appears 'dead'. (Which is a good rule of thumb for any tree.)

■ Yew grows best on chalky soil but for garden purposes it will grow anywhere, although good drainage is essential. A good helping of manure and compost when planting is usually enough to guarantee this but it may be necessary to put a 6-inch layer of stones in the bottom of the trench or hole before filling with soil. Whatever happens, the roots do not want to sit in water. Having ensured this, do not make the mistake of letting the young plants dry out. They need lots of water to grow well.

■ Christmas trees can be planted in the garden but you must keep the roots moist while they are in the house. Pack damp sand around them when you put them in a container, and keep it moist. Keep the tree as cool as possible and never put it by a radiator. If it starts to drop its needles it means that it is too warm and drying out.

24.12.95 **The Garden at Christmas**

Although it is unadventurous to admit it, most of us strive after good taste in our gardens. We want them to be soft, calming, crisp, ordered, flowing, symmetrical – some or even all of these things, but rarely garish, playful or vulgar. But Christmas, especially if you have children, is a very vulgar time indeed. Every year my wife and I gather swags of ivy, cloudy bunches of mistletoe taken from the mass growing on the hawthorn on our boundary, and large bunches of holly to be placed in earthenware jars. All in the best possible taste. Then the children take a look, roll their eyes and groan and set to with baubles and streamers to jazz it all up as much as they can. The holly is raided to dot around the place, a sprig here and a sprig there, and as for the mistletoe – urrgh! Kissing! Yuk!

It is pretty much the same in our garden the year round, but whereas the garden and I triumph from June till October, subsuming the more blatant accoutrements of the children in the weight of foliage and flower, their bikes, footballs, hula hoops and the mysterious constructs that the youngest strings across every path dominate the garden all winter. The bright paintwork of their toys is splattered outside like tinsel on the tree. The poor garden can hardly compete, not being mature enough to have barriers of neatly clipped hedges (talking of which, I have just been looking through Tony Lord's new book, *Sissinghurst*, and there is a picture of the famous White Garden in full midsummer regalia juxtaposed against the same shot taken in midwinter. I prefer the latter for its perfect austerity of the maze-like box hedges around the borders) and having very little by way of blowsy good taste to challenge the inevitable detritus of childhood. It is sort of tasteful, I suppose, inasmuch as there is a distinct harmony of brown on sodden brown on brownish-green.

This Christmas we are having gardening friends to stay. That is to say, they are friends who also happen to garden with knowledge and seriousness – even intensity. Luckily they also have plenty of children to temper their own high horticultural standards. Nothing is worse than the withering politeness of childless gardeners contemplating our chaotic ménage under full sail. But if I cannot hope to enthral them with the riches and surprising range of our garden in midwinter, I shall at least try and pick a few flowers for their bedside.

Ever since reading Rosemary Verey's *The Garden In Winter* I do go round the garden on Christmas Day rather self-consciously collecting a (very) small bunch of flowers. In 1988, the first year I did this, the posy was pretty sizeable because we had had a freakishly warm December that brought primroses, snowdrops, crocuses, jasmines and choisya all into flower by Christmas Day. Forgetting the previous thirty-three Christmases of miserable grey dampness or freezing cold, I based my expectations the following year on that freakish bunch and was duly disappointed.

This year looks a bit thin too – I might get one or two flowers off the inappropriately named Christmas roses (*Helleborus niger*) and more likely a couple off its hybrid *H. nigercors*, although it will be too early for the other parent of this cross, *H. argutifolius*. The winter honeysuckle *Lonicera fragantissima* usually provides a sprig of impossibly dainty and sweet-smelling flowers, but this year it has been moved and had cement dripped all over it and is sulking. I have two *Clematis cirrhosa balearica*, neither of which has ever flowered or looks like breaking the habit of a lifetime this year, although, to be fair, Christmas is a bit early even for the most virile specimens of this lovely clematis. The rose 'Felicia' is a pretty fair bet to produce at least one flower,

Every year my wife and I gather swags of ivy, cloudy bunches of mistletoe taken from the mass growing on the hawthorn on our boundary, and large bunches of holly to be placed in earthenware jars. All in the best possible taste.

albeit a small, limp one, and *Viburnum bodnantense* 'Deben' is bound to have masses of flowers. And that is it, from my garden at any rate. Not much of a bouquet. Thank God for holly.

However, the garden usually provides me with purgative exercise rather than aesthetic riches. An hour or two's hard slog before either eating, or drinking too much eases the guilt a little. This is where I stretch the term 'gardening' to its broadest sense. One year I ploughed up the lawn with a two-wheel tractor, which was very sweaty and wonderfully dramatic. Usually I reserve a pile of logs to be split or some fencing to be done. Failing that, the compost heap can be turned. It hardly matters what the job is as long as it involves being outside and makes you puffed, ache and sweat a lot. I appreciate that the scope for doing this amongst you townies is fairly limited, but then, you have chosen your bed and must lie unhealthily on it.

Just as I am glad that the children take over the house at Christmas, glad that the sophistication of the place is swept aside with a pagan brashness, so secretly I am glad that the garden always has a bike not put away and left dropped across a path or in the middle of the lawn, glad that the vermilion football lies nestled amongst the massed fragility of the hellebores and that Tom has carefully tied orange nylon baler twine in a cat's-cradle between the pleached limes. Gardening is altogether too grown-up and tasteful at any time, and at Christmastime especially, the Lords of Misrule should hold anarchic sway. Here's wishing you a very vulgar Christmas.

■ If you have large pots or urns in the garden it is a good idea to weigh them down with stones or sandbags and then wrap them in sacking or tarpaulins. This will stop them being blown over and their porous surfaces damaged by frost.

■ If you have conifers with an upright habit (clean-living, right-minded types), then they are very susceptible to damage by heavy snowfall. The best way to avoid this is to wrap them around with string so that the branches cannot be bent down and the snow finds it harder to settle.

■ Although it is important to make a hole in a fish-pond so that toxic gases can escape, never smash a hole as the shock waves will kill the fish. Put a saucepan of hot water on the ice and let it melt its way through.

■ Prune as and when you can, tidying up as you go. I have long wanted a chipper to deal with prunings so that I can compost them rather than burn them, but it seems that the only ones big enough to be worth having are petrol-driven and expensive, and from an environmental point of view I suspect that the petrol consumption and fumes do more harm than the bonfire. Such are the agonies of environmental correctness.

This Christmas we are having gardening friends to stay...
Luckily they also have plenty of children to temper their
own high horticultural standards. Nothing is worse than the
withering politeness of childless gardeners contemplating
our chaotic ménage under full sail.